The Medium and the Magician

CRITICAL MEDIA STUDIES
INSTITUTIONS, POLITICS, AND CULTURE
Series Editor
Andrew Calabrese, University of Colorado
Advisory Board

Patricia Aufderheide, American University
Jean-Claude Burgelman, Free University of Brussels
Simone Chambers, University of Toronto
Nicholas Garnham, University of Westminster
Hanno Hardt, University of Iowa
Gay Hawkins, The University of New South Wales
Maria Heller, Eötvös Loránd University
Robert Horwitz, University of California at San Diego
Douglas Kellner, University of California at Los Angeles
Gary Marx, Massachusetts Institute of Technology
Toby Miller, New York University
Vincent Mosco, Queen's University
Janice Peck, University of Colorado
Manjunath Pendakur, Southern Illinois University
Arvind Rajagopal, New York University
Giuseppe Richeri, Università Svizzera Italiana
Kevin Robins, Goldsmiths College
Saskia Sassen, University of Chicago
Dan Schiller, University of Illinois at Urbana-Champaign
Colin Sparks, University of Westminster
Slavko Splichal, University of Ljubljana
Thomas Streeter, University of Vermont
Liesbet van Zoonen, University of Amsterdam
Janet Wasko, University of Oregon

Recent Titles in the Series
Changing Concepts of Time
  Harold A. Innis
A Fatal Attraction: Public Television and Politics in Italy
  Cinzia Padovani
Entertaining the Citizen: When Politics and Popular Culture Converge
  Liesbet van Zoonen
The Medium and the Magician: Orson Welles, the Radio Years, 1934–1952
  Paul Heyer

Forthcoming
Mass Communication and American Social Thought: Key Texts, 1919–1968
  Edited by John Durham Peters and Peter Simonson
Global Electioneering: Campaign Consultants, Communications, and Corporate Financing
  Gerald Sussman
Contracting Out Hollywood
  Edited by Mike Gasher and Greg Elmer
Raymond Williams
  Alan O'Connor
Democratizing Global Media: One World, Many Struggles
  Edited by Robert A. Hackett and Yuezhi Zhao
The Film Studio
  Ben Goldsmith and Tom O'Regan
Raymond Williams
  Alan O'Connor
The Blame Game
  Eileen Meehan

The Medium and the Magician
Orson Welles, the Radio Years, 1934–1952

Paul Heyer

ROWMAN & LITTLEFIELD PUBLISHERS, INC.
Lanham • Boulder • New York • Toronto • Oxford

ROWMAN & LITTLEFIELD PUBLISHERS, INC.

Published in the United States of America
by Rowman & Littlefield Publishers, Inc.
A wholly owned subsidiary of The Rowman & Littlefield Publishing Group, Inc.
4501 Forbes Boulevard, Suite 200, Lanham, MD 20706
www.rowmanlittlefield.com

P.O. Box 317, Oxford OX2 9RU, UK

Copyright © 2005 by Rowman & Littlefield Publishers, Inc.

All rights reserved. No part of this publication may be reproduced, stored in a retrieval system, or transmitted in any form or by any means, electronic, mechanical, photocopying, recording, or otherwise, without the prior permission of the publisher.

British Library Cataloguing in Publication Information Available

Library of Congress Cataloging-in-Publication Data

Heyer, Paul, 1946–
 The medium and the magician : Orson Welles, the radio years, 1934–1952 / Paul Heyer.
  p. cm. — (Critical media studies)
 Includes bibliographical references and index.
 ISBN 0-7425-3796-X (cloth : alk. paper) — ISBN 0-7425-3797-8 (pbk. : alk. paper)
 1. Welles, Orson, 1915– I. Title. II. Series.

PN1991.4.W44H49 2005
791.4402'8'092—dc22

2004018363

Printed in the United States of America

∞™ The paper used in this publication meets the minimum requirements of American National Standard for Information Sciences—Permanence of Paper for Printed Library Materials, ANSI/NISO Z39.48-1992.

To the memory of Florian Morelli

A man may see how the world goes with no eyes. Look with thine ears.

—Shakespeare, *King Lear*

My big inventions were in radio and the theatre. Much more than in movies.

—Orson Welles

Contents

Acknowledgments		xi
Introduction:	A Man for All Media	xiii
Part I. The Road to CBS		
Chapter 1	A Voice Is Born	3
Chapter 2	Theatrical Notoriety, Radio Anonymity	15
Chapter 3	*Mercury Theatre on the Air*	45
Part II. Mercury Does Mars: The Panic Broadcast		
Chapter 4	Genesis	75
Chapter 5	Exodus	81
Chapter 6	Revelation	95
Part III. The Sound in the Fury		
Chapter 7	Campbell Playhouse	115
Chapter 8	Orson at RKO	151
Chapter 9	The Last Radio Shows	191
Epilogue		211

Selected Radiography	217
Notes	223
Bibliography	233
Index	239
About the Author	255

Acknowledgments

Orson Welles's papers, correspondences, tapes (in both reel-to-reel and cassette formats) and the acetate disks of many of his radio programs are housed in Indiana University's Lilly Library as the "Orson Welles mss. collection." It is an extraordinary resource. Seeing the original scripts of the Mercury Theatre on the Air programs and the disks that transcribed them was like gazing upon a Rosetta Stone of broadcast radio. I wish to thank Lilly staff members Sue Presnell, Helena Walsh, Elizabeth Powers, and David Greenebaum, who patiently and graciously guided me through the archive during my visits. Helena's assistance in helping me track down and select photographs for this book has been invaluable.

Welles's radio work was so diverse and prolific that not all of it has found its way to the Lilly repository. A good deal of what he did for the CBS and the Mutual Networks is housed at the Museum of Television and Radio in New York, where I made good use of my membership. Other broadcasts, especially those he did in Europe, I was able to acquire from Original Radio Classics in Vancouver, British Columbia, and from Radio Yesteryear in Sandy Hook, Connecticut. Alas, both outlets no longer operate, but much of what was in their extensive collections can still be found through a diligent search of the Internet. I hesitate to list specific sites, since they tend to come and go like summer squalls.

Anyone who tries to fathom the Welles legacy is indebted to those who have come before, and there have been many, as my bibliography attests. Nevertheless, special mention must be made regarding the work of Jonathan Rosenbaum and Bret Wood, whose biographical bibliographies guided me through well-charted but not fully explored territory. Jonathan, along with Welles scholars

Michael Anderegg and Jim Naremore, have been unusually generous in giving me their time, constructive criticism, and encouragement. I, of course, bear complete responsibility for the various positions and opinions contained herein.

A high point of the project has been the invitation to write and narrate a radio documentary for Australia's national network, ABC, commemorating the sixtieth anniversary of Welles's infamous *War of the Worlds* broadcast. *When Mars Attacked* (1998) was made possible through the support of Matthew Leonard, the producer of ABC's *Radio-Eye*, who also allowed me to suggest material for their monthlong tribute to Welles's radio legacy. During what turned out to be two Welles-related trips to Australia, Hart Cohen was a gracious host and valuable source of ideas and encouragement. Terry Guthridge, Andrew Preston, and Sue Turnbull in Melbourne, and Collette Snowdon in Adelaide, provided unlimited hospitality and superb itinerary arranging.

Special thanks must go to my research assistant, radio documentary coproducer, and Welles aficionado extraordinaire, Blair Davis. Blair's editorial reading of each draft, diligent fact finding, and ongoing supportive critique have sustained this project every step of the way. Carole Akazawa provided me with life support and my debt to her is beyond words.

Throughout the writing of this book, friends and colleagues in Canada, the United States, and Australia have provided sustained encouragement, especially Jan Anderson, Patricia Anderson, David Black, Howard Blue, Aniko Bodroghkozy, Bill Buxton, Robert Campbell, Frank Chorba, Ian Chunn, David Crowley, Abby Dancey, Dominique Darmon, Peter Davis, Ian Dawe, Melissa Fennell, Elaine Fenton, Jonathan Finn, Philippa Gates, Rick Gruneau, Evelyn Hassen, Vincent Hayward, Karla Hennig, Penelope Ironstone-Catterall, Iwona Irwin-Zarecka, Liss Jeffrey, Barbara Jenkins, Yasmin Jiwani, Rowland Lorimer, Oya Majlesi, John Max, Gary McCarron, Rick McCormick, Eric McLuhan, Lucie Menkveld, Holly Moist, Vanneau Neesham, Maria Paule, Gary Porter, DeNel Sedo, Neena Shahani, Matt Soar, Steven Stack, Will Straw, Paul Tiessen, Iqbal Velji, Robert Walker, Julian Weaver, James Wong, Denyse Zenner, and Ania Zofia. Sylvia Hoang has provided invaluable computer assistance and Julie Pong has been once again my indexer extraordinaire.

And finally, I am fortunate to have such a supportive editorial team. Andrew Calabrese, Erica Fast, and Brenda Hadenfeldt at Rowman & Littlefield have been a delight to work with for this, my second book under their aegis. Their sense that the work of Orson Welles fits within a tradition of critical media studies has helped add valuable new emphasis to my project. Erica's editorial guidance was always astute and her encouragement inspiring. April Leo perceptively and efficiently handled the production process.

Introduction: A Man for All Media

Few twentieth-century artists have achieved renown in such a variety of media as Orson Welles. If we consider first, as most do, his work in film then the renown is threefold: director, actor, writer. Major creative outpourings are also a result of his involvement in theater and radio. Noteworthy minor contributions mark his forays into sound recording and television. And all this from someone who seriously contemplated becoming a painter, co-wrote *Everybody's Shakespeare* at eighteen, and had a lifelong career as a stage magician. A learned commentator, let us call him or her critic X (since the observation has no doubt been made independently several times), once noted with reference to artist Y, that Y's major achievement is his or her reputation. Well, for Orson, that too.

Needless to say there is no shortage of biographies. And, although there is no book-length autobiography, we do have a comprehensive volume of interviews conducted by Peter Bogdanovich, who has a knack for asking perceptive questions. Nevertheless, we are still not ready to declare "that's a wrap" to our assessment of the legacy of this multimedia legend. At least one chapter remains unfinished: radio.

No Welles commentator has failed to mention its importance, yet none have placed it center stage as they have with film or theater. This is understandable. Welles's movies are bigger. They combine a high art aesthetic with the entertainment conventions of popular culture and endure in regularly accessible formats. Theater, his first love, although more elusive than radio (since performances are not usually recorded), is usually privileged above it artistically in assessments of his work.

Even in the field of radio studies, important recent works, such as Susan Douglas's *Listening In* and Gerald Nachman's *Raised on Radio*, while readily acknowledging Welles's broadcast legacy as significant, give it only fleeting consideration apart from the obligatory assessment of his *War of the Worlds* broadcast. Michele Hilmes's *Radio Voices: American Broadcasting, 1922–1952* goes somewhat further. It contains a perceptive ten-page section on Welles, replete with a plea for a fuller assessment of his radio career, one that the present study endeavors to answer.

In making a case for radio, my contention is simple and I hope suggestive. From 1934 through 1952, as an innovator and personality, Welles had an impact on broadcast radio as great as the one he exerted on film and theater, an observation he made himself on several occasions. This career can be seen as being composed of four phases, which subsequent chapters explore: the first, 1934–1938, saw him make the transition from an anonymous voice to a rising star; the second, 1938–1940, is comprised of the CBS years, in which his *Mercury Theatre on the Air* and *Campbell Playhouse* set new standards for radio drama; the third phase encompasses the diverse array of broadcasts he did during, and on behalf of, the war effort; and finally we have his sporadic postwar output in the United States, later augmented by work in two British-based syndicated series.

Numbers often prove little, yet it is worth pondering how many years it took for the audience who saw his most famous film, *Citizen Kane* (1941), to equal the listenership of even one episode of the *Mercury Theatre on the Air*, *Campbell Playhouse*, or *The Adventures of Harry Lime*. Hilmes is of a like mind with respect to the influence of radio as a whole when she declares that it has far exceeded what most media commentators would lead us to believe.

Today, of course, classical radio does seem an ephemeral medium for the public at large—despite the many taped broadcasts now available, especially on the Internet, to collectors—while film has become *the* art form of the past one hundred years and Welles one of its greatest practitioners. Yet even here there is radio. Conventions he employed in sound broadcasting profoundly influenced his cinema, as I try to show by assessing the feature films he made during the years in which he worked in radio.

However, what has inspired me most in writing this radio portrait is the appropriateness of Welles's genius to the medium: the unique marriage of voice and imagination. On stage he could be awkward and the audience at times unresponsive to his productions. With film he was managing a collaborative endeavor that often proved unmanageable. But on the podium for CBS, conducting and acting in a *Mercury Theatre* presentation for an invisible audience, he had a time deadline that could not be circumvented. He also had more artistic control than in any other performing art; sometimes diabolical control, as evidenced in the infamous *War of the Worlds* broadcast on 30 October 1938. My analysis of this broadcast serves as a centerpiece for this study.

A major reason why Welles was so effective on radio, and other media, was his grasp of the nature and possibilities of those media to further what he always called "the illusion of the story." The *War of the Worlds* broadcast turned radio on itself by simulating a live on-the-spot newscast, something I call *radio vérité*, complete with overlapping and awkward dialogue, microphone feedback, and those chilling moments of dead air when the Martians attack—techniques virtually unheard of in previous radio drama. Putting it in terms that media theorist Marshall McLuhan might favor, we could say that the Panic Broadcast made the medium of radio news the content in a story presented through the medium of radio drama.

My invocation of the name McLuhan in the name of Welles has another basis. In his classic work, *Understanding Media*, McLuhan discusses the Panic Broadcast as a key auditory text in revealing aspects of the nature of radio in general. Although he did not write about Welles elsewhere, conversations I have had with his son, Eric, indicate that Marshall's fascination with Orson extended even beyond the infamous radio play. It could be argued that just as McLuhan, a polymath intellectual and major figure in the media studies or media ecology tradition, understood media perhaps better than any intellectual of the twentieth century, so Welles, as a practicing artist, seemed to grasp better than any of his contemporaries how the properties of various media could be used to further his creative intentions.

This grasp of media led to the multimedia aspect of many of his productions: the unusual lighting and use of African drummers in his Voodoo *Macbeth*; the radio-inspired use of loudspeakers positioned in various parts of the theater (early surround sound) in his production of Marlowe's *Faust*; and of course, the use of radio-inspired sound, along with elements of painting and photography, in *Citizen Kane*.

If Welles can be seen as a media theorist by way of his artistic practice, he can also be seen as a critical media theorist. Throughout his life he was a strident advocate for social justice, speaking out regularly against racism, anti-Semitism, and fascism. He would do this allegorically in his stage and radio plays, and directly in print and radio editorials. Although never a socialist per se, he was pro-labor, a strong supporter of Roosevelt's New Deal, and a critic of monopoly capitalism (an implicit theme in *Citizen Kane*). As Howard Blue points out in his excellent study, *Words at War: World War II Era Radio and the Postwar Broadcasting Industry Blacklist*, an FBI file was opened on Welles in 1942 and his name would appear later on several blacklists. One surprising and unsettling aspect of my archival research into Welles's radio career was to uncover among his papers life-threatening hate mail triggered by his political commitments.

In the pages that follow, a great variety of Welles's broadcasts are assessed—to comment on all of them would require several volumes. Some are discussed extensively, others briefly, while a few must unfortunately be passed over entirely. The criteria for those programs warranting fuller coverage are these: artistic merit and/or popular appeal. These two criteria of course sometimes converge, as in the case of *Dracula* (11 July 1938), which was Welles's *Mercury Theatre* radio debut; the *War of the Worlds*; and *A Christmas Carol* (23 December 1938 and 24 December 1939). Less an artistic than a ratings success, programs such as *Rebecca* (9 December 1938), the first broadcast in Welles's *Campbell Playhouse* series, merit assessment on that basis. On the other hand, less well-known but brilliantly conceived productions such as *Hell on Ice* (9 October 1938) are introduced to the reader.

Finally, to foreground radio while backgrounding Welles's work in theater and film is an admittedly inaccurate reflection of his artistic priorities. I beg indulgence on two counts. First, an ample biographical literature already exists showing the relevance of various parts of his artistic output to the whole (readers familiar with any of these writings might want to skip the overview of his early life outlined in the first chapter and the summaries I provide of some of his more well-known films). Second, this study is as much about radio during a time when it was our dominant mass medium as it is about this visionary artist who contributed so greatly to radio's prominence.

PART ONE

THE ROAD TO CBS

CHAPTER ONE

A Voice Is Born

He knew that he was precisely what he himself would have chosen to be had God consulted him on the subject.

—Micheál MacLiammóir

We have no record of the first words he spoke, but we do know that he spoke early and often. Verbally, Welles was a prodigy who read and recited passages from Shakespeare before he began formal schooling. He amazed all who attended him; he performed before he knew it was only one vocation among many. What Mozart did at the same age with piano and violin, Welles did with an instrument that has elicited endless adjectives and enduring awe: his voice.

An extraordinary configuration of DNA must have underscored such precociousness, but the circumstances that fueled and tapped this potential were no less important. A host of biographers have made much of the push and pull exerted on his psyche by an unusual family life in the Midwest, the personalities and intrigues rivaling anything in the novels of Booth Tarkington (one of his favorite authors). However, in this brief background chapter for a book primarily about radio, my main concern with Welles's early years resides in a different but related area: what he experienced and accomplished during this time that would influence his ability to conjure effective ways of storytelling in various media, especially radio.

George Orson Welles (1915–1985) was born on 6 May in Kenosha, Wisconsin, to Richard Head Welles and Beatrice Ives. Richard was an inventor and entrepreneur, prone to the bottle and the boudoir, who mended his ways temporarily when he married Beatrice. If Orson's father opened him to worldliness and opportunism, his mother exposed him to the arts with such insistence that he became an aesthete while still in short pants. By all accounts she was a skilled pianist who gave up full-time concertizing for marriage and family. Although more of a disciplinarian than Richard, she always insisted on the best for young Orson, socially and culturally. An ardent suffragette and effective public speaker on a variety of topics, she sometimes invited him to hear her perform. He basked in her eloquence, and absorbed it. By the age of two he was speaking in complete sentences and astonishing adults with how he could converse with them.

Whether entertaining at the family home in Kenosha, or attending a soirée in nearby Chicago, the Welles family surrounded themselves with celebrities and patrons from the performing arts. Yet, of all the artistic influences on his childhood, perhaps none was more profound than his mother teaching him what French literary critic Roland Barthes would later call the "pleasure of the text." She read to Orson regularly and taught him to read before he began formal schooling. The works that her lyrical voice imparted to him were not lightweight fare. Shakespeare was central, first in the form of condensed adaptations, which he quickly eschewed in favor of the real thing. Captivated by hearing these texts he yearned to read them on his own. To facilitate his acquisition of literacy at such a high level, Beatrice gave him Shakespeare's *A Midsummer Night's Dream* for his third birthday. The Bard would exert more influence on his later careers than any other figure. Welles would go on to co-write a students' introduction to the plays, perform in and produce them for the stage, radio, and television, and direct and star in three notable film adaptations, *Macbeth* (1948), *Othello* (1952), and *Chimes at Midnight* (1966).

The young Welles also received inspiration at this time from an unusual interloper to the household, Dr. Maurice Bernstein. He was a charming and intense young osteopath exiled from Chicago medical circles for physically attacking a colleague. His fascination with Beatrice soon extended to Orson. The precocious child's artistic bent inspired him to encourage it with gifts. He gave Orson a violin at age three. It was an experiment that at least proved Orson was not Mozart reincarnated. A conductor's baton soon followed. As Orson mounted a makeshift podium and waved it in time to recordings of classical music, the seeds of his later directorial talents began to sprout—in photographs of him taken twenty years later, during broadcasts of his *Mercury Theatre on the Air* and *Campbell Playhouse* at CBS, we see him standing on a podium, arms raised in the manner of a symphonic conductor. A set of oil paints and canvases soon followed and so enthralled Orson that for a time during his adolescence he gave thought to a career at the easel; a glimpse of how far advanced the modern European masters were relative to his own skills would eventually nix that idea. Painting, in any case, would remain a lifelong passion. A posthumously published collection of his watercolors, *Les Bravades* (1996), although somewhat lacking in originality, reveals a fine eye and an identifiable style.

Other gifts included a magic set and a puppet theater. With the former he relished conjuring and beguiling an audience through illusion—magic would become a lifelong stage vocation as well as a metaphor underscoring his work in virtually every medium. With the puppet theater, he became producer, director, actor, set designer, and by the age of four, writer, since he was scripting original story ideas. These creative forays helped the young prodigy create imaginative spaces that linked what he experienced in life with what he was learning through literature and history.

During this time Beatrice and Richard quarreled often and, shortly after the family moved to Chicago in 1918, they began the first of several separations. Bernstein, although not the cause, was a major catalyst. Relocating in Chicago gave mother and son, and whatever Bernstein was becoming to them, more frequent access to the artistic circles they enjoyed. During a trip to New York orchestrated by Bernstein to attend a Stravinsky concert, Orson managed to immerse himself in conversation about the music with a group of people in a lounge at the Waldorf Hotel. An attractive brunette in her mid-teens, aspiring to a career in theater, found his company a delight and his person unforgettable. She was Agnes Moorehead.[1] The two would meet again in the same city fifteen years later and engage in numerous radio collaborations—she would become "the lovely Margot Lane," his companion in *The Shadow*. They would reunite in Hollywood as well, where "Aggie" would begin an illustrious film career with appearances in *Citizen Kane* and *The Magnificent Ambersons* (1942).

When he was with Beatrice, home had been all things to Orson. Following her untimely death in 1924 from hepatitis when Orson was nine years old, he was passed around among relatives and friends to assuage his grief. He then spent several months with *both* Richard and Bernstein in a house they had rented in Chicago. They decided he should now attend public school, which he did in Madison, living with the family of a psychologist friend of Bernstein's who would have the chance to observe a boy genius at close quarters.

The experiment failed on both fronts. Although Orson learned a few things by attending public school, he also preached about the inadequacies of the system to any and all within earshot. He may have acted belligerently, but not out of malice. For those not directly in his line of fire there must have been a certain charm to it all. The media took note, and on 19 February 1926, *The Madison Journal* ran an article on the wunderkind: "Cartoonist, Actor, Poet, and only Ten." This account of his exploits seems exaggerated—how could any summary of such activities by a ten-year-old *not* make him seem larger than life?—but it is for the most part factual. The article is a landmark bit of memorabilia in the archival material pertaining to his early life, charting the first eruption of his persona beyond the circle of his family and their acquaintances; it may have also given him an early awareness that his ideas could reach an audience beyond that milieu. As for boarding with the psychologist, the man's more than academic interest in the boy led Orson to flee back to Bernstein in Chicago.[2]

The next step again found Richard Welles and Bernstein in accord. Orson would be sent to the Todd School in Woodstock, Illinois, about fifty miles outside of Chicago. Richard Jr., Orson's elder brother by ten years and only sibling, had gone there, although he had been expelled for unruly behavior.[3] The school, although not a perfect match for Orson's sundry talents, was perhaps the best of all educational worlds available to him, since it had a reputation as a progressive institution. However, the key ingredient that made Todd work for him was its headmaster, Roger "Skipper" Hill, who had inherited the position from his more austere father. He became mentor, confidant, and as it turned out, a lifelong friend, and he survived Orson by several years.

Hill was a rare blend of noble gentility and earthy pragmatism. He accepted the boy's commitments and encouraged him to pursue them further, especially theater and all things pertaining to it. As a result Orson virtually commandeered the drama program at Todd. When he found the reigning curriculum too lightweight he began injecting liberal doses of Shakespeare. He also performed in the occasional musical review. However, even before he began these activities he was beguiling the boys in his dormitory with nightly storytelling sessions. Many of his tales were ghostly and terrifying. All were delivered with dramaturgical gusto—a harbinger of the Shadow persona he would bring to radio.

Terror of a sort also came to Orson on 28 December 1930. On that date Richard Welles was found dead in Grand Detour. Bernstein was called in to issue the certificate. The cause was listed as heart and kidney failure. In later years, Welles would suspect suicide. On one level he knew that Richard's death probably resulted from the protracted taking of one's life that can result from acute alcoholism. Nevertheless, he felt he was partly to blame; if only he had been more attentive to his father in the months leading up to Richard's demise.[4]

With this personal loss, the Todd School, now more than ever, became for Orson a refuge as well as a kingdom. Protected from the vicissitudes of a tumultuous decade, he immersed himself in his artistic interests. Most of them involved the past. The dramas he acted in and directed were never contemporary, and his reading focused mostly on the classics. He spoke and wrote using a discourse imbued with late Victorian and Edwardian phrases and seemed disinterested in the popular culture of his day. Although the arts curriculum he pursued was theatrically focused, it did have other dimensions. Being a financially well-endowed institution, Todd provided students with access to a small radio station. As a result, Orson acted in a Sherlock Holmes radio play that he also scripted.[5] A decade later he would reprise the experience for CBS. We can only wonder what the young teenager thought about the medium and whether he sensed it was on the threshold of becoming a major entertainment forum.

Graduating from Todd as Welles did in 1931 left those leaving suspended between two academic worlds. Todd only went up to the tenth grade. Skipper's father, Noble Hill, wanted the school to be a unique but not a terminal educational experience. Two years at another institution, public or private, were necessary to achieve high school matriculation. For most of the boys a good prep school would follow and ease their transition into university, but it did seem possible that Orson's extraordinary achievements at Todd might allow him to bypass the remainder of secondary school and enter university directly. Skipper thought Harvard might be willing to accept him, since it had a strong concentration in theater arts. Bernstein pinned his hopes on Cornell and Orson's possible entrance into a more rounded program of studies. The boy felt otherwise. He wanted to work in theater, not study it in a classroom. His performances at Todd had been noticed. Prominent people in the field, such as Whitford Kane, director of Chicago's Goodman Memorial Theater, had offered encouragement; Welles would later reciprocate by using the name Kane for the lead character and in the title of his first film.

Hoping to thwart Welles's desire to rush headlong into an uncertain theatrical career, a compromise emerged. He would take a break and travel to Europe—Bernstein suggested Paris but was not averse to Orson's notion that Ireland and Scotland might be equally rewarding. Ostensibly this would be a pleasure trip, a chance to sightsee, paint, and keep a diary. Bernstein no doubt hoped it would take the boy's mind off theater for a while and maybe instill in him a desire for further education. Orson, cunning as ever, knew that somehow, some way, he would find thespian niches on those far shores. When he landed in Galway that summer he was quite content to do what today would be the equivalent of a backpacking and youth hostel tour.

The backpack contained, in addition to the requisite survival gear, painting paraphernalia, notebooks, and a recently acquired guide to the region, *Field and Fair: Travels with a Donkey in Ireland* by Cormach Dreathnach. Orson soon purchased a donkey cart for himself and set off on his own Celtic odyssey. He slept where he could, in inns, homes, and at times under the stars. His writing consisted of letters home, which both Bernstein and Hill copied and circulated. He was unsatisfied with his paintings, but on occasion they were good enough to exchange for food and lodging. There was spiritual comfort in the journey. Fortunately, he was at ease meeting people, perhaps because he had usually impressed them enough to get his way. Also, the situation of being a stranger in a strange land was one he had prepared for by having traveled extensively with his father. But as summer ceded to fall, the chilly and sometimes wet evenings on the road became obvious. He had done his rustic thing. It was time for the city—for local culture to give way to high culture. Dublin loomed, and therein the Abbey and Gate theaters.

He chose the Gate. More precisely, he decided to spend a precious part of his dwindling funds to attend a performance there, since on his travels he had befriended a young man, Cathral O'Callaigh, who was part of the company. The play was Edward the Earl of Langford's *The Melians*. It was not particularly memorable, nor was the acting, but what happened in the aftermath was. Welles connected with his friend backstage, and then by chance or (more likely) by design, briefly met the Gate's founders, Micheál MacLiammóir and Hilton Edwards. Three years earlier they had been drawn together by a passion for the theater and each other. They decided to establish the Gate as an alternative to the Abbey. The new theater was to be more eclectic and less nationalistic in its repertoire. Edwards concentrated on producing, while MacLiammóir became the resident star. It did not take Orson long to decide that he wanted in. The next morning he re-encountered Edwards, whose reaction is recorded in MacLiammóir's autobiography: "Somebody strange has arrived from America; come see what you think of it." When Micheál queried, "What is it?" Hilton replied:

> Tall, young, fat: says he's been with the Guild Theater in New York. Don't believe a word of it, but he's interesting. I want to give him an audition. Says he's been in Connemara with a donkey, and I don't see what that's got to do with me. Come and have a look at him.[6]

MacLiammóir's subsequent description took in Orson's large physical stature, his "disconcerting Chinese eyes," and that inimitable voice "with its brazen transatlantic sonority." It was, he wrote, the voice of "a preacher, a leader of men, of power," which "boomed and boomed its way through the dusty air as though it would crush the little Georgian walls and rip up the floor."[7] Welles, who was learning to make a specialty of first impressions, pulled out all stops on this occasion. Brazen and audacious, he also knew when to be respectful. His hosts were impressed, but wary. When he told them he was eighteen, adding two years to his actual age, it may have been the only thing he claimed that they believed. He was simply too full of bluster to be taken at face value; yet too unique to be dismissed. They gave him an audition.

By their standards he was still an amateur, and although a risk, one they deemed worth taking. He was cast as Duke Karl Alexander, the anti-Semitic aristocrat in *Jew Süs*, Ashley Dukes's adaptation of the Lion Feuchtwanger novel. It was a major role, especially for a debut. Fortunately, because it was a villainous one, the characteristic Welles tendency to overact worked to his advantage. The audience despised the character—Welles could always play the heavy—and transposed this into an appreciation of the performance. The kid's panache also impressed. When, during the suicide scene, he could not pull his sword from its scabbard and then compounded the embarrassment by flubbing his lines, he improvised a new end for the Duke by flinging himself down a flight of steps. The audience was ecstatic. Looking back at that night decades later, he remarked: "I had *all* the applause I needed for my life, I got more acclaim for that than *anything* I've done since."[8]

The performance was both more and less than MacLiammóir expected: "wrong from beginning to end but with all the qualities of fine acting tearing their way through the chaos of inexperience." He conceded that although the diction was remarkable, there was considerable overacting. Yet amid the bravura, MacLiammóir sensed authenticity. The following comment is one of the most telling ever written about Welles's acting:

> One wanted to say, "now, now, *really* you know," but something stopped the words from coming. And that is because he was real to himself, because it was something more to him than a show, more than the mere inflated exhibitionism one might have expected from his previous talk, something much more.[9]

Reviews of his performance were also favorable and he was an asset to the company in other ways. He could do public relations, paint sets, and deliver great lines off-stage as well as on, making him instant entertainment at any social gathering. Other, mostly minor roles followed in which he showed a decided penchant for exotic character parts. These became convincing early examples of the myriad exotic voices he would bring to the stage, radio, film, and television. Nowhere would this potential be more manifest than on radio. Not having to look the part he was acting gave him more latitude in character than he would have in the other performing arts, where his physical stature might preclude roles he could easily vocalize. He finished the season at the Gate to positive notices. True, the roles had gotten smaller, but they were still significant—his ghost in Hamlet drew much praise.

Returning stateside in March 1933, he stopped off first in New York, excited by the prospect of entering the world of Broadway theater as easily as he had accessed the Gate in Dublin. With all those favorable reviews of his work in Ireland, including one in the *New York Times*, doors would surely open—as it turned out, not even enough for him to get his foot in them. He could have persisted, but now was not the time. Home beckoned, and that meant returning to Todd and the Hill family. Skipper, supportive as always, hired him as the school drama coach. With his life as a stage actor on hold, he also used the hiatus to write. He decided, with Skipper's encouragement (and help), and over Bernstein's insistence that he should be thinking about college, to draft a play. This proved almost as difficult as landing a role on the New York stage, but he persevered; at least here he had some semblance of control over his fate.

The subject matter came easily. He had always been fascinated by the life of John Brown, and while at Todd had researched the historical circumstances of the notorious abolitionist. A large part of the script was written on the Ojibway reservation in Lac Flambeau, Wisconsin . . . in a wigwam. Yes, Orson in a wigwam, and a year earlier on the Irish roads in a donkey cart. These scenarios are hard to imagine in contrast to the four-star hotels and *dolce vita* of his later years. Nevertheless, popular images of Welles the gourmand and bon vivant should not mislead. Although he may have spent extravagantly on his immediate personal pleasures, very little went toward acquiring things, and no major director has ever put as much of his own finances into his films.

The John Brown play, eventually titled *Marching Song*, is a sprawling and ambitious effort. Parts of it shine, but ultimately the whole is less than the sum of those parts. He hoped it would wind up on Broadway and went there to flog it to producers, but without success. It was eventually performed at Todd forty years later without Welles's participation. The most intriguing thing about the play in retrospect is not what it is, but where the ideas in it would lead. Barbara Leaming has highlighted some similarities in conception between *Marching Song* and *Citizen Kane*, a film where Welles's input on the screenplay has been called into question.[10] In both stories we have an inquisitive journalist trying to piece together the life of an enigmatic headline maker; in both, the investigator gleans a variety of accounts about his subject, some of them conflicting.

Frustrated by the failure of *Marching Song* to find a producer, Welles, the aspiring playwright, nevertheless aspired again. He started, but never seems to have completed, a commercial potboiler called *Dark Room*, but soon shifted his energy to a shorter and exceedingly unusual piece, *Bright Lucifer*. Set in a lonely cabin on an Indian reserve, it begins as Gothic melodrama gone primitive, and then mutates into a scenario of ghoulish horror worthy of Stephen King. The play is risqué, even by today's standards. It has references to child homosexuality, incest, and necrophilia, and is imbued with what we would now label "coarse language." Still, Welles tried to have it produced, revising and submitting the manuscript over a several year period. There were, understandably, no takers . . . until the fall of 1997, when the Madison Community Theater staged it. The producer-director Jay Wrath, when interviewed on CBC radio, admitted the play was "corny" but that it provided insights into Welles's life and was accompanied by fascinating stage directions.[11] From these stage directions he concluded that the play might be more effective if performed on radio and hoped to mount such a production in the near future.

It is also worth noting that Welles himself would eventually bring Gothic horror to the airwaves with his version of Bram Stoker's *Dracula* on 18 July 1938, the debut broadcast of his Mercury company. In listening to that performance, and reading the stage directions to *Bright Lucifer*, the connections indicate he had an ear for the medium before he even entered a sound studio. The same auditory richness also characterizes the script of *Marching Song*, with its military music, sound effects, and multilayered dialogue—a period evocation he would reprise on radio with the *Mercury Theatre* presentation of John Drinkwater's *Abraham Lincoln* (15 August 1938). These early efforts at play writing also tells us about the nature and limits of Welles's artistic genius: that creating compellingly original story ideas would not be his forte. His greatness as an artist lay in adaptation, in interpreting the work of others. With his Mercury cohorts he would transform one type of theater into another; on radio he made novels and short stories come alive; and in cinema, he was able to create both great films from great literature, as he did with Shakespeare, and a great film, like *Touch of Evil* (1958), from a work of pulp fiction, Whit Masterson's *Badge of Evil*.

Writing plays was not the only writing he did during this in-between period in his life. Given his interest in Shakespeare and a more than passable publishing setup at his alma mater, the Todd Press, a new project emerged. It would be called *Everybody's Shakespeare* and co-authored with Skipper Hill.

The idea was simple and timely: reprint several of the plays with staging directions. The books would also include a general introduction on the relevance of Shakespeare written by Hill, along with a collaborative essay on each play accompanied by Welles's illustrations. What resulted was the same general essay for each volume with Welles's drawings only implying how the plays should be staged.

The first installment, *Twelfth Night*, was soon followed by *The Merchant of Venice* and *Julius Caesar*. In 1934 Harper and Brothers brought out the three volumes in a single edition. The book sold steadily if not spectacularly. In 1939, Welles's notoriety prompted Harper to republish it as *The Mercury Shakespeare*. A year later a related project, the Mercury Text Records, was released as part of the Columbia Masterworks series. They contained the same three plays as the book. What a boon to educators this multimedia concept must have been.

These projects led Welles to think of himself more as a writer rather than an actor. And that is how he introduced himself to Thornton Wilder at a party in Chicago in the early autumn of 1933. Wilder, not yet forty, was a novelist and playwright whose star was ascending. After they conversed for a while, he asked "the writer" if he was also Orson Welles "the actor"?[12] Welles was surprised that someone so renowned would have heard of his exploits, but Wilder had not only read the *New York Times* reviews of the Gate Theatre, he had corresponded with people who had mentioned the promising young thespian. The future author of *Our Town* then took Welles out on *the* town. Wilder was impressed enough to give Welles a list of theater names that he would contact on Orson's behalf and advised him to get on the next train to New York.

One name led to another. His first meeting was with Alexander Woollcott, an Algonquin Round Table founder, literary critic, and radio personality. His show, *The Town Crier*, featured literary reviews interspersed with anecdotes. It was popular with a wide audience and de rigueur for anyone in or aspiring to café society. To say the hugely overweight, androgynous, and squeaky-voiced Woollcott—he resembled a learned eunuch—was a character is an understatement. No doubt he thought the same of Welles; he also believed there was enough talent to fuel the ambition. And that voice, how it enthralled Woollcott: dark, resonant, authoritative; quite the opposite of his own. Through Woollcott, Welles connected with theatrical producer-director Guthrie McClintic and his wife the noted actress Katherine Cornell. After giving him the once over, followed by a brief audition, they made him a member of their company. He began his stint by playing Mercutio in *Romeo and Juliet* in Buffalo.

McClintic and Cornell took the train to New York and Welles joined them there in December, after having spent the summer organizing a drama festival at Todd which saw him arrange for the participation of Micheál MacLiammóir and Hilton Edwards, and then meet and later marry (that November) Virginia Nicolson. The company opened with their road-tested version of *Romeo and Juliet*. One minor change was in effect. Mercutio would be played by Brian Aherne, with Welles reassigned (he believed demoted) to the lesser role of Tybalt, although he also got to voice the chorus. This was supposedly done to ensure that in later productions Aherne would agree to play certain roles for which he was particularly well suited. The play was well received. As Tybalt, Orson attracted a modicum of notice, but he clearly wanted to be in the media shower that descended on Aherne, Basil Rathbone (Romeo), and Kit Cornell (Juliet). His performance was noticed, however, by someone who would exert far more influence over his artistic life than New York theater critics.

In the audience opening night was John Houseman (née Haussmann), an urbane multilingual émigré from Romania via England. Today we know him primarily for his Academy Award–winning performance in *The Paper Chase* (1973), which was his acting debut at age seventy. When he saw Welles play Tybalt, Houseman was just starting out as a theatrical producer-director after a successful but uninspiring sojourn in the business world. A few months earlier he had mounted, to much acclaim, *Four Saints in Three Acts*, an experimental modernist opera composed by Virgil Thompson with a libretto by Gertrude Stein.

Houseman enjoyed the McClintic-Cornell rendering of a play he knew well. Nothing about it seemed exceptional or out of the ordinary . . . until

> the furious Tybalt appeared in that sunlit Verona square: death, in scarlet and black, in the form a monstrous boy—flat-footed and graceless, yet swift and agile; soft as jelly one moment and uncoiled the next, in a spring of such furious energy that, once released, it could be stopped by no human intervention.[13]

He was mesmerized, not by Welles's Tybalt, but by Welles as Tybalt, and by "a voice of such clarity and power that it tore like a high wind through the genteel, modulated voices of the well-trained professionals around him."[14]

Yearning to get a closer look at the "monstrous boy," he went to the reception backstage but Welles had already left. In the days that followed, Houseman thought about him incessantly and gleaned information wherever he could regarding the legend growing around this nineteen-year-old newcomer to the New York stage. A rendezvous would occur in three weeks, but the pretext for it had been months in the making. Houseman and his partner Nathan Zatkin had just established the Phoenix Theater and agreed to produce a rather uncommercial play by the renowned poet Archibald MacLeish. Titled *Panic*, it deals with the Wall Street crash as experienced by a larger-than-life tycoon in his late fifties, McGafferty, who goes down with the market. *Panic* is a verse play with overtones of a Greek tragedy. It required a unique lead, someone physically large with a voice to match, who could also alliterate MacLeish's poetics. The part had not been cast, although Paul Muni and Alfred Lunt had been approached unsuccessfully. For Houseman, the "monstrous boy" was a deus ex machina.

They met backstage following Tybalt's exit scene and then retired to a bar. After a few drinks, Welles was told about the project and given a copy of the script along with Houseman's phone number. He called at noon the next day to say he was willing to leave the McClintic-Cornell company and throw his lot in with Houseman—for the part of McGafferty. It was one of the most important artistic decisions of his life, one destined to profoundly shape his future in both theater and radio. An audition was arranged.[15] When MacLeish saw how young Orson was, he gave a look of frustration; when he heard the voice, his jaw dropped in awe.

CHAPTER TWO

Theatrical Notoriety, Radio Anonymity

> Nothing about him encouraged any hope that he had got his comeuppance; on the contrary, the yearners for that stroke of justice must yearn even more itchingly.
>
> —Booth Tarkington, *The Magnificent Ambersons*

Panic became Welles's New York theatrical breakthrough. Written in the manner of a classical drama, it is Sophocles and Shakespeare come to Wall Street—a ticker tape tragedy. The role of McGafferty would also anticipate a persistent theme in his later films: the fall of a seemingly omnipotent patriarch. Never one to embrace contemporary plays with enthusiasm, Welles was nevertheless pleased with MacLeish's idea of using classical form to frame a twentieth-century situation. He must have also had a sympatico with the playwright who, coming from Glencoe, Illinois, was a fellow midwesterner. They would come to share a similar politics: a stridently antifascist, pro–New Deal position, which lent an ear, but nothing more, to socialism.

Although by 1935 MacLeish was a major name in poetry, having won a Pulitzer prize, *Panic* was only his second play and the first to be produced. Houseman, knowing there could be no guarantees in staging such a production, arranged only three performances. This would keep costs down, since no major profit was expected in any case. It would also allow his Phoenix Theater to briefly borrow the services of excellent actors (for twenty-five speaking parts and a chorus of twenty-three) and a skilled production crew, some of whom volunteered their services gratis, for the arty venture. Directing this "monster on a shoestring," as Houseman called it, proved so daunting that he passed the reins to Janet Light and concentrated on production and promotion.[1] Perhaps he also feared the reputation of his "monstrous boy," well founded, for terrorizing rehearsals. Welles, however, with his first Broadway lead at stake, was courteous, helpful, and for one of the rare times in his theatrical career, punctual.

The three performances played to entirely different audiences. The first was staged for subscribers and friends of the cast, who were appreciative but not overwhelmed. The second performance, the official opening on 15 March, played to those who could afford the $5.50 admission price. A half-full theater of well-heeled socialites did not appreciate the play's glimpse of capitalist misdeeds. The final presentation was to a leftist audience. The magazines *New Theater* and *New Masses* sponsored the production and arranged a debate, cum interrogation, with MacLeish after the final curtain. Reaction to the play was enthusiastic. The subsequent exchange pitted the Marxist notion that the Wall Street crash was the result of inexorable historical laws heralding the collapse of capitalism against MacLeish's view that it derived from excessive greed and a failure of will. The Left had come hoping to enlist him in their ranks; they departed with the realization that, although sympathetic to their cause, he was still his own man.

Those in the theatrical know found the text of the play stilted. McGafferty was held to be rather one-dimensional as he sees his world collapsing and is abandoned by a previously devoted legion of capitalist lieutenants. "It's every man for himself in a sea, McGafferty," one of them shouts. MacLeish suggests that if they had more resolve the catastrophic tide that eventually sweeps McGafferty out of an office window—a little too quickly for some critics—could have been stemmed.[2] If the story enthralled neither the majority of the audience nor professional commentators, the production values and the performances did. The expressionistic lighting, which anticipated what Welles would employ on Broadway with *Caesar* and in Hollywood with *Citizen Kane*, along with the stark but effective sets and diverse sound effects, created a compelling atmosphere. And his performance, if not lauded as brilliant, was seen both as convincing and the harbinger of an important new theatrical voice.

If MacLeish's plays were less than stellar as material for the stage, the poetic and auditory aspects they embodied would make for effective radio drama. Two years later Welles would again be involved, when he starred in *The Fall of the City* for the *Columbia Workshop*. By that time he had become an experienced radio performer. How and when he got his start in the medium is not altogether clear, but it appears to have occurred around the time of *Panic*, and in anonymity.

According to Welles, his broadcasting career began as a result of the encouragement and recommendations of Paul Stewart, who would later be an integral part of the *Mercury Theatre on the Air*.[3] Before he encountered Stewart, Welles was aware that there was money, if not notoriety, to be earned on radio. He turned up for auditions regularly. That he was unsuccessful at first seems remarkable, since his talent and voice seem, and must have seemed even then, so suited to the medium—who could have beaten him out for a part? Finally, with Stewart's help, he landed a role on NBC's *Cavalcade of America*, a Sunday night show sponsored by Du Pont, which dramatized key events in American history. He claimed, in an interview with Peter Bogdanovich, that he debuted with a rather unflattering portrait of John D. Rockefeller, which displeased the sponsor and set back his radio career.[4] If it did it was only briefly, since for the next several years he would be invited back to do the show on a fairly regular basis.

Welles also mentions appearing on a sustaining program (an unsponsored, network-funded show) around the same time called *School of the Air of the Americas*, also known as *The American School of the Air*. According to that meticulous chronicler of Welles's career, Jonathan Rosenbaum, an episode of this program broadcast in 1934 was in fact Welles's radio debut, made possible by the redoubtable Paul Stewart who introduced him to the director, Knowles Entrikin.[5] This CBS offering, as the name suggests, was educational radio. It served up dramatizations from history, literature, and current events, which were piped into classrooms run by more enterprising educators. The pay was $18.50 per episode and Welles lined up regularly with numerous out-of-work actors hoping to get a call. One of them was Joseph Cotten.

Cotten first encountered Welles when the two of them were waiting to rehearse an episode of the program and Welles accidentally set fire to Director Entrikin's wastebasket with his pipe ashes. During their ensuing conversation, Welles asked Cotten, ten years his senior, about the New York stage; and "Jo," as it turned out, was curious about Orson. In his autobiography Cotten says that he impressed Welles with the fact that he had read Orson's *Everybody's Shakespeare* the previous year.[6] The rehearsal in question was for a program about colonial Africa. Both men came down with a serious case of the giggles every time the line "barrels and barrels of pith" was uttered. Entrikin took a dim view of these schoolboy shenanigans. Not oblivious to their talents, he would continue to hire the two of them, but they would never again appear together on the same episode of the program. Separated on the broadcasts, they would nevertheless meet together often after hours. Although of opposite temperaments, each saw in the other complementary qualities.[7] Before emerging as a major star in his own right, Cotten would do important work for Welles in theater, radio, and film.

Entrikin also employed Welles's services in another documentary series dealing with national history and culture, *America's Hour*. However, the biggest radio coup Welles landed at this time, again as an anonymous voice, was *The March of Time*. It was an unusual program, born during a period when radio was both beginning to present live drama and testing the waters as a news medium. *The March of Time* took major news stories and, using anonymous actors to portray the figures in question, attempted a condensed recreation of events. The program originated with this name and format on CBS in 1931, but the idea had begun in 1928 when Roy Edward Larsen, a manager at *Time* magazine, teamed up with radio executive Fred Smith to create a ten-minute weekly offering called *Newscasting*.[8] Ostensibly it was a dramatic reading of news stories drawn from *Time*. Within a year the program underwent a name change to *Newsacting*, expanded to fifteen minutes, and began doing dramatic recreations of the material using actors and sound effects. The show was syndicated to over one hundred stations and financed by the czar of *Time*, Henry Luce.

Larsen and Smith, however, were convinced that their modestly successful venture had even greater potential and decided to pitch it as a half-hour weekly series to CBS. They changed the name to *The March of Time*, after the Harold Arlen tune, and in turn adopted the piece as a musical signature. A powerful narrator was thought essential to the show, with his commentaries highlighted by the soon to be legendary phrase, "Time—Marches On!" The enthusiasm Larsen and Smith showed over their program was not shared by the network, which did not quite know how it fit in with traditional radio genres. Several executives at *Time* were also uncomfortable with sensationalism done in the name of their magazine. Despite these reservations the program got qualified approval, along with sponsorship money from *Time*, and went on the air on 6 March 1931.[9]

The March of Time enjoyed a modicum of popularity, and was born at a time when radio as a whole began challenging the domination of news reporting traditionally exerted by print. But Luce soon felt that the near half-million *Time* subscribers should not have to pay for raising the cachet of a medium he perceived as a serious rival. With the withdrawal of its sponsor, the show was canceled in early 1932, only to be resurrected as a sustaining program that September after twenty thousand listeners sent letters to CBS asking for its return. This kind of popularity soon drew other sponsors, such as Remington Rand and then Wrigley's, in doubtlessly one of the first instances whereby a sponsor gave free publicity to another company, in this case one whose very name, *Time*, was in the title of their show. In any case, in late 1933 Luce, perhaps realizing that radio no longer posed a threat, at least to his news magazines, came back on board.[10]

The March of Time, which initially aired one to three times a week, shifted to a five times per week, fifteen minutes per episode format during the 1935–1936 season. It was on 22 March 1935 that Welles made his debut on the show. He performed a short excerpt from *Panic*, and then, according to legend, volunteered his services for the baby babble of all five Dionne quintuplets when the actor scheduled to do it canceled.[11] During the 1937–1938 season, the program moved to NBC and returned to its once weekly format. Most of the surviving examples of Welles's work on the series, now ensconced in the Museum of Television and Radio in New York and Los Angeles, date from this period. The series went off the air from 1939 to 1941, owing to restrictions on what could be broadcast during the outbreak of war in Europe, but it returned in October 1941 with more direct news reporting and less drama. During its last season, 1944–1945, *The March of Time* aired on the fledgling ABC network, which the FCC (Federal Communications Commission) had created by forcing NBC to divest itself of one of its two network divisions, the Red and the Blue. The Blue became ABC, and *The March of Time* had the rare distinction of being a program that had appeared on all three major networks.

The March of Time on radio is perhaps less well known than its movie alter ego, which was a newsreel that ran from 1935 to 1951 as a ten-minute filler between segments of double features.[12] It had several forerunners and rivals such as Fox's *Movietone News* and the *Hearst Metrotone News*, but distinguished itself from them by providing more context and commentary on its stories. The newsreel version of *The March of Time* did not feature dramatizations, but sometimes clips of places other than the one in the story were used when location footage was unavailable; and occasionally events were restaged with either the original participants or their likenesses. What both the radio and film versions of *The March of Time* featured was the "Voice of Time," also known as the "Voice of Doom," Westbrook van Voorhis, who on radio had succeeded Ted Husing and Harry von Zell. He spoke in what was sometimes called "Timespeak" or "Time-ese," a relentless, breathless, and apocalyptic tone of voice—in a given segment bombs might be dropping on cities, but never van Voorhis's voice at the end of a sentence.

A brilliant send-up of the newsreel was done by Welles in the "News on the March" sequence that comes near the beginning of *Citizen Kane*. Knowing van Voorhis from radio, Welles sought his services for the experiment. When the Voice of Time's fee turned out to be prohibitive, Mercury Theatre stalwart William Alland did the voice-over, and brilliantly, right down to the type of word reversals, "Legendary was Xanadu," that were a van Voorhis trademark. In the 28 November 1936 issue of the *New Yorker* Wolcott Gibbs parodied the style: "Backward ran sentences until reeled the mind. . . . Where it will all end, knows God."

The March of Time may appear hokey today, but it was an important episode in the history of radio. Broadcast historian Erik Barnouw credits it with helping define radio's news niche as something distinct from the journalistic formats of print.[13] Few expenses were spared in staging each episode, which would often have a production staff of up to seventy-five, an orchestra, and employ the services of some of New York's finest actors. Welles always had a fond regard and respect for the show. It doubtlessly appealed to his love of dramatic improvisation and odd character roles. Reminiscing about the program with Peter Bogdanovich, Welles observed, "It was a marvelous show to do. Great fun, because half an hour after something happened, we'd be acting it out with music and sound effects and actors. It was a super show—terribly entertaining."[14] The program also introduced him to some fine actors, such as Martin Gabel, Agnes Moorehead (whom he had met informally fifteen years before), and Ray Collins, who would later become a part of his *Mercury Theatre* ensemble.

Over the next two years his appearances on *The March of Time* would be numerous, but they are not easy to identify in those episodes that have survived. In March 1938 he was particularly busy. Among his dozen-plus portrayals he did Leopold Stokowski, rumored to be betrothed to Greta Garbo, who, unbeknown to listeners, played herself; Sigmund Freud, distressed by the Nazi occupation of Vienna; and New York Mayor Fiorello La Guardia, declaring that the city, not the presidency, was the limit of his political ambition. For this latter role, Welles squeezed his voice up half an octave and effected a rapid-fire delivery.

Although Welles's attempts to break into radio began at about the time he began his collaboration with Houseman, the latter paid little heed to broadcasting. This is ironic, given the enormous contribution he would later make to radio as a producer and writer after he and Welles established *The Mercury Theatre on the Air*. Their relationship, following the debut collaboration of *Panic*, was the most cordial it would ever be. Much time was spent, according to Houseman, imagining the kinds of projects they might wish to collaborate on in the future, some viable, some harebrained. He recognized Welles's enormous talent and was prepared to follow and nurture it almost anywhere. Welles knew that his partner could, with rare acumen, open theatrical doors, raise money, and arrange publicity.

Their partnership, especially when it experienced a tumultuous and final ungluing five years later during the filming of *Citizen Kane*, has been much assessed by Welles biographers. Most side with Houseman. Barbara Leaming is an exception. As Welles's official conduit to posterity her ear was understandably sympathetic to her subject. She mentions that his wife Virginia was suspicious of Houseman's motives. Since Welles was the source of this information there are three possible contradictions here: first, Houseman always spoke highly of Virginia and seemed to enjoy a good working relationship with her when they were involved in the same project; second, Welles would later tell Leaming Virginia was an opportunist who latched on to him to escape small town U.S.A. and whose word was not to be trusted;[15] and finally, his animosity toward both Virginia and Houseman dates from approximately the same time, 1937–1938, the period in which he emerged as a major theatrical and radio star.

No one helped Welles break into the limelight more than Houseman and Virginia. That he turned on them, perhaps out of resentment, while being more forgiving toward his earlier supporters, Dadda Bernstein and Skipper Hill, is an issue I will let more psychologically oriented biographers ponder. Veterans of theater and radio who worked with both Houseman and Welles have remained puzzled by Orson's animosity toward John. In a 1988 audiotape, *The Mercury Company Remembers*, several of them describe the way the two men complemented one another with their differences, and how Welles's career was never the same after his final split with Houseman.[16]

In the beginning however, all was bon ami and promise. When their plans to do Marlowe's *Faustus* and John Ford's *'Tis a Pity She's a Whore* fell through because of funding setbacks, they parted amicably. The Phoenix Theater would be no more, but out of its ashes the Mercury would emerge two years later. Orson and Virginia headed to Wisconsin for the summer. He tried to write another play but mostly relaxed and contemplated possible futures. Returning to New York that fall, he found theatrical work surprisingly difficult to secure. But, as before, and now more than ever, there was radio, especially *The March of Time*.

The program had Welles doing a plethora of voices, many of them involving foreign accents. He would listen to recordings of the personalities in question, or watch film clips if available. In lieu of these resources he would conjure the voice by meditating over a picture of the person and reading whatever background material was available. Many of these voices were of people whom the average person had never heard speak, making Welles's renditions all the more convincing. He supplemented this work with appearances on CBS's *Musical Reveries*, reading poetry between musical segments. It is hard to imagine a more compelling reader of literature than Welles, a talent he may have acquired from his mother when he accompanied Beatrice on her recitals. From the Bible, through Shakespeare, Melville, and beyond, Welles would ply this talent his entire life. We find it much in evidence, for example, in the radio variety shows he did during the war. He would first entertain the audience—often composed of military personnel—with farcical sketches featuring major movie stars, then end with a trenchant literary reading that would keep everyone enthralled. A further inkling of his impressive ability in this area can be found in the documentary film *Orson Welles: The One Man Band* (1996).

Welles's early forays into radio paid the rent but promised to yield much more given the recognition he was achieving among broadcasting's insiders. Notoriety on the airwaves, however, would have to take a back seat to theatrical enterprise. Houseman was back in the picture with an offer Welles could not refuse. Houseman had just been appointed, along with the black actress Rose McLendon, as joint head of the Negro Theater Project in Harlem, a branch of the Federal Theater Project, which was in turn administered by the Works Progress Administration. The theater division was a "make work," "make culture" enterprise organized by the dynamic Hallie Flanagan, head of Vassar's Experimental Theater. She hired Houseman, and he in turn assembled a team that included composer Virgil Thomson, lighting expert Abe Feder, and Welles as artistic director. Their first assignment was to adapt a play from the classical repertoire. Welles chose *Macbeth*. To be more precise, it was Virginia who suggested what became known as the Voodoo *Macbeth*—Shakespeare's classic set in early nineteenth-century Haiti during the regime of the slave turned emperor, Jean Christophe.[17]

The play opened on 14 April 1936 and became a theatrical cause célèbre. The all-black cast performed with enthusiasm and occasional brilliance. The staging was spectacular, as was the music, which incorporated African and African American elements. Reviews were mixed but generally favorable. It was an auspicious directorial debut. Not since his days at Todd had Welles so controlled a theatrical production. If there were any doubts before, there were none now: this is what he was born to do. So committed was he to the project that when the play went on the road and Macbeth (Maurice Ellis) took sick in Indianapolis, Welles jumped on the first available flight and filled in, in blackface.[18]

Welles's Voodoo *Macbeth* also became a topic covered in a remarkable episode of *The March of Time*. Who but those in Welles's immediate circle could have realized that the anonymous actor being interviewed as Orson Welles was the self-same newsmaker? It was a media event Marshall McLuhan might have well appreciated. Reminiscing about it to Peter Bogdanovich, Welles called it "the greatest thrill of my life . . . the apotheosis of my career."[19]

Sensing that the success of the Voodoo *Macbeth* would be a phenomenon not easily repeated, Houseman and Welles beseeched Hallie Flanagan to cede more control of the Negro Theater Project to blacks, and to let the partners try another form of theater under her auspices. She consented to their proposal to do lively and accessible (artistically and financially) versions of classic plays. The partners were given the Maxine Elliot Theater on 39th Street between Broadway and 5th Avenue and called their new venture Project 891, after the number assigned to it by Washington.

On 26 September 1936, *Horse Eats Hat* became their opening production. The play was an Edward Denby–Orson Welles adaptation of the period farce, *Un Chapeau de paille d'Italie* (literally, *An Italian Straw Hat*) by Eugène Labiche and Marc-Michel. The music was composed by Paul Bowles and arranged by Virgil Thomson. Besides Welles, the large cast included his new comrade in arms, Joseph Cotten, and wife Virginia. The production might not have been experimental theater, but it was far from orthodox. Both conservatives and the Left took offense, not just to the sexual innuendo (the WPA censor asked for changes that were probably never made), but to the seemingly undisciplined staging. The action occasionally spilled over into the audience. The intermissions yielded comic activity, which although scripted, seemed spontaneous. In one scene, where stage props were supposed to be smashed, the actor also demolished part of the set, while in another, a prompter made himself obvious by arguing a cue with the actor. This transgression of traditional conventions and boundaries made the play akin to a happening, or to use that ubiquitous contemporary term, postmodern. *Horse Eats Hat* did not endear itself to traditional theater critics, but with the best seats going for fifty-five cents, a curious and often delighted public kept attending until December.

As busy as Welles was at this time, he did not let his involvement with radio suffer. Quite the opposite. *The March of Time* was experimenting with a five day per week, fifteen minutes per episode format that led to frequent calls. And, from 6 September to 11 October he did *The Wonder Show* for the Mutual Broadcasting Network. In these *Wonder Show* melodramas he both narrated and played a recurring character, the Great McCoy. The contract indicates he was to be paid $150 for the first episode, which was broadcast from New York, and $200 plus expenses for each remaining program, slated to air from Chicago.[20]

Shortly after *Horse Eats Hat* opened, and without much fanfare or later recognition regarding the significance of the debut, Welles got a chance to adapt and star in his first radio play. It was a two-part (thirty minutes each) adaptation of *Hamlet* produced by Irving Reis for an early version of his *Columbia Workshop*. It is a straightforward adaptation—more theater than radio.[21]

Project 891 followed farce with tragedy. On 8 January 1937, they began the new year with *The Tragical History of Doctor Faustus* by Christopher Marlowe. It was a complex project, filled with elements of magic and the supernatural. According to Houseman, it was the most brilliantly executed of the eight theatrical collaborations he and Welles would do together. Welles accessed his bag of tricks, literally, to make things transform, rise, and disappear. He also incorporated techniques gleaned from radio drama. Paul Bowles was instructed to compose a bizarre and otherworldly score. In so doing, he made use of odd instrument combinations, something Bernard Herrmann was pioneering at CBS in his collaborations with Irving Reis. Welles arranged for the mysterious sound effects and piercing screams that punctuate to be amplified and projected to various parts of the theater using radio loudspeakers. This gave the production the aura of a psychological thriller— *The Shadow* foreshadowed—especially given the black backdrop used in many scenes. When bright lighting was employed during a scene, for example, in the illumination of Helen of Troy or the fires of Hell, it was scintillating, and the work again of Abe Feder.

Welles not only modernized the production, he edited the text down to ninety minutes of the most salient scenes. This gave the play a universality that seemed to be enhanced, rather than offset, by the retention of Marlowe's vivid Elizabethan language. Not surprisingly, *Faustus* received mostly glowing reviews, although a few dissenters grumbled over what a government-funded production should or should not try to accomplish. The fifty-five cents or less ticket price helped ensure a remarkable four-month run, with the house averaging ninety percent. But it did not offset production costs, nor did the government money, which had to be justified with elaborate paperwork and took forever to arrive. Houseman filled in the forms as quickly and thoroughly as he could when something was needed. Welles, however, was not prepared to wait for Krishna to provide. He spent enormous amounts of his own money on the production, as he did with other Federal Theater projects: "I was the only operation in history who ever illegally siphoned money into a Washington project."[22] This personal expenditure was made possible through his work in radio. He was entering the busiest on-air period of his life, and although at the outset he was far from a household name, it was not unusual for him to pull in a thousand dollars during a given week.

To accommodate the demands of his numerous broadcasting commitments, Welles arranged for *Faustus* to start at 9:00 P.M. This allowed him to do radio shows that ended as late as a few minutes before the hour. Fortunately, the studios were not too far from the Maxine Elliot Theater, and his appearance as Faustus came several minutes after the opening chorus. On some occasions, after his immolation by Mephistopheles, Welles would leave the theater and dash back to the studio for a show being rebroadcast to the West Coast. And more often than not, he would also have a morning call for one of the educational programs.

In addition to his regular radio assignments, he did *Living Dramas of the Bible* for CBS, *Standard Brands Presents* and *Roses and Drums* for NBC, and *Parted on Her Bridal Tour* for Mutual. He also became the voice for My-T-Fine Chocolate Pudding. Most of the dramatic performances and text readings were done without rehearsal. He would often enter the studio at the last minute, receive brief instructions, and then go on the air—he was that good, as well as familiar with the auditory necessities and personnel of each studio. Some of these commitments were so close in time that traveling even a short distance through New York traffic posed a problem. It was one he solved by using an ambulance with sirens blaring and lights flashing, instead of a limousine or taxi, once he found out it was not illegal to do so.[23] Amid these myriad radio appearances during the first half of 1937, two would become legendary: the recurring role of Lamont Cranston in *The Shadow*, and his performance as the announcer in Archibald MacLeish's verse play *The Fall of the City*.

Contrary to some sources, Welles was not the first, nor was he the most renowned Shadow, but he was unquestionably the most famous actor to play the role. Prior to his two-year stint, James La Curto, Robert Hardy Andrews, and Frank Readick enacted the sinister voice. Welles would not only succeed Readick in the genealogy, he would eventually make this multi-talented radio actor a integral part of the *Mercury Theatre on the Air*. When Welles departed the role, Bill Johnstone took over until 1944. His somewhat thinner, older voice proved adequate but lacked the panache that his successor, Brett Morrison, had in abundance. Morrison proved to be the quintessential Shadow—yes, better even than Orson. He built on the Wellesian legacy but added a touch more humor and intensity to the character in a reign that saw the show to its conclusion in 1954.

If Welles was not the first Shadow he was, nonetheless, the first to make the character a recurring and integral part of the stories. Previously the Shadow was the voice who introduced and narrated the episodes in a program first known as *Street and Smith's Detective Story Magazine Hour* for the Mutual Network. The famous sign-on, "Who knows what evil lurks in the hearts of men? The Shadow knows . . . ha, ha, ha," dates from this period. Thus the Shadow, even before Welles played him, was a memorable character; the program itself less so. It was slipping in the ratings and in need of a new format.

Mutual explored several options and came up with the idea of making the Shadow the centerpiece of each story—a crime fighter with a split persona. By day he was "wealthy man about town, Lamont Cranston," a sophisticated if somewhat effete playboy. By night, availing himself of "secrets learned in the Orient" through which he could "cloud men's minds" into thinking he was invisible, he becomes the "relentless Shadow." The Shadow therefore never actually became invisible, as was the case with the protagonist in H. G. Wells's *The Invisible Man*; he only convinces, through a form of collective hypnosis, those in his presence that he is unseen. This idea was perhaps inspired by the fakirs of India who, in their most legendary trick, could disappear in front of an audience, usually after climbing a rope suspended in the air. It was also, of course, an inspired gimmick for a radio thriller—an invisible protagonist known to both his quarry and his audience through voice alone.

The origins of *The Shadow* are diverse. Most obviously, Lamont Cranston and his companion Margot Lane are an updating of Sir Arthur Conan Doyle's dynamic duo, Sherlock Holmes and Dr. Watson, although Miss Lane seems more adept at interpreting clues than Watson. There is also, in several Charles Dickens stories, a nocturnal avenger named the Shadow. As regards the character's dual personality, so integral to the 1937 radio version and its source, the William B. Gibson stories in Street and Smith's publication, *The Shadow Detective Magazine*, there are several possibilities. In 1920, with Douglas Fairbanks Sr.'s spectacular movie rendering of Zorro, this Shadow of the Hispanic West began delighting audiences; by 1937, several sequels and a Republic Pictures serial had been released. In *The Scarlet Pimpernel* (1935) Leslie Howard played a similar weak-kneed bon vivant, who when not sipping Chablis in the salon was leveling his steel at tyrants.

The dualism of these characters, a kind of Jekyll and Hyde personality in the service of justice, has continued to manifest itself in popular culture. The nerdish Clark Kent as Superman and foppish Bruce Wayne as Batman have become recurring staples of television and film. They first appeared in comic strips in 1938 and 1939, respectively, and were probably influenced by the Shadow. The Shadow, however, is different. He is closer to Jekyll and Hyde than all the above characters. He "knows what evil lurks in the hearts of men," to quote from the opening lines of the show, because he shares aspects of it. Apprehending criminals may in part be a noble calling, but it is also a dark compulsion in which he takes sadistic glee—somewhat like a feeding Dracula, whom Welles would play a year later in the very first *Mercury Theatre* broadcast. The Shadow's signature laugh is that of a dungeon master. He toys with and terrifies his criminal victims before handing them over (sometimes, it seems, reluctantly) to the authorities.

The scripts for *The Shadow* (never Welles's doing) were simplistic half-hour fare geared toward a young audience, as was the Sunday 5:00 P.M. air time. Nevertheless, Welles reveled in playing the character. It was his best-known role, until the release of *The Third Man* (1949) fixed him in the public mind as Harry Lime. Perhaps Welles saw something of himself in the invisible trickster whose nefarious machinations were ultimately for the greater good. He probably put up with the naiveté of the stories because of an arrangement he had with the sponsor, Blue Coal, whereby he did not have to be present at rehearsals.[24] Not knowing how events in each episode would turn out prevented complacency and must have appealed to his sense of dramatic spontaneity. He earned $185 per week for the series, and under the terms of the contract received no on-air credit. This program, along with his other, mostly anonymous radio commitments, was a financial boon to his theatrical ventures with Houseman. He would later tell Peter Bogdanovich, "without a single radio listener having ever heard my name, I was taking home $1,500 weekly."[25] When doing promotions for the program and its various spin-offs—the magazine, a comic strip, and various fan clubs—he would appear in black, with a Lone Ranger type of mask, a cape, and wide-brimmed hat. By year two of the series, with his theatrical notoriety burgeoning, it behooved both the network and sponsor to let the media know that the famous Orson Welles was indeed the infamous Shadow.

The format of the show begins with the Shadow's sneering introduction and subsequent basso cackle. It is accompanied by the strains of "Le Rouet d'Omphale," literally, "Omphale's Spinning Wheel" by Camille Saint-Saëns, a brooding, dirgelike piece with an indistinct melody—at times it sounds like a cat walking tentatively over the keys of an organ. In some programs the "Who knows what evil lurks in the hearts of men" is dropped, and only "The Shadow knows," followed by the laugh, is heard. The actor responsible in almost all instances is not Welles. He has both claimed and disclaimed credit for doing the show's opening sequence—sometimes noting that the laugh was simply impossible for him to do in a convincing way. After listening to a great many—probably too many—episodes, my ear concludes thus: In a few instances it might be Welles doing the introduction, but in most cases the laugh sounds like the overdub of another voice. We do know that Frank Readick's previous introduction was retained and used often. However, in several 1937 episodes there is another, very familiar, and distinctive voice doing the sign-on. My guess is Burgess Meredith, a radio, theater, film, and television actor with a long series of credits, many of them distinguished, some merely famous, like the Penguin in television's *Batman*. He was in New York City doing theater and radio in 1937; in fact he would later co-star with

Welles in *The Fall of the City* and eventually become an occasional member of the Mercury Theatre.

How Welles operated as the Shadow can perhaps best be appreciated by looking at two representative episodes, one from 1937, the other from 1938. The first is called *The Death Triangle*. It should be noted that over half of the episodes of *The Shadow* have *death* or *dead* in their titles; we are therefore usually not dealing with any crime less than murder most dastardly. This particular episode is more complex than most. It opens in 1913 with a prisoner on Devil's Island getting the lash; his escape plan has been betrayed. We then flash forward to a program of organ music, which is soon interrupted by news that a doctor has treated the Shadow for a bullet wound and does not expect the man to live; then back to the music, a technique that directly anticipates the first part of the infamous *War of the Worlds* broadcast a year later. When the story resumes we find out that the doctor faked the report to attract the attention of the real Shadow, whose help he needed.

The doctor was one of four men who escaped from Devil's Island twenty years previously. Three, including the doctor, were innocent of the crimes that put them there and eventually exonerated; the fourth was reported to the authorities by one of the three and recaptured. His recent escape was followed by death threats to the three. A meeting is arranged between them and the Shadow. Stunned by radio reports of an allegedly wounded Shadow, Margot Lane goes to the doctor's office for more information, is denied entry, but manages to follow his car to a country estate were she meets Lamont Cranston just before he transmogrifies into the Shadow—unlike Superman's Lois Lane, Margot is well aware of her man's dual persona. He explains the situation. As Cranston, Welles speaks in a breathy English accent, "I drove the cahh heah this ahftanoon. . . ." When he becomes the Shadow, his voice is modified through the use of a sound filter and takes on a deeper, more characteristically Wellesian tone, replete with midwestern inflections.

Margot departs and the Shadow enters the house to discuss the situation with the three anxious men. He seems suspicious of the various clues that indicate they are being stalked and threatened. One man bolts to his room, grabs a gun, and is confronted by the knife-wielding escapee. The Shadow enters—this time his intimidating laugh is the actual voice of Welles. The victim somehow convinces his assailant that they should dispense with this auditory apparition before dealing with each other. The Shadow dodges a knife, and then bullets, by throwing his voice. The gunman then turns and shoots his previous attacker, now unarmed, only to be in turn skewered by a second knife the man was carrying. The doctor enters and finds out what the Shadow has discovered after the mayhem: that the real escapee died shortly after leaving Devil's Island, and it was one of the three men, jealous of the other two's successes, who donned a disguise that evening and tried to kill them, succeeding in the case of the man who went for the gun and shot him. He was also the convict who was whipped in the first scene, and subsequently carried with him the belief that his escape attempt had been revealed to the authorities by his compatriots.

The intricate story is enhanced by persuasive sound effects. Several Blue Coal commercials also punctuate the episode. Among other things, we learn how warm and cozy it can make us in winter, especially in places like Buffalo that are experiencing heavy blizzard conditions—some things never change. The Shadow's characteristic sign-off, almost as famous as his introduction, was no doubt geared to convince younger listeners to stay on the straight and narrow: "The weed of crime bears bitter fruit. Crime does not pay. The Shadow knows . . . ha, ha ha." Again, it is not Welles's voice, but the one that opened the program.

Early the following year an episode titled "Sabotage" played on the tensions with Germany and the threat of a possible war. It begins with several navy vessels being destroyed with bombs placed by a saboteur. Lamont and Margot head for the shipyard, where the stricken vessels were either built or repaired. He stops off at a bar and, playing a drunk, confronts a man, a ship inspector, who, through the Shadow's mind-reading abilities, is revealed to have planted the bombs for money. They leave and the Shadow confronts the man, who will not reveal who he is working for. The Shadow lets him go but later follows him when, after being threatened by his evil boss, the man plants another bomb. The Shadow removes it and contacts Margot through a form of telepathy that allows him to transmit to the wireless she has in her car! They follow the mercenary bomber to his doctor boss's sanitarium. The Shadow goes in while Margot calls the police.

When the man demands his payment, he is shot and dies muttering that he should have listened to the Shadow. The evil doctor, speaking with a decidedly German accent, knows that the Shadow is in the room and challenges him to speak. When he does, the doctor taunts him, and then turns on some noxious but not lethal gas, hoping this will destroy the Shadow's invisibility so he can then be shot. However, the police arrive and the man flees through a secret passageway to a waiting speedboat. A choking Shadow pleads with him to surrender, declaring that he has placed the bomb he removed from the navy ship on the speedboat. The man scoffs, then . . . KABOOM (the explosion sounding like mallets on a bass drum) . . . followed by our hero's self-satisfied and sinister laugh.

If *The Shadow* was perhaps the quintessential example of pulp fiction on radio, then *The Fall of the City* for *The Columbia Workshop* took the medium to dramatic heights it had rarely if ever experienced. The verse play was broadcast on 11 April 1937 and lasted only thirty minutes. Like *Citizen Kane* four years later, it effectively brought together some of the most talented people in their respective fields. When MacLeish wrote the play he had Welles in mind for the central role of the announcer/reporter, along with "the everywhere of radio as a stage and all of history as time."[26] Because it was a CBS production, Bernard Herrmann was available to provide the music. Ultimately, it was producer/director Irving Reis who fused these elements into a seamless and stunning production.

Reis was a studio engineer at CBS who, in 1936, suggested an experimental series to the newly appointed vice president in charge of programming, William B. Lewis. He was given the go-ahead and *The Columbia Workshop* made a tentative start in July. Reis knew the technical potential of radio, having worked on *Buck Rogers*, but he was also coming to appreciate how sound effects could enhance a high-level dramatic presentation. The opportunity to stage one on a large scale landed in his lap, literally, when MacLeish mailed him a copy of *The Fall of the City*. It may have been written in high-blown verse, but the self-conscious newsreel style and applicability of the story to contemporary world events, even though the setting was in a fictitious preindustrial society, made the challenge of broadcasting it worth accepting. Too many people, MacLeish felt, were deferring to tyrants such as Hitler, Mussolini, and Stalin. The American public needed a wake-up call. Reis and Welles gave them one.

The Fall of the City was the first verse play written for radio. With a cast of over two hundred, many of them high school or college drama students, it was also the largest radio play broadcast up to that time—and done on the proverbial shoestring of a sustaining program. The students were volunteers and the actors received minimal salaries. Most of the action takes place in a crowded city plaza. To achieve the expansive acoustics, Reis secured the Seventh Regiment Armory at 67th and Park in midtown Manhattan. To create the illusion of a large crowd, he enhanced the student voices by recording them, followed by a playback several seconds later. The effect is extraordinary. Not only does the crowd sound like it numbers in the thousands, the listener can envision the multitude covering a vast area. Whether Reis knew it or not, the technique of overdubbing the sound of a cheering crowd with recorded cheers was a technique Goebbels had begun employing through the use of strategically placed loudspeakers at Hitler's rallies.

The story told in *The Fall of the City* is quite simple, but the simplicity harbors the power of a parable. A mythical city stands in the path of an invading army. The situation is chronicled by a reporter from contemporary times. Amid the din of the crowd we hear the organ tones of Welles's voice literally pull us into the unfolding spectacle:

> We are here on the central plaza.
> We are well off to the eastward edge.
> There is a kind of terrace over the crowd here.
> It is precisely four minutes to twelve. . . .
> I wish you could see all this as we do.
> The whole plaza full of these people.
> Their colorful garments, the harsh sunlight.

His voice is intense, almost breathless. He speaks the new discourse of live, on-the-spot radio reporting and therefore provides an unusual counterpoint to the citizenry who speak in verse. To keep Welles's narration from being overwhelmed by the crowd sounds, Reis placed him in a special booth in the center of the armory so a proper auditory mix could be effected.

The drama in the street begins with a recently deceased woman returning to give a prophetic speech punctuated by a phrase that will recur throughout the play: "The city of masterless men shall take a master." At first this fate seems ambiguous. Might it not be a good thing to have strong leadership? But then, at what cost? Another speaker, played by Burgess Meredith, argues that democracy and peace must be maintained through reason and truth. He is supported by a priest who warns of the dangers of succumbing to a tyrant. The people's will, however, is eroded by a general who lectures on the futility of resistance as he points to smoke rising from several decimated towns in the mountains. His views are echoed by retreating defenders who urge the people to give the approaching conqueror what he wants and save the city.

As the tyrant approaches the plaza, members of the nervous populace renounce their liberty with words that would have made Rousseau and Byron shudder:

> Freedom's for fools.
> Force is the certainty.
> Freedom has eaten our strength and corrupted our virtues.
> Men must be ruled.

They prostrate themselves before the armored figure entering the square. The reporter describes the scene with incredulity, which rises to a crescendo as he points out that the conqueror has raised his visor:

> There is no one.
> No one at all.
> No one.
> The helmet is hollow.
> The metal is empty.

But the servile populace sees only his feet.

No synopsis can do justice to such a radio play, especially since the power of *The Fall of the City* lies not on the page but in the performance. The speeches are delivered with clarity and conviction, and the entire production is enhanced by the technical achievement of near perfect balance. The eminent broadcast historian Erik Barnouw has called it a landmark in radio history. Frank Brady argues that it was "the most famous radio show in history up to that time."[27] Clearly, if the Golden Age of Radio can be said to have produced a *Citizen Kane*, *The Fall of the City* is a leading candidate for the honor.

The broadcast also helped Welles, who was gaining increasing renown for his theater work, move out of the domain of radio anonymity. It would now behoove future programmers to use his name as a drawing card. He also learned much from working with Reis, which would later be incorporated into his own radio productions—*The War of the Worlds*, for example, and even theatrical stagings such as *Caesar*. David Thomson goes even further and suggests that *The Fall of the City* influenced Welles's cinematic sensibility:

> He was deeply moved by the giving of witness and the voice and mood of a man urging you to see. . . . There has never been a moviemaker who was more shaped and driven by radio—nor a director who had mined his own ambiguous soul in radio first.[28]

Somehow, millions heard the broadcast and millions more heard about it, despite the 7:00 P.M. time slot opposite Jack Benny on NBC. Serious radio got a boost. Even NBC took note and realized there should be a niche for such programs amid their panoply of fluff. Not surprisingly, verse plays poured into network offices, but nothing measured up to the original, except perhaps MacLeish's own *Air Raid* broadcast a year later. By that time, with H. V. Kaltenborn and Edward R. Murrow reporting on events in Europe for CBS, the scenario of *The Fall of the City* was becoming all too real.

Less than a month later, on the first two Sundays in May, Reis's *Columbia Workshop* presented a Wellesian version of *Macbeth*. On this occasion Welles eschewed his earlier voodoo conception of the play in favor of the original Highland context. Bagpipes replaced drums. The broadcast, although uneven at times, was a reasonably successful attempt to "air" high culture. It did not, however, attract the ratings or the response of *The Fall of the City*.

These experiences with Reis gave Welles an appreciation of the way radio could project drama through a mass medium. The possibility of someday having top-to-bottom creative control over such a production must have appealed to him. Without actively seeking it, a debut opportunity would come that summer courtesy of the Mutual Network. But before undertaking the project, another unorthodox stage venture called for his directorial talents. If the Voodoo *Macbeth* had raised him to the status of a theatrical enfant terrible, then *The Cradle Will Rock* would affirm it with a vengeance.

Written and composed by Marc Blitzstein, *Cradle* was something totally different artistically and politically for Project 891. It was contemporary, not traditional, and involved musical sequences. Dedicated to Bertolt Brecht, it has often been labeled a labor opera. *Cradle* was substantially left of the New Deal, which in 1937, with the economy slowly on the mend, was subject to vociferous attacks from the right and on the threshold of dissolution. However, bad timing was not, nor would it ever be, an impediment to Welles's attempt to stage a production. In this case, he was enamored by the possibility of directing musical theater for the first time; Blitzstein, for his part, was enamored by Welles's unconventional artistry. Houseman was less enthusiastic. He sensed that the time for such strident political statements in the arts had passed—staging *Cradle* could only invite trouble. It did, in spades, but it also yielded a notoriety that would take both their theatrical careers to new heights.

Cradle was originally planned as a production for the left-wing Actors' Repertory Company, but a funding shortfall led to cancellation. Hallie Flanagan, perhaps sensing that the end of government-sponsored theater was drawing nigh, seemed to have no hesitation approving it as 891's next production. Houseman has described *Cradle* as a mix of Brecht and Kurt Weil, Gilbert and Sullivan, vaudeville, and political oratory. Much has been written about this moment in Welles's career, and shortly before his death he had planned to direct a motion picture dealing with the events surrounding it— Rupert Everett would play him, and Amy Irving, Virginia. The effort came to naught, but the story was later dramatized in Toronto playwright Jason Sherman's *It's All True*, and by Tim Robbins, whose *Cradle Will Rock* film was released in 1999.

The incidents surrounding 891's attempt to stage the production are too complex and distant from the radio theme of this book to be given more than a brief mention here. Suffice to say that *Cradle* was planned during a time of considerable labor unrest, even within the WPA, since a campaign was being waged in Washington to end government subsidies to anything that smacked of a make-work project, especially in the arts. When the powers that be realized the controversial nature of *Cradle*, rather than banning it outright, they issued a bureaucratic memorandum saying that no new FTP could begin before 1 July (*Cradle* was due to open 16 June).

Opening night saw the theater seized by uniformed guards who also confiscated the props and costumes. Welles and Houseman found an alternate venue across town, but the Musician's Union and Actor's Equity decreed that their members could not perform since the original contract had been terminated. A piano was rented and Blitzstein made ready to do the production solo. The audience and cast, in defiant celebration, marched from the Maxine Elliot Theater on 39th Street to the Venice Theater on Seventh Avenue and 58th Street. As Houseman put it, "There was the smell of history in the air."[29] Both he and Welles gave brief speeches from the stage, then Blitzstein began. He was soon joined by some of the cast members performing from their seats as audience members—therefore not violating their union's ruling. The event was a political if not an artistic success and made the front page of all New York newspapers the following day.

Welles followed the rebellious triumph by resigning from the FTP. Houseman was not so rash, but he wound up being dismissed anyhow, by an appreciative Hallie Flanagan, who in turn offered him a one-year teaching post in Vassar's theater department. With a modicum of hesitation, he accepted the post, but the chance to turn the New York theater world on its ear a second time would again cause him to again seek out Orson, whom he was now calling "Wonder Boy."

The media attention over *Cradle* also helped bring Welles's radio work to wider public attention. Not surprisingly, it was the Mutual Network who first approached him with an offer to produce, direct, star in, and write his own series, or in this instance what we would today call a mini-series. He was, after all, their Shadow, and had been their Great McCoy. No other network had such a regular claim on his services. And although CBS and NBC appreciated Welles's talent, it was the folks at upstart Mutual who were willing to take a risk on a quality dramatic program with him. They hoped it would help them elbow their way into the top echelons of radio—the network's two big hits, *The Shadow* and *The Lone Ranger,* being decidedly lowbrow, lacked the necessary cachet. The offer was made (as would be the one from CBS the following year) for the broadcasts to air during the 1937 summer season. Strategically, this meant that competition from NBC and CBS would be weaker; also, if the production flopped, it would not be as detrimental to the network as a failure in fall prime time; finally, if the initial broadcasts succeeded, there would still be several weeks left in which to attract a larger audience. The safe scheduling may have also been prompted by Welles's reputation for artistic risk taking.

With Mutual giving him creative carte blanche, he chose to dramatize a novel, Victor Hugo's *Les Misérables*. It was a relatively safe choice; one imagines the network breathing a sigh of relief when he informed them. The story lent itself to serialization, possessed auditory potential, and had been made into a successful film two years earlier.

In a surprising number of Welles's later radio plays, the novels they are based on had been filmed previously. A direct influence seems unlikely. Not being a cinephile at this point in his career, he was probably unaware of anything but the fact that such films existed, and maybe whether or not they had been successful. This was a time in cinema history when film versions of great novels, as well as what we now call bio-pics, flourished. The situation was partly a response to sanctions imposed on the industry by the Hays Office in 1934. Contemporary depictions of crime and the erotic were severely censored, or prohibited outright, and the industry was encouraged to pursue more noble and uplifting themes. Audiences, for their part, loved it. Weary of the economic malaise of the 1930s, they relished traveling to Sherwood Forest, revolutionary France, or the South Seas on the *Bounty*.

But Welles would not let them forget completely the poverty and injustice that earmarked the decade. One of the reasons he chose *Les Misérables* was because it played out themes of the past relevant to the present. It also contained one of the great hooks in literary history: Jean Valjean undergoes his protracted and painful ordeal by virtue of the simple, but not so simple as it turns out, act of stealing bread to feed his widowed sister's children, and since Valjean himself was unmarried and childless, the crime takes on added nobility. Welles sensed that Hugo's gigantic but compelling novel would make a sizable and equally compelling radio play.

In adapting it, he employed the trademark style of his more renowned, later radio productions. Of particular importance is the voice of the narrator, who describes the context of each episode, summarizes past events, and bridges incidents essential to the plot but impossible to dramatize because of time restrictions. Despite Welles's later claims, the technique (Rick Altman has called it "the intrusive episodic narrator")[30] was not new. In fact it was a staple of Mutual's program, *The Lone Ranger* (the program most likely to have given birth to that notorious radio cliché, "Meanwhile, back at the ranch"). But this earlier form of narration that uses a disembodied voice from the present, a kind of "once upon a time" voice, was not what Welles wanted. For him, the narrator should, whenever possible, be a character or characters in the story. When this is not feasible, such as in the bulk of *Les Misérables*, Welles then makes him a kind of demi-character. The voice we hear is clearly not in the events described. As listeners, we might wonder about its origins. Speaking with the tone of the time and with the authority and emotions of an eyewitness, the voice seems to upwell from the past and draw us into it.

Les Misérables was a daunting production to orchestrate. The writing itself was time consuming—in the later Mercury radio plays, Houseman, Howard Koch, and others would often do the initial drafts, with Welles editing and revising what he received. His writing credit for *Les Misérables* was made clear to audiences at the outset, with the announcer touting him as the "distinguished young actor, writer, and director" who will do all of the above in the series, plus narrate. The rest of the cast is not cited and receives only sporadic mention at the end of several episodes; and sometimes, probably because of time constraints, no mention at all.

Welles did, however, have formidable help. If there is one constant in Welles's career, from his theatrical and radio ventures in the Depression, through the early days at RKO when purse strings were loosed, to his later scuffling in Europe to make films on a shoestring, it was the ability to draw talented people into his orbit. *Les Misérables* featured a large and excellent cast. Martin Gabel would play the relentless Inspector Javert and appear in many later Welles productions, as would Ray Collins, Everett Sloane, and Betty Garde. We also find a young, pre–film noir Richard Widmark, and Orson's wife Virginia, now donning the stage name of Anna Stafford, perhaps to secure her own artistic identity or simply to protect Welles from accusations of nepotism. There is also an intriguing Shadow connection: beside the specter of the current Shadow, Welles, we have the Shadow past, Frank Readick, the Shadow future, William Johnstone, and "the lovely Margot Lane," Agnes Moorehead. If that were not enough, excerpts from the theme music of *The Shadow* are used in several episodes.

The mini-series opens with the plight of Jean Valjean being suggested, through his desperate wanderings, then told, via flashbacks to the trial that decided his fate. We are also introduced to the Bishop who would come to believe in him. Welles's voice as the narrator perfectly captures the simple profundity of Hugo's characterization of this cleric as someone, "who when he had money, visited the poor; when he had none, visited the rich." When Welles voices Valjean in the early episodes, it is a portrayal devoid of sentiment. He is gruff, belligerent, and downright nasty. At this point we sympathize with Valjean's plight but not with his person.

The turning point comes in the second episode, when Valjean absconds with the Bishop's silver plates. When he is caught and brought to face his victim, the man tells the authorities that he *gave* the plates to Valjean. Shocked at this belief in him, Valjean goes on to do good works. He eventually changes his identity and becomes the mayor of a small town, only to be self-compelled to reveal his true identity to protect an innocent man from being indicted for crimes allegedly committed by him. When the relentless Inspector Javert gets wind of the situation, the chase is on.

The sound effects to this point are minimal, but evocative. In several scenes to come they would be all-enveloping. When Valjean escapes in a coffin from a mission in which he was hiding, and then is buried, we feel the claustrophobia. Our breath shortens with his; then deepens with relief when he is rescued. And in the legendary chase through the sewers of Paris, eerie sounds make us feel the dank and smell the stench. To achieve the right sonority, the scene was played in a washroom with the actors at floor level. Welles would use this porcelain studio again in a later *Mercury Theatre on the Air* presentation of *The Count of Monte Cristo* for CBS.

Javert's pursuit succeeds and Valjean is caught. But the Inspector—Martin Gabel is brilliant in the role—has undergone a crisis of conscience during the ordeal. He realizes that in Valjean's case formal justice is injustice, and he remains bewildered by the accused having earlier saved his life when Javert was captured by insurrectionists and faced with execution. He grants Valjean a brief visit with Cossette (Orson's wife Virginia), the daughter of a victim of poverty whom Valjean has raised and is now trying to reunite with her betrothed. True to his word, Valjean returns to Javert after the visit to face his fate, only to find that the Inspector has decided his own by plunging into the Seine—a haunting sequence in the film version (1935), where we actually see Javert (Charles Laughton) commit the act.

Les Misérables is one of the most ambitious and successful adaptations of a literary classic that Welles, or radio itself, would ever broadcast. The production format and aesthetics provided a template he would use for his more well-known *Mercury Theatre* and *Campbell Playhouse* programs over the next several years.

Prior to his spectacular auteur entry into the field of radio drama with *Les Misérables*, the genre had not been a dominant one—music and comedy had reigned since the establishment of the networks in the late 1920s. The kind of dramatic programs that were on the air lacked the essentials Welles felt were necessary for effective broadcast storytelling.

The most influential early radio drama anthology program was *The First Nighter*, which began on NBC in December of 1930. Sponsored by Campana Balm, it endeavored to create the illusion of attending a Broadway premiere, with ushers giving directions, discussions about the production, the orchestra tuning up, and of course the ambience of an enthusiastic live audience. Welles, although steeped in theatrical tradition, could not abide this format. *First Nighter* specialized in light romantic comedy and melodrama. John Dunning has aptly called it "an audio version of the old Saturday Evening Post."[31] The program constantly moved among the networks but never found a permanent home. It expired on NBC in 1952.

First Nighter spawned minor imitators, such as *Curtain Time* (1938, Mutual; 1945, ABC; 1946–1950, NBC) and *Knickerbocker Playhouse* (1939, CBS; 1940–1942, NBC Red). It also inspired a major rival that would trump it at its own game, *The Lux Radio Theatre* (1934, NBC; 1935–1954, CBS; 1954–1955, NBC). *Lux* started by using material and a format similar to *First Nighter* but soon expanded its repertoire. In June 1936, it moved from New York to Hollywood and the sponsor's agency, J. Walter Thompson, hired Cecil B. De Mille as host/impresario. Under his aegis, *Lux Theatre* began broadcasting radio adaptations of successful motion pictures, although on occasion the show used as its source novels that would only later be made into motion pictures, provided they were studio property at the time. This was the case with *Dark Victory*, *How Green Was My Valley*, and *This Above All*.

Lux Theatre began with a modest listenership and some skepticism within the industry over the viability of its formula.[32] When De Mille was hired, insiders told him that nobody wants to listen to a one-hour drama on radio. Someone who did was Bill Paley, who had earlier lured *Lux* to CBS. A year later, with De Mille on its masthead, it became the number one show, with an audience of thirty million. It filled an expanding niche for serious but accessible radio plays. *Lux Theatre* aired Monday night at 9:00 P.M., a time when most people would be at home, since De Mille did not want to raise the ire of his Hollywood colleagues by broadcasting on the prime movie-going nights of Friday, Saturday, and Sunday.

De Mille, who served as host, narrator, and commercial pitchman, was set up by the agency to project the illusion of being producer/director as well. He brought to the airwaves a sense of Hollywood grandiosity and theatrical intimacy. Listeners felt they were ear witnesses to a lavish production, which De Mille cultivated with lines such as "the audience is buzzing in anticipation . . . the curtain is going up . . . Miss Davis is resplendent in a blue taffeta gown," etc. This kind of audience pandering Welles would disdain, although when called upon he was not averse to being a guest star on *Lux Theatre* (*Jane Eyre* on 5 June 1944 and *A Tale of Two Cities* on 26 March 1945).

As Michele Hilmes has shown, Welles was also quite willing to bite the hand that once fed him when he thought its politics was tainted. This occurred in 1945 when De Mille refused to support the AFRA (American Federation of Radio Artists) opposition to an antilabor bill passed by the California Legislature. As a spokesman for the AFRA and former guest on *Lux Theatre*, Welles wanted to set the record straight regarding De Mille's credentials as a radio artist:

Mr. De Mille never conducted the program, nor did he produce nor direct it. Mr. De Mille was a narrator on the program, came to dress rehearsal on Sunday, read his lines which were prepared for him, and returned on Monday evening to read them over the air.[33]

Needless to say, Welles's 1937 production of *Les Misérables* was quite different from anything *Lux Theatre* had done up to that time. It was high literature, tragedy rather than melodrama, and used extensive narration. The soundscape he created privileged the story, not the actors. The *Lux Theatre* aesthetic was almost the reverse. It showcased the voices of glamorous stars, with De Mille occasionally reminding us just how glamorous they are. This emphasis diminished the role of sound effects, a signature ingredient in Welles's productions. More significantly, in listening to a number of *Lux Theatre* recordings, it is clear that most of them were drawn from movie adaptations, and there is little concession in the script to the medium of radio. *The Thin Man* (8 June 1936) is typical. It is scaled down to fit, rather than adapted for a live broadcast. The story becomes almost impossible to follow without knowledge of the film. However, the captivating chemistry of William Powell and Myrna Loy, who reprise their film roles, must have easily dissuaded listeners from struggling with the plot.

Lux Theatre, although it did not provide a model for what Welles wanted to achieve in radio drama, may have at least suggested to him that extended (one hour or more) dramatic radio plays were a viable broadcast option. The program that most certainly influenced the way he thought they should be produced was *The Columbia Workshop*. Irving Reis—about whom surprisingly little has been written given his influence on Welles, Bernard Herrmann, and Norman Corwin—had already offered Welles a glimpse of the power of Reis's kind of radio when he had asked Welles to perform in the *Columbia Workshop* rendering of *The Fall of the City*. In his productions, Reis wanted to "do almost anything that lends itself to unique treatment and interesting experiments with sound effects and voices."[34] *The Columbia Workshop* was probably as close to an avant-garde offering as network radio ever got. Its penchant for unsettling productions led CBS to pull the program during the war years (it was briefly reinstated for the 1946–1947 season). Although Welles admired Reis, he saw his own artistic mission in more crossover terms. He wanted to bridge the edge of high art with the center of popular entertainment. With *Les Misérables* his ambitious opening gambit in that direction had succeeded.

Not surprisingly, but amazingly, during the seven-week run of *Les Misérables* Welles was involved with other programs. On 15 and 22 August, he played the lead in the *Columbia Workshop* version of John Galsworthy's *The Escape*, a story he would reprise two years later for the *Campbell Playhouse*. And on 30 August, he acted in his third Shakespeare production for radio, *Twelfth Night*, this time under the aegis of another sustaining program called *The Columbia Playhouse*.

The play was the last in a series of experiments with the Bard by CBS. It featured Orson as Orsinio, Tallulah Bankhead as Viola, Cedric Hardwicke as Malvolio, and Helen Meincken as Olivia. The condensed production, written by Brewster Morgan, is episodic and delightful. Conway Turl's informal narration explains the story, indicates transitions, and sets up each scene of this complex gender bender. Victor Bay's music meshes well with the tempo and zany antics of the story. Tallulah Bankhead shows a flair for farcical comedy in a role totally unlike the vamp persona she would be called upon to effect in movies. Welles articulates his speeches with a captivating resonance that overrides the sometimes difficult to grasp meaning of numerous lines—legend has it that he once read excerpts from a phone book and listeners were enthralled. An unusual aspect of the performance is that it was done before a live audience, something he would eschew in later programs under his control.

In the middle of August, in the midst of all this radio work, Welles had a visitor drop by his Sneden's Landing home. It was Houseman returning from Vassar, where he was preparing to take up the position Hallie Flanagan had offered him. But his heart was not in it. Doing live theater was preferable to teaching it. Nevertheless, two days out of his week would now be given over to academe. At this point, Welles, despite his successes in radio, yearned for more theatrical exposure. So much so that a few months earlier he had turned down an offer from Warner Brothers to join their coterie of actors—a supporting role in *The Adventures of Robin Hood* was used as a lure.[35]

A somewhat different offer to join filmdom also came his way. David O. Selznick tried to lure him with a position whereby Welles would select literary properties and then turn them into screenplays. An additional perk was the possibility of eventually acting and directing. It was not enough to lure him. He wanted more guarantees—of the kind RKO would provide two years later. It is also possible that he felt these two early offers were just part of the general and sometimes desperate scouring of Broadway by Hollywood in the quest for stage-trained actors for the talkies, along with writers who could script decent dialogue.

Not wanting to cut off completely the possibility of future dealings with Selznick, Welles, in turning down the offer, did so in a gracious letter dated 19 May 1937.[36] In one-and-a-half single-spaced pages he indicates his appreciation of the offer, adding that he thinks he could do the proposed job very well, but says his ultimate goal is to begin his film career as an actor-director. The letter concludes with a sterling assessment of Houseman's suitability for the position. Did Welles feel that the best way to end his dependency on Houseman was to have him a continent away? How seriously Selznick took this recommendation at the time is not clear, since he probably had little if any idea who Houseman was. However, by 1941, he would come to know enough about Houseman to make him an executive producer.

When Houseman landed on Welles's doorstep that August, he found that he was not alone in feeling dissatisfied with his current lot. Welles had just seen plans for a production of *King Lear* collapse. The venture was to be produced by Broadway doyen Arthur Hopkins, with Welles to star. Frustrated by the paucity of thespian projects, he suggested something—it was almost a challenge—that stopped Houseman dead in his tracks as he was leaving: "Why the hell don't we start a theater of our own?" Houseman's quick retort was, "Why not?"[37] He returned to the house and did not leave that evening, nor the next day, nor the day after. Thus was the Mercury Theatre born. The name was taken from a radical literary magazine, the *American Mercury*, founded by H. L. Mencken and George Jean Nathan, which often featured the work of aesthetically knowledgeable social commentators such as Lewis Mumford.

The venture was announced publicly in "Plan for a New Theater," a declaration of principles published in the 29 August issue of the *New York Times*. (An inspiration, perhaps, for the declaration of principles sequence in *Citizen Kane*?) The perpetrators mentioned their previous work and promised a commitment to "classical plays excitingly produced . . . which have emotional or factual bearing on contemporary life." Mercury would schedule four or five productions for its first season and be a people's theater, with a top price of $2 and many seats going for less than $1. It would open that November with *Julius Caesar*. The announcement attracted considerable attention.

Much of this attention came from the Popular Front. This was an alliance of workers, unions, people involved in the arts, and the American Communist Party, with which the Popular Front was, especially in the postwar years, often and too narrowly identified. According to Michael Denning, who has undertaken a definitive study of the movement and its creative end, the Cultural Front, Welles was "the American Brecht, the single most important Popular Front Artist in theater, radio, and film, both politically and aesthetically."[38] Although certainly no communist, or even a socialist, Welles was an independent left-liberal, pro-union, and at the forefront of the fight against racism and fascism. This led him to court the entire spectrum of the American Left. Less than a year after the above cited position statement in the *New York Times*, he wrote another, "Theatre and the People's Front," for the 15 April 1938 edition of the *Daily Worker*. Ostensibly a Communist Party organ, the paper strove for a wide sympathetic readership through its discussions of culture. Welles hoped that they, as well as the hard-liners, would come to and react favorably to his theatrical productions.

As the all-black production of *Macbeth* had attacked racism in a compelling but indirect way, so Mercury's debut effort to mount *Julius Caesar* would attack fascism. Deft lobbying by Houseman also attracted enough funds to mount the first production, now simply titled, *Caesar*. Mercury's venue would be the rundown but spatially excellent Comedy Theater on 41st and Broadway. A large luminous sign with *Mercury* spelled out vertically in block capitals was erected atop the marquee. Recruiting a talented cast from the large pool of available candidates was not difficult. Welles selected several, such as Joseph Cotten and Martin Gabel, on the basis of having worked with them on radio.

He also did an extraordinary adaptation of the play, which set it in a hypothetical, but all too real contemporary fascist state—something similar was tried in a 1995 film version of *Richard III*. The lion's share of the set designs was also Welles's handiwork, most notably what became known as the Nuremberg lights, which came straight from below and illuminated the actors moving upstage. Marc Blitzstein, following Welles's suggestions, composed a multi-textural musical score. It evoked the sounds heard on both radio and in newsreels that reported the very theatrical public displays of Hitler and Mussolini. It is possible, but unlikely, that some members of the Mercury production team had seen Leni Riefenstahl's Nazi propaganda extravaganza, *Triumph of the Will* (1935). If not, they were certainly familiar with incidents depicted in it.

Rehearsals were uneven and anxiety ridden, but the play turned out to be a smash. It yielded sold-out houses through the end of the year, then ran in repertory until June. Reviews at the time were overwhelmingly positive. The impact of *Caesar* has also withstood the test of time. In a recent interview, theatrical commentator Richard France described it as the single most important production of Shakespeare in the history of the American stage.[39]

Welles, of course, wanted to try other things. Believing that it was always a good idea to follow a tragedy with a comedy, and vice versa, Mercury staged Thomas Dekker's *Shoemaker's Holiday*. The cast featured a pre–ghoul meister Vincent Price. At one point during the first quarter of 1938 the company was mounting four productions in three theaters. There was *Caesar* in New York, and a version that went on the road, as well as *Shoemaker's Holiday*, along with a resurrected oratorio version of *The Cradle Will Rock*. The three New York theaters used were within a two-block stretch of 41st Street, leading Mercury's founders to erect their own street signs that said "WELCOME TO MERCURY STREET." Today this stretch, which in its heyday must have seemed like the theatrical center of the universe, has been given over to more mundane businesses and is dotted with loading ramps instead of marquees.

On 29 April, Mercury launched its next production, which would enjoy a six-week run, George Bernard Shaw's semiautobiographical play, *Heartbreak House*. Welles played the very Shavian Captain Shotover, a cantankerous octogenarian. It was another success. With triumphs in both theater and radio raising his profile, Welles, in the makeup of Captain Shotover, made the cover of the 9 May issue of *Time* magazine. The article was titled "George Orson Welles: Shadow to Shakespeare, Shoemaker to Shaw," and played up his iconoclastic boy wonder persona.

Amid these triumphs he did significant work in a less touted medium. He recorded *Caesar* for Columbia Records, the first time a full-length play had been put to disc in the United States. Musicraft soon followed with an offer to wax *The Cradle Will Rock*, the first time an entire Broadway production had been so preserved. True to his ability to understand the medium in which he worked, he did not merely transcribe the stage versions of these pieces. He made small but significant alterations to each, so that when recorded with a single microphone and without benefit of visuals, they would require nothing more than the listener's imagination. During these experiments with sound recording, Welles further developed skills that would prove invaluable to his work in broadcasting. Good thing, because the supernova that Mercury had created in the universe of theater was about to diminish, but radio would give it an opportunity to blaze forth again.

CHAPTER THREE

Mercury Theatre on the Air

With his magnificent voice, he could become the perfect storyteller.

—James Naremore

Welles's theatrical notoriety helped bring even more attention to what he had already, and could, accomplish on radio. His forays into broadcasting spanned the medium's cultural spectrum: *The Shadow* prompted discussions in playgrounds, *The Columbia Workshop* did the same in the corridors of another Columbia—the university. It seemed only a matter of time until he was awarded his own show.

In the late spring of 1938 CBS began making overtures. The network had been contemplating the possibility of a Welles series for several months. The catalyst that may have finally prompted the offer was the *Time* magazine cover story. The article lauded his theatrical achievements but emphasized how the earning power and audience access he had in radio were far greater, often providing a financial source for his stage ventures. A contrasting profile several months later in the *New Yorker* (8 October), written when the *Mercury Theatre* radio program was attracting wide notice, nevertheless devoted most of its coverage to his work as a stage director and actor.

CBS was not just interested in Welles per se. They wanted to move their programming in new directions, away from vaudeville-influenced variety shows and more in the direction of extended live drama. The network, which was founded in 1927 by the Columbia Phonograph Company, had started out with a commitment to music and comedy. Under the auspices of William Paley, who at twenty-six took the helm shortly after CBS's inception and would guide its destiny into the television era, light entertainment was nurtured and developed. It dominated most radio stations during the first half of the medium's Golden Age and prompted intense network rivalries, especially between upstart CBS and the more venerable (founded a year earlier) NBC. During the early 1930s, Paley had managed to woo Al Jolson, Eddie Cantor, and a number of other major stars from the rival studio.[1]

CBS's acquisition of *The Lux Radio Theatre* from NBC in 1935, and the addition of Cecil B. De Mille as host a year later, also turned out to be a major coup. Over the next several years it became the most popular program on radio. And with the more high art *Columbia Workshop* also in his stable, Paley had the most innovative and critically acclaimed drama as well. When *Lux* went on summer hiatus in 1938, Welles's *Mercury Theatre* became its designated replacement. The offer CBS made clearly capitalized on Welles's name and growing reputation. He would be the program's centerpiece, its producer, director, writer, and star—at least this is the way things would be sold to the public. In reality, save for playing the lead and directing, he would have considerable help with the other tasks. Houseman, as it turned out, was apportioned a lion's share of the production and writing labors. Davidson Taylor of CBS would serve as executive producer. He was as superb a liaison between Columbia and Mercury as Welles could have hoped for.

Excited but not surprised by what the network was offering, Welles commandeered Houseman—literally, on the highway as John was driving to Welles's house in Sneden's Landing with Orson headed in the other direction—to attend the negotiations with CBS.[2] Unlike Welles, Houseman had no radio experience. Even as a listener, his exposure to the medium was limited primarily to news and Orson's projects, most notably *Les Misérables*, which impressed him considerably. Always the worrier, Houseman tried to restrain his anxiety over the fact that their first program was slated to air less than two weeks after the contract was finalized; he must have also sensed that much of the burden of making it happen would be his.

The contract was negotiated by Paley's executive right hand, William Lewis. He offered Welles a budget of $50,000 to produce nine one-hour programs. CBS would provide the orchestra. Orson did not quibble. This was far from the production budget of *Lux* but it was a substantial endowment for an unsponsored sustaining program, especially compared to the paltry $400 per episode Irving Reis drew for the *Columbia Workshop*.

CBS must have also been impressed with Welles's ability to be his own publicist. Together with Houseman, he drafted a manifesto for the new venture and published it in the *New York Times* that July. The *Times* had in the past assiduously followed the fortunes of the Mercury Theatre, often allowing its founders to write position statements. In this most recent one, Welles insisted that the upcoming broadcasts not recapitulate the format of stage plays, which De Mille was trying to do with his *Lux Theatre*. Welles found it anathema when De Mille would say things like, "Ladies and gentlemen, the curtain is going up," and various other phrases geared to make listeners feel they were privy to an exclusive theatrical production. Time and again Welles wrote, and mentioned at press conferences, that radio drama is more akin to a novel than a play.[3] He insisted that it is as dependent on storytelling as it is on performance and therefore requires a narrator to help guide the listener through the experience. In Welles's view this narrator must not be some kind of disembodied voice telling us about what happened long ago and far away—the "once upon a time" format—but whenever possible should be a character or characters in the story, capable of establishing an intimate rapport with the listener. An effective first person narration, he believed, should make us feel events are unfolding as they are being described.

This emphasis led to the show's initial and somewhat pompous title, *First Person Singular*. It was awkward and often went unmentioned in subsequent commentary, where the program was usually referred to by using either Welles's name or the *Mercury Theatre* label. By the tenth broadcast, *First Person Singular* was no longer a replacement for *Lux*. It became a regular sustaining program with a new, Sunday 8:00 P.M. time slot and a new, more apropos name, *Mercury Theatre on the Air*, which would be widely cited. In doing *First Person Singular* Welles was fortunate enough to have at his disposal the CBS orchestra conducted by Bernard Herrmann. It was an auspicious and effective teaming; also a very collaborative one. Over the next few years most of Welles's radio dramas and his first two films, *Kane* and the *Magnificent Ambersons* (1942), would be scored and underscored by Herrmann's participation.

How and when they first met is uncertain, but it appears that the initial project that involved both of them was Irving Reis's *Columbia Workshop* two-part rendering of *Hamlet* in the fall of 1936, which was adapted and directed by Welles. In that instance he had to serve as peacemaker when Herrmann broke his baton and tossed the script in the air over a disagreement with Reis.[4] With only seconds until air time, Welles persuaded Herrmann to remount the podium; but the script and score were not replaced in the correct order. As a result the musical cues were off throughout, which Welles found amusing and Reis distressing. The three reunited for *The Fall of the City* on Sunday evening, 11 April 1937, which was an artistic triumph.

On 2 May, Reis handed the reins to Welles for a two-part reprisal of *Macbeth*, this time in Scottish rather than a voodoo mode. In lieu of exotic drums, Welles opted for bagpipes, which were not a part of the orchestral ensemble. He showed up late with his piper, and with a script twice too long. Editing it precluded rehearsing with the orchestra using Herrmann's music. According to Houseman, just before air time Welles told Herrmann, "No music! No music at all!"[5] What Welles meant was that he would cue the music and assume the role of conductor as well as director almighty. With one hand he invoked the bagpiper to play a dirge at various points in the story; with the other he pulled a fanfare out of the trumpets and drums when needed. With which hand he cued the sound effects is uncertain, but he effectively managed that task as well. His "Trust me, Benny! Just trust me!" did not allay the conductor's annoyance over this intrusion into his domain. He vowed never to work with Welles again. I suspect that he was also impressed with Welles's creative audacity.

After Welles brought a reluctant Herrmann to Hollywood in 1940 to do *Kane*, the composer/conductor remained and became one of the leading musical practitioners in cinema history. Among his credits are eight films with Alfred Hitchcock, including *Vertigo* (1958) and *Psycho* (1960). His final effort, released a year after his death, was Martin Scorsese's *Taxi Driver* (1976). He also scored television shows such as *Have Gun Will Travel* and *Gunsmoke*. Nevertheless, it should be remembered that many of the musical innovations he brought to film and television resulted from his work at CBS radio in the 1930s with Welles, Reis, and Norman Corwin. In a 1971 interview in *Sight and Sound*, he was explicit about this: "I learned to be a film composer by doing two or three thousand radio dramas. . . . Radio was the greatest place to train one's dramatic sense."[6]

Herrmann started with the requisite classical training, occasionally dabbling in composition. His chance to do radio resulted from a lucky break. In 1934 his friend Johnny Green (composer of the classic *Body and Soul*), who was then working at CBS, urged the head of the studio, William Paley, to hire Herrmann as Green's assistant. Radio was a thriving musical medium at the time and Herrmann soon got his first show, *Music in the Manner,* a program of classical and popular concert fare. He injected into the program his fondness for twentieth-century American composers such as George Gershwin and Charles Ives. After musically overseeing several programs involving literature readings, Herrmann became staff conductor in 1935. He soon went on to provide music for *School of the Air*, an educational anthology that occasionally featured a young Edward R. Murrow. This was followed by several performance-oriented offerings, such as *Exploring Music* and *Famous Musical Evenings*. Nevertheless, Herrmann constantly lobbied for more opportunities to showcase his compositional side. In the fall of 1937 *The Columbia Work-*

shop provided a valuable one. His work with Reis on that program set the context for what he would later accomplish with Welles, Hitchcock, Scorsese, and others.

Herrmann treated composing for radio, and later film, as a primary art form, not the mere addition of mood music. His approach eschewed using the full orchestra for every musical moment in favor of employing whatever combination of instruments would achieve the appropriate auditory complement—even if it meant hiring additional instrumentalists for the occasion or using nonmusical paraphernalia. His success in making musical motifs and sonorities serve dramatic purpose was and still may be without equal—the shower sequence in Hitchcock's *Psycho* being perhaps his most renowned musical segment.

In addition to his work in a variety of media, Herrmann had aspirations as a "serious" orchestral composer. However, his efforts in this area were primarily neo-Romantic rehash and not widely appreciated. He was also not a tunesmith, a fact he was painfully aware of when fellow film composers began to produce a series of hits beginning in the late 1940s; this failing was partly behind his falling out with Hitchcock in 1965. And, although from the outset to the end of his career he harbored the desire to be a leading conductor, his volatile personality mitigated against the possibility. It would also, on occasion, cost him a chance to work on a major film.

Herrmann's explosive temperament was present from an early age. When his first violin teacher disapproved of the way he played a particular piece, young Benny promptly broke the fiddle over the man's head.[7] In 1935 this orneriness could have very nearly cost him his job at CBS. When network head William Paley expressed reservations about some of Herrmann's musical ideas, the response was, "You're assuming the public is as ignorant about music as you are."[8] Rather than lashing back, the unflappable Paley seriously pondered whether Herrmann might in fact be right. Perhaps as much to understand himself as well as to explore links between the emotions and music, Herrmann became a devotee of psychology, especially Freud. Yet, in stark contrast to his incendiary public persona, his letters and essays reveal an exceptionally composed and rational intellect.

Welles handled Herrmann in stride, and vice versa, after some initial hesitation. Orson realized that in this collaboration, unlike the festering cold war with Houseman, disagreements would be immediate and open—the clash of two similar temperaments resulting in a kind of balance of power. Herrmann, for his part, always insisted that he found difficult people like Welles the easiest to deal with, while he was constantly suspicious of the friendly types he called "glad-Harrys." And clash they did, but with an unwavering mutual artistic respect. After one set-to while working on *Kane*, Herrmann delivered a litany of insulting remarks about Welles to eager reporters, then checked himself to remind them that he was referring to Orson the man, not Orson the artist.⁹

Herrmann welcomed the by-the-seat-of-the-pants experience that working with Welles on a regular basis entailed.

> Welles's radio quality, like Sir Thomas Beecham's in music, was essentially one of spontaneity. At the start of every broadcast Orson was an unknown quantity. As he went along his mood would assert itself and the temperature would start to increase till the point of incandescence. . . . Even when his shows weren't good they were better than other people's successes. He inspired us all—the musicians, the actors, the sound-effects men and the engineers. They'd all tell you they never worked on shows like Welles's. Horses' hooves are horses' hooves—yet they felt different with Orson—why? I think it had to do with the element of the unknown, the surprises and the uncomfortable excitement of improvisation.¹⁰

It did not take Herrmann long to tune into these traits and to prepare radio scores on very short notice. This did not require starting from scratch for each performance, since he had a bag of musical tricks composed for just about every dramatic occasion. In working with Welles it became a matter of selecting and modifying the appropriate motifs, then composing the necessary transitions. It may have been hectic, but it was also inclusive and intimate, as indicated in an interview taped shortly before he died.

> Orson is an improviser. Orson hasn't any one way to do anything. It's an ensemble performance. Everybody who works with Orson is part of everything. You're with him at meals and on the holidays. Your life and his become one for the time you work together. Welles was almost a precocious child when you worked with him. It was an instantaneous intuitive understanding of what should be done.¹¹

According to Houseman, the idea to team Welles and Herrmann came from the lanky and articulate executive producer of *First Person Singular*, Davidson Taylor. It was more than a marriage of CBS convenience, since the musically trained and well-read Taylor sensed immediately the creative chemistry a Welles/Herrmann collaboration might unleash. Fortunately, his openness to innovation was tempered by enough patience to keep his two charges in check . . . most of the time. That he got them together at all, after the *Macbeth* incident a year previous, testifies to his administrative adroitness and interpersonal skill.

First Person Singular had to have a theme, an identifiable musical signature. Houseman notes that it was Taylor who suggested the memorable Tchaikovsky Piano Concerto in B Flat Minor. Neither Welles nor Herrmann seemed to object or suggest alternatives, but the CBS brass was not enthusiastic. A lively big band piece, they thought, would be more appropriate to the medium and the era. Nevertheless, it was ultimately Taylor's call and his choice was inspired. The sonorous melody, recognizable by almost anyone today—although the title of the piece and the composer's name might be hard for a nonmusically trained person to recall—washes over the listener through a series of evocative orchestral chords. Here is music of a high order steeped in an emotionalism that has mass appeal . . . for a program trying to do the same with literature.

One of the criteria Welles insisted on was that there be no studio audience. Radio was for him a conjuring act. To glimpse its behind-the-scenes infrastructure was tantamount to observing the wires, false bottoms, and other devices used by a magician when performing his act. The absence of an audience also liberated his actors to perform without inhibition and to dress and gyrate in whatever way was necessary to be effective.

In the other notable prime time drama anthology series, C. B. De Mille's *Lux Radio Theatre*, a live audience was de rigeur. One imagines (no doubt accurately) his movie star actors dressed in their finery, struggling to play an emotional scene, script in hand, without looking too disheveled before their public. CBS, in any case, did not object to *Mercury's* radio stage remaining private, nor would Campbell Soup when they assumed sponsorship of the program in December. For Welles's public—those who had seen him perform on stage, or the many who just wanted a glimpse of the legend in the making—it was another story. He was besieged with requests to attend the broadcast. His response was humorous and worth citing at length:

> Frankly, this is what is known as a form letter. Many people like yourself have written us asking for tickets for our forthcoming broadcasts on the Columbia Network—too many for us to accommodate without setting up some silly system of selection and rejection—and they are all, every one of them receiving this answer: We have written it into our constitution in large black letters that no one, no family friend or family enemy, no representative of the Radio Industry, or of the radio laity, shall be allowed within visiting distance. . . . [ellipses are his] This is flat; this is final; and this is probably a little foolish. We of the Mercury are going crazy as it is, and, what with records, our new fall production, Summer Theatres, the hot weather and things, the puzzle of picking a studio audience is a problem in precedence we can't solve, and a positive pain in the neck. I am quite certain you cannot fail to understand where this would end, that is, if it should ever end.

Thank you, anyway; thank you and you, and you my cousin Laura, and you Mr. Flinkinirons, the Vice-President of CBS, and you Mrs. Somebody who will never come to see another Mercury play again, and you—you who are tearing up this particular letter at this particular minute; thank you for asking to come, and for wanting to come, and for not coming. Thank you and please understand.

Yours sincerely,[12]

With the agreement of all parties *Treasure Island* would launch the series. In retrospect it was a sensible decision. The book is an accessible literary classic imbued with adventure, although devoid of any love interest. In 1934 it had yielded a successful movie starring Wallace Beery and Jackie Cooper. For the radio play Welles would narrate, provide several voices, and play the role of Long John Silver. As to a suitable script, well, that July he was busy on a film segment for the stage play *Too Much Johnson*, and having, or trying to have an affair with renowned ballerina Vera Zorina, so he sentenced Houseman to scriptorial labor.

A radio neophyte, Houseman did the best he could via a scissors and paste condensation of the book. Welles popped in on occasion to suggest changes. Then, with less than a week to go, Orson suggested another project, *Dracula*. Why the switch? Granted, he had always had a fondness for the story, which after debuting in Bram Stoker's novel was successfully adapted to the stage and then made into a movie in 1931 featuring Bela Lugosi's memorable performance. But CBS had already expressed enthusiasm for the *Treasure Island* project and *Time* magazine had listed it as the first program in the series. *Newsweek* did not mention what the new series would broadcast first, but they gave it great advance billing, mentioning Welles's history of successful adaptations for different media and his innovative approach to radio storytelling.

Looking at this relatively sudden change of stories in the context of Welles's overall career, it does not appear surprising. The substitution is consistent with his gnomic unpredictability and suggests that he wanted to begin with something more ambitious than *Treasure Island*. Perhaps he thought that since the novel is often associated with children's literature, a more adult-oriented story was preferable for the initial broadcast. Also, proposing the more daring *Dracula* to CBS initially might have met with resistance, while springing it on them at the last minute would make it harder for them to question the choice. A similar switch would occur two years later. After several false starts on other projects he began shooting *Citizen Kane* without a preliminary go-ahead from RKO, telling the studio he was only making tests.

Houseman, now aware he was facing Gothic horror instead of piracy, put aside his Robert Louis Stevenson collage. With the assistance of honeymoon returnee Augusta Weissberger, he pointed his scissors at Bram Stoker. Welles, as per Welles, gave brief instructions as to how the bloodsucking count should be portrayed, then he vanished. When he returned two days before rehearsal, he joined Houseman for a scripting session at Reuben's restaurant on 59th Street.[13] Never one to subscribe literally to the adage that hunger fuels artistic creativity, Welles ate and created. On they went past midnight, with coffee and cognac lubricating the flow of ideas until another meal was warranted: steaks, very rare in honor of the occasion, followed by cheesecake, coffee, and brandy. Sometime during this gastronomic and literary binge, Augusta was roused from slumber to bring some cash and to pick up copy for typing. At dawn a massive breakfast was ordered. At nine they fed a stake to the count and the draft was completed. Three days later, on 11 July, the results were broadcast.

Welles was insistent that the Mercury *Dracula* be based on the 1897 novel, not the play written two decades later by Hamilton Deane and John Balderson, which became the basis of most subsequent interpretations. (He later told Peter Bogdanovich that he had once played Dracula in the stage play,[14] but if such a performance took place it has gone unnoticed by some very thorough biographers.) The problem with a faithful rendering of the original novel is that the story is told from multiple points of view. This is complex for the listener to be sure, but rewarding for those who tuned in for the entire broadcast.

It was a stunning debut, brilliant in conception, if not always in script and execution. The complexity of the story and diversity of sound effects resulted in a juggling act that Welles was barely able to manage. Directing the ghoulish pandemonium was not made any easier by the fact that he played two major roles in the story, Dr. Arthur Seward, the principal narrator, and the sanguine count himself. The other Mercury players included George Coulouris, Martin Gabel, Ray Collins, Karl Swenson, Elizabeth Farrell, and the redoubtable Agnes Moorehead.

The show began with an introductory flourish. Dan Seymour announced that the Mercury Theatre would be presenting a unique new summer series. For whatever reason, the *First Person Singular* title was not mentioned until the conclusion, and then only in passing. It was also absent in most newspaper listings, which referred to the program as *Mercury Theatre* or *Mercury Theatre on the Air*, the name it would eventually assume. Perhaps *First Person Singular* was just too pompous or academic a title—a grammatical category after all. Following Dan Seymour's sign-on, Welles is touted by a series of voices:

> In a single year, the first in the life of the Mercury Theatre, Orson Welles has come to be the most famous name in American drama. Says *Collier's* magazine: "Twenty-three-year-old Orson Welles threw a bombshell into Broadway." Robert Benchley writes in the *New Yorker*, "The production of the Mercury is, I should say, just about perfect." *Time* magazine declares, "The brightest moon that has risen over Broadway in years, Welles should feel at home in the sky,

for the sky is the only limit which his ambition recognizes." And finally the United Press remarked, "The meteoric rise of Orson Welles continues unabated."

I cannot help recalling, in response to words such as "bombshell," "Moon," and "meteoric," what Welles would unleash a few months later with *War of the Worlds*. In any case, the introduction switches back to Seymour's voice and continues:

> With four hit shows in the first year, the Mercury Theatre can well close its doors on a season unparalleled in Broadway history, but Mr. Welles has long been working on a project for a greater audience, the Broadways of the entire United States. The Columbia network is proud to give Orson Welles the opportunity to bring to the air those same qualities of vitality and imagination that have made him the most talked about theatrical director in America today. And it is this project which Columbia brings you this summer; the first time in its history that radio has ever extended such an invitation to an entire theatrical institution. But here is Orson Welles himself to tell you about it.

We then hear the master's voice speaking in serious and sincere tones, although a bit too fast. He tells us what we can expect in the coming weeks and presents a litany of famous authors whose works will be adapted. This is highbrow fare for radio to be sure, but it should be noted that six of the ten initial program ideas had already been done as motion pictures, so maybe it is not so highbrow after all. Besides *Dracula* and *Treasure Island*, film versions of *A Tale of Two Cities* (1916; 1935); *The Thirty-Nine Steps* (1935); *Abraham Lincoln* (1930); and *The Count of Monte Cristo* (1934) were well known. Welles goes on to introduce George Coulouris and Martin Gabel, and then touts *Dracula* as the best story of its kind, before bidding us adieu as he slips into the character of Dr. Seward.

The musical segue to Seward's first speech consists of crashing minor chords accompanied by chimes. It anticipates the opening sequence of *Kane*, which itself plays like the introduction to a Gothic horror story. Seward's light English accent tells us that ominous events have occurred, which will be revealed through the journal of Jonathan Harker. George Coulouris's voice continues the story. Harker is Transylvania bound to consummate a deal whereby Count Dracula will purchase an abode in England. His journey is accompanied by sound effects, including a train, horse-drawn coach (the clippity-clop sounding surprisingly artificial), howling wolves, and thunder. It is overkill, too loud and fast paced. Critics might contend, as they have with Welles's films, that this is yet another example of his use of technique that draws attention to itself. However, the sound in subsequent Mercury broadcasts would improve considerably.

Harker soon finds that he is a prisoner in Castle Dracula, despite his host's insisting the contrary. In portraying the count, Welles creates one of his most riveting characters in radio drama. He uses a deep voice that is simultaneously sinister and reassuring. It owes little, if anything, to the Bela Lugosi characterization that has so etched Dracula in our mind's ear. The timbre and accent employed seem to foreshadow the way he would speak as Colonel Haki of the Turkish police in *Journey into Fear* (1942). If Lon Chaney's sobriquet was "the man of a thousand faces," then Welles's should be "the man of a thousand voices."

Before Dracula leaves for England and the Harker entries temporarily end, there is a humorous incident whereby Harker cuts himself while shaving, and the count, trying to show restraint, warns him that "doing such a thing in this country could be dangerous." Seward continues the story by reading newspaper accounts of a shipwreck in which the captain's corpse was tied to the helm and a black dog was seen to leave the wreckage as it washed ashore. What happened on board is revealed through yet another point of view: an account found in a bottle in the Russian captain's (Ray Collins) pocket, who now takes over the narration and tells us of Dracula's shipboard machinations.

We return to Seward, who passes the story via telegram to his Viennese mentor, Dr. Van Helsing (Martin Gabel). It seems that Seward's fiancée, Lucy (Elizabeth Farrell), is down on her blood, so to speak. Van Helsing assures us that since "she's not anemic," those two puncture wounds on her neck just might be the cause. While Seward goes to London to visit a patient, Lucy gets a visitation of her own. The story shifts to her voice and a memoir she wrote at 2:00 A.M. Sound effects put us in the mood: wind, a window breaking, and a wolf howl. The last entry has Dracula's voice saying, "You shall be flesh of my flesh, blood of my blood," followed by an orgasmic sigh from Lucy.

When the two doctors return they find her on the floor dying. An explanation of why they left her alone in the first place is not provided; perhaps it was lost in the scripting session at Reuben's restaurant somewhere between the cheesecake and the brandy. There are other gaps in the story, but it must be remembered that these radio plays, in contrast to written fiction, and even film scripts, were prepared on extremely short notice—usually in less than a week—and therefore should not be judged by the same standards.

After an unexplained lapse of time, we find out Lucy is dead and buried, but the local children are showing up with incisions on their necks similar to hers. They tell of a beautiful woman who lured them with chocolates. Van

Helsing takes up the narration. He explains the strange events via a lesson from Vampirology 101. Taking a crucifix, Bible, and stake, the two doctors head for the local graveyard to liberate Lucy. Seward does the deed, Van Helsing the reading. Lucy's scream is worthy of Fay Wray's best effort in *King Kong* (1933). It must have led more than one 1938 family member to exhort, "Turn down the radio!"

The saga continues with Seward's chronicle of how a dazed Harker was found wandering the Transylvanian hills only to be returned by medical authorities to England. It was Harker's wife Mina (Agnes Moorehead) who brought his diary to light. She now takes up the story, although Seward's and Van Helsing's perspectives soon reenter. The three of them form a vampire hit squad and, with holy water in hand, douse the resting places of native soil the count has stashed in England. Unfortunately, Mina soon gets a nocturnal visit similar to Lucy's, after which Dracula grabs passage on the first steamer home.

Under Van Helsing's hypnosis, Mina provides further information on the count's plans. Taking the faster overland route, the trio try to head him off at the pass, literally. They close in just before he reaches Castle Dracula, whereupon his coach crashes. Seward moves in with the stake, but it is sunset and the count is up for the challenge. He snarls that Mina is his, and reels off a shopping list of diabolical incantations. Mina then snatches the stake away from Seward, "with the strength of an animal." We hear a piercing scream . . . it fades out . . . and then after a lapse of time, the voice of Seward as narrator tells us that it was Mina who ultimately skewered the count.

This finale is exceptionally well done. By that point in the broadcast the glitches had been worked out, the sound effects were in balance, and the voices clearly audible. Welles delivers Dracula's final diatribe in a poetic basso worthy of a Shakespeare reading—the Voodoo *Macbeth*, with its male witches, might have been an influence.

As announcer Dan Seymour signs off, he mentions that the program we have just heard is the first of a series to be presented "in the immediacy of the first person singular." The cast is announced, as is Davidson Taylor and Seymour himself. However, it is Welles who has the last word. He mentions that next week's episode will be *Treasure Island*, and if listeners have any additional story preferences they should write to him. He goes on to assure us that the specter of Dracula should not cause us worry . . . and is interrupted by a wolf howl. . . . "Just the sound effects," notes Orson, who quickly slips into character and, in the voice of the count, insists that there *are* wolves and vampires. A similar playful epilogue (perhaps an aspect of his Shadow persona) would follow the *War of the Worlds* broadcast, only in that one he would reassure us that there are no Martians.

Reviews of *Dracula* were favorable, and although the audience was not large, increased public awareness of the program would expand listenership the following week. *Dracula* was an auspicious debut for Mercury, not on a par with *Julius Caesar* on Broadway and *Citizen Kane* in cinema, to be sure, but a broadcasting landmark nonetheless. Comparisons with *Kane* reveal some intriguing parallels. In both productions Welles pulls out all stops technically; both stories use flashbacks based on multiple points of view, a technique that would reach its cinematic apogee in Akira Kurosawa's *Rashomon* (1950); and both deal with the downfall of a powerful figure who overreaches his grasp. This latter theme would reemerge in later Welles films, such as *The Stranger* (1946), *Macbeth* (1948), *Mr. Arkadin* (1950), *Touch of Evil* (1958), *The Immortal Story* (1968), and some would say it emerges in his own life after *Kane*.

Preparing *Dracula* and *Treasure Island* set a pattern for future programs. Welles and Houseman would pick a story for adaptation. This would often be a classic, but it had to be sufficiently reducible to a radio drama format—epics such as *War and Peace* would have to remain between the covers. Most of the initial writing, up until Howard Koch became a regular with the 9 October broadcast of *Hell on Ice*, was done by Houseman. This usually took place on less than a week's notice. He winced under the pressure but remained stoic. As a result Welles often took him for granted. Had Houseman been more assertive and argumentative with him, as Bernard Herrmann was, it is possible that the terrible confrontations that occurred later in their partnership might have been avoided.

Given his lack of experience in radio, Houseman did a more than credible job. Not surprisingly, his later memoirs and essays reveal a substantial writing ability. As Houseman scripted each program, Welles might, or might not, provide further input; and he might, or might not, show up for the preliminary rehearsals conducted by Paul Stewart. These sessions used only the most basic sound effects and no music. An acetate recording was usually made and given to Welles, who would then begin revising. In a day or two another rehearsal would follow the format of the first. On broadcast day, Monday until the switch to Sunday on 11 September following the series' renewal, a dress rehearsal would be held with Herrmann's orchestra and a full complement of sound effects. Houseman has noted that these final run-throughs were apparently something to behold. Welles would revise right up until the eleventh hour, paying particular attention to the integration of music and sound effects with the story. Tantrums were common, so were insults and things thrown. But when the red light went on at 9:00 P.M., the task at hand voided all other considerations.

Treasure Island aired on 18 July. It was a much more straightforward story than *Dracula*. Only one first person narrative guides it, that of Jim Hawkins. Welles played him as a adult, and fourteen-year old Arthur Anderson voiced the young Jim. Orson of course also had the plum role, Long John Silver. Unlike *Dracula*, which was brilliantly conceived but only a partial success in production, *Treasure Island* was performed almost flawlessly. From the outset, the balance of first person narration, music, sound effects, and character acting seizes the listener. All thoughts that this might be a story primarily geared for children must have vanished in the windblown Gothic sequence that opens the drama.

Welles introduces the radio play by talking about the origins of the novel: a young boy asking his stepfather (Robert Louis Stevenson) to tell him an interesting story. It is doubtful, however, that there were many young listeners tuned in, given the 9:00 P.M. Monday air time. Children whose parents let them listen must have been both thrilled and unsettled by the program. The violence, moral ambiguity of the characters, and actions of young Jim Hawkins would not have been permissible if this were broadcast solely as children's fare. The same moralistic pressures that in 1934 had imposed a stringent enforcement of the film production code also led the Federal Communications Commission to a similar taming of radio, especially with youth-oriented programs. *Treasure Island* is, however, a dark tale in any medium. The violence and death at close quarters in it even led to censorship of the Disney version as late as 1975; the sequences were restored in the 1994 home video release.

Arthur Anderson is particularly effective as young Jim. To have someone the same age as the character play the role was fortunate, and a rarity for Mercury. Most future productions would utilize adults "playing down" for such parts, with indifferent results. Young Jim's transformation, from wide-eyed naiveté to tempered worldliness, is done in gradual and convincing increments. Throughout the drama the first person voices (adult and then young Jim) come in at just the right intervals to guide the story and bridge the inevitable gaps in such a condensation. As for the condensation itself, kudos should have gone to Houseman. Welles might have directed the production, but Houseman scripted most of it. This was his initial effort at writing for the medium—he had started to work on *Treasure Island* before the switch to *Dracula*—and one he was able to spend more time on than would be the case with later programs.

Of Bernard Herrmann's music, not enough can be said. If pressed I would pick it as the best radio drama score of that era. Never one for modesty, the composer might have felt the same way. There is reason behind my speculation. When Herrmann was asked to pick what he thought was his best work in film, *Citizen Kane* got the nod, and, to my ears, at least, there are notable parallels between that score and the one for *Treasure Island*. Several motifs in the movie occur first in the radio play, in particular when the muted brass section plays minor key passages to evoke a Gothic mood. In both productions the music of course accomplishes much more, but in remarkably similar ways. It evokes place and character, and effects transitions, without unduly drawing attention to itself. Other ears might disagree and find the scores intrusive; if so, they would probably say this is more apparent in the film than in the radio play. It is possible that the music in *Treasure Island* might seem clichéd to contemporary listeners habituated to what would come later in cinema. But this is a testament to Herrmann's creativity. Far from using hackneyed techniques, he pioneered a musical style for radio drama, which *he then brought to film*, where it would set influential standards.

Welles, along with Norman Corwin, Irving Reis, and Arch Oboler, also used radio sound in ways that would later influence motion pictures. *Treasure Island* is rife with blatant and nuanced effects that help vivify place: the wind and sea; the tapping of blind Pew's cane; the ebb and flow of jungle noise; and the casual sounds of period interiors, chairs, doors, windows, and the like. From the outset Welles knew exactly the kind of sound he wanted for a given scene. However, his knowledge of how to achieve it was not always as astute.

In his revealing account of the history of radio sound effects, Robert Mott notes that when Welles started in radio he was a "visual director," in other words one who believes that a sound over the air should match the image of how it is produced.[15] Possibly this was a legacy from his work in theater. In one unnamed Mercury production that Mott recalls, Welles required the sound of footsteps in the desert. During rehearsal, the sound effects people delivered it convincingly with cornstarch in a box. Welles was not satisfied: "I'll be damned if you're going to do the footsteps for my desert story in a box cats use to poop in." Numerous bags of sand were then trucked in from Coney Island—only to demonstrate that walking on real sand does not sound very convincing over the air. Attempts to amplify it only distorted the voices. Welles had the sand removed and went with the cat box. More important, he gained increased respect for those sound effects people who helped him conjure the Mercury broadcasts each week. Rarely cited in the program's credits, Mott lists them as Bill Brown, Henry Gauthierre, Ray Kremer, Ora Nichols, and Jim Rogan.[16]

The concluding salutation of *Treasure Island* has Welles appearing out of character to pay tribute to the cast: Ray Collins, George Coulouris, William Alland, Richard Wilson, Agnes Moorehead (who is especially good in her few scenes as Jim's mother), et al. Singular kudos are bequeathed to fourteen-year-old Arthur Anderson. In praising the young man's work with Mercury,

Welles must have remembered the incident a year before whereby the lad touched off the sprinkler system during a performance of the funeral scene in *Julius Caesar*—probably the result of playing with matches. As Brutus, Welles bore the brunt of the soaker, and Anderson became for a time persona non grata.[17] However, he more than redeemed himself as young Jim.

As for the actor who played Jim Hawkins senior, Welles wryly notes that he "bear[s] no comment." A *Tale of Two Cities* is announced as next week's offering. Then, as was the case the previous week, listeners are asked to write in with story suggestions. This is a paean to the openness of a sustaining program, free of commercials, funded by the network, and ceding almost complete artistic control to the producer. With Campbell Soup taking over sponsorship in December, program ideas would often be suggested, and at the very least scrutinized, by the Ward Wheelock advertising agency. Although it would be the notoriety stemming from *War of the Worlds* that would eventually bring the soup empire on board, they had already given thought to sponsorship six months earlier. *Treasure Island* had served as a kind of audition broadcast. Why a deal was not consummated then seems baffling in light of the quality of the production and favorable critical response. Perhaps the powers that be wanted to see in what direction the series would head and its viability with the public.

Welles also managed to ad-lib some comments to fill in what remained of the hour, a technique that would reach its apogee a few weeks later, on 5 September, in *A Man Who Was Thursday*. Far from the result of bad planning, finishing early was prudent and easily handled; the opposite would have been disastrous. Orson had the ability to pull engaging words out of the air as easily as he did rabbits out of a hat in his magician's persona. Several decades later he would flaunt this skill on television while substituting for Johnny Carson on the *Tonight Show*.

These first broadcasts of *First Person Singular* were a valuable creative outlet for Welles. The new artistic direction helped offset problems in the previous one. As Mercury geared itself to the airwaves, its theatrical incarnation was experiencing setbacks. The second season was supposed to unfold with *Five Kings*, an ambitious Shakespeare adaptation, and William Gillette's Gay Nineties farce, *Too Much Johnson*. Reversing the order seemed wise. *Five Kings* was an elaborate and expensive production, which, it was thought, would benefit from a lighter and commercially successful segue. If *Too Much Johnson* could have done what *Horse Eats Hat* did two years previous, the strategy might have worked.

July 1938 turned out to be one of the most artistically remarkable and frustrating periods in Welles's career. If a debut in which he had creative control of his own radio series was not enough, he decided to test his relatively untried abilities at filmmaking. He conceived a forty-minute cinematic prologue to set the stage, so to speak, for *Too Much Johnson*. Only one effort with the medium had preceded it, *Hearts of Age*, the four-minute experimental spoof of symbolist films he made in the summer of 1934. The film segment for *Too Much Johnson* was far more ambitious. It involved slapstick humor and a protracted chase in the Mack Sennett tradition. Unfortunately, the only surviving copy of the film was destroyed in a fire at Welles's home in Spain in 1970. However, thanks to Frank Brady's 1978 interview with him and subsequent biography, we have a detailed description of most of the scenes.[18]

To finalize this cinematic overture, Welles put himself under veritable house arrest at the St. Regis. "Knee deep in twenty-five thousand feet of combustible nitrate film," according to Houseman, Orson glued himself to a Moviola. He struggled to make the sequence make sense—a labor as frustrating as it was daunting. Whether his occasional forays to CBS to rehearse and perform episodes of *First Person Singular* were a welcome diversion or a resented interruption is uncertain. During this period, Welles had to learn, largely on his own, a good deal about the basics of film editing. Unencumbered by the heavy hand of orthodoxy, aspects of his unique cinematic vision must have been born of the experience. If found, a copy of the *Too Much Johnson* sequence would no doubt be a boon to the legion of commentators who have tried to fathom that vision.

The play was due to begin its pre-Broadway trial at the Stony Creek Connecticut Summer Theater on 16 August. Several days before, a test run with the available segments of the film was attempted. The footage was woefully incomplete and the venue itself not consonant with film projection. The project was abandoned, as was the play after a two-week run. Welles was distraught. It was his first major theatrical setback. Houseman describes him as retreating to an air-conditioned refuge at the St. Regis and brooding for a week in a room still darkened from his film editing efforts. Wracked by asthma, self-doubt, remorse, and who knows what else, he managed to surface on the seventh day to face his commitment to CBS and to begin planning *Danton's Death* for Mercury's theatrical season opener.

Somehow, during the entire *Too Much Johnson* episode, from mid-July to mid-August, radio programs got done and done well. On 25 July, the choice of *A Tale of Two Cities* for the third Mercury broadcast was prompted, according to Dan Seymour's introduction and Welles's sign-off, by listener requests. Condensing Dickens's lengthy novel into a one-hour drama was no easy task. The radio version, by necessity, had to delete secondary characters and a few subplots. First person narration, as per usual, provided the transitions. However, there are several leaps in the radio play that would probably have been best negotiated by listeners familiar with the novel or the 1935 film.

If the script is not as effective at scaling down the novel as the writing would be in subsequent broadcasts, the performance more than makes up for it. Welles plays two roles. He is Dr. Manette, who is unjustly imprisoned for giving medical attention to several peasants after they have an altercation with the aristocracy. And in London, he is Sydney Carton, a debauching, misanthropic lawyer who redeems his life through an avowed, "far, far better thing I do than I have ever done before." The thing he does is rescue from the guillotine Charles Darney (Edgar Barrier), the fiancé of Doctor Manette's daughter, Lucie (Mary Taylor). Darney is a former French aristocrat, now an émigré to England, who is imprisoned when he returns to France to clear the name of one of his former servants. Carton saves Darney by knocking him out in prison and trading places. The above quote is uttered just before he ascends the scaffold. During this moving finale, Carton's redemption is twofold, since he consoles an innocent seamstress whose execution precedes his. Through the horror, the crowd cheers and keeps count, "21 . . . 22 . . . 23 . . . " while the infamous Madame de Farge (Betty Garde) knits her legendary scorecard.

The sound effects, as in the previous week with *Treasure Island*, were both realistic and in balance with the dialogue. The prison, ship, and courtroom scenes are particularly compelling. They were also relatively easy to do, since similar sequences had been created for previous radio dramas. What was new was the guillotine. The sound of the mechanism seems to derive from the closing or sliding of a metal door. As for the chop and drop of the head, Houseman has said that this took a bit more time to figure out. After numerous experiments, what worked best was a meat cleaver slicing a cabbage in half, with the severed part dropping into a wicker basket.[19]

The following week, the reign of terror that gripped France in the throes of revolution was supplanted by fear of domestic terror in World War I Britain. *The Thirty-Nine Steps*, John Buchan's popular novel (made even more popular as a result of Alfred Hitchcock's 1935 film), was transformed into a successful radio play. It was a challenge for both Mercury and its audience. The various locations and accompanying sound effects required diverse and especially well-timed production values; and the complexity of the story again favored those listeners with some familiarity with either its earlier print or celluloid incarnations. Playing both Richard Hannay and, later in the story, Marmaduke Jopely, Welles opens with Hannay's first person account of how the bizarre espionage saga began. Falsely accused of murder, he is pursued by both the authorities and dastardly Germans. A cross-country chase ensues. Although these events were supposed to have happened during the previous war, the drama was presented in a way that must have made them seem somewhat contemporary in 1938. Welles's hostility and suspicions regarding what the Axis powers were up to was not tempered. Isolationists and pre–World War II admirers of the Reich, such as Charles Lindbergh, would no doubt have construed his interpretation of the story as extreme and unwarranted.

The closing sequence exposes Lord Sterling as an impostor and spy. The thirty-nine steps are revealed as the escape route from his villa to the sea. As British agents prepare to close in on the villa, Hannay stalls his lordship's plans by engaging him in a tense game of billiards. I suspect the stalling had to do with more than just the story. The pacing and dialogue suggest the timing of the production had come up just a bit short and needed to be stretched. As the drama ended, Welles appeared at the microphone for his typical sign-off. Knowing that Hitchcock's film must have been in the minds of many listeners, he remarked, "If you missed Madeleine Carroll you should blame Hitchcock; if you were surprised by anything you should blame us." The idea of Hannay having a romantic interest was solely Hitchcock's. In their versions of the story neither Buchan nor Welles made this concession to popular sentiment. Welles's reference to the audience missing Miss Carroll would be rectified in the 10 February 1939 edition of *Campbell Playhouse*. She would play Lucilla Crespin in Mercury's version of William Archer's *The Green Goddess*.

The format of the program changed for the next broadcast. Instead of the usual one-hour drama, Mercury presented a triptych of short stories: *The Little Boy* by Carl Ewald, *The Open Window* by Saki, and *I'm a Fool* by Sherwood Anderson. The program went off smoothly thanks to some effective scripting by Houseman and Welles's unyielding capacity to play as many characters as the scripts required. The multistory format would be tried again on 6 November, a week after *War of the Worlds*, but for the next three months the one hour, one drama mode would predominate. The following week's subject, however, would take this format in a somewhat different direction. Rather than interpreting a novel, Welles and Houseman went with a play, John Drinkwater's *Abraham Lincoln*. I suspect the selection resulted from the relative ease with which this theater piece could be adapted for radio. It also allowed them to spend time elsewhere: doubtlessly in final preparation for the Stony Creek opening of *Too Much Johnson*.

The presentation of *Abraham Lincoln* was accompanied by a sudden increase in Mercury's radio audience. From now on, it was announced, *First*

Person Singular would be picked up by the Canadian Broadcasting Corporation coast to coast. Clearly the program's reputation for doing accessible artistic fare must have prompted its selection by public broadcasters north of the border. Welles and company should have perhaps chosen another Mercury offering to showcase the series to Canadian listeners. *Abraham Lincoln* is a pastiche of monologue, speeches, and recreated conversations that comes off as a sentimental history lesson with very little drama. That it could have been otherwise is suggested by one previous and two later film versions of the life of the great man: *Abraham Lincoln* (1930), which featured Walter Huston in a rare D. W. Griffith talkie; *Young Mr. Lincoln* (1939), with John Ford directing Henry Fonda; and *Abe Lincoln in Illinois* (1940), directed by John Cromwell, with Raymond Massey, a Canadian, in *the* definitive screen portrayal of the president.

The Mercury version deals with events just before, during, and immediately after the war. Welles is forceful, if not historically convincing, when he voices Lincoln's views on "the rights of Negroes," a monologue probably fueled by his own strong advocacy of civil rights. The music is maudlin throughout, mostly variations on "John Brown's Body" and "When Johnny Comes Marching Home." The actors, Ray Collins, George Coulouris, Karl Swenson, Agnes Moorehead, et al., seem to lack energy.

The format of adapting a play rather than a novel would continue for another week with *The Affairs of Anatole* by Arthur Schnitzler. It was more melodramatic and adult oriented than previous broadcasts, and had Houseman and Welles adding diary and letter readings, along with some additional monologues, to enhance the adaptation. Although sound effects were not of paramount importance for this theater piece, save for the music used to evoke the Viennese locale, their role would resurface significantly in the tour de force to follow on 29 August, Alexander Dumas's *The Count of Monte Cristo*. The period depicted, settings, and accents had already been field tested in July and August the previous year in *Les Misérables*, presented over the Mutual Network. Welles introduces *The Count of Monte Cristo* with more zest and verbiage than usual, gleefully noting how the immensely talented Dumas nevertheless went bankrupt because of his theater ventures, a fate Orson could well appreciate. He also mentions, no doubt as a challenge to racial prejudice, that Dumas's grandmother was a negress.

Welles would of course play Edmund Dantes. Falsely accused of treason by the jealous cousin, Montego, of his betrothed, Mercedes, Dantes is incarcerated in a seaside prison, the Château d'If. He nearly goes insane bearing the weight of his innocence. In desperation he digs a tunnel to a neighboring cell and encounters the "mad priest," who gives him scholarly and emotional council for eight years. The legacy includes a map to find a lost treasure buried on the isle of Monte Cristo. When the priest dies, Dantes takes his place in the burial sack and is thrown into the ocean. He escapes, finds the fortune, becomes a count, and returns home to clear the name of Edmund Dantes after a total lapse of time of fourteen years. Using his wealth and wiles, Dantes arranges for his enemies, foremost among them Montego, to swindle one another; and in so doing, they clear him.

Welles again strikes an effective balance between the first person narration of part of a story and the dramatized sequences. His reflections as Dantes are delivered with the emotional resonance of Shakespeare soliloquies. The villain in the story is not just the diabolical Montego, but a corrupt government capable of imprisoning the innocent because of the influence of men like him. Too rigid to be changed through reason, it must be righted through individual acts of defiance. Welles revels in this Byronic theme. The part of Mercedes was played by Anna Stafford, in actuality Virginia Welles. By this point in their strained marriage she must have been feeling that his role in this story should have been that of Montego rather than Dantes.

In a period piece such as this, music and sound effects are crucial. For whatever reasons, Bernard Herrmann was unavailable for the production. It was musically arranged by Alexander Semmler. His style here is so faithful to Herrmann's that I suspect the maestro may have provided him with several motifs to work into the score. A major use of sound in the drama was the acoustic environment in which Dantes digs toward and eventually encounters the mad priest. According to Houseman, Welles did this with a special microphone placed at the base of a toilet in the men's room. The actors spoke into it at floor level, their voices reverberating convincingly. A second microphone, placed inside a toilet that was periodically flushed, provided an effective simulation of waves breaking at the base of the prison wall.

The ninth and last airing of *First Person Singular* occurred the following week, 5 September, with a broadcast of G. K. Chesterton's *The Man Who Was Thursday*. Dan Seymour introduces the show by noting that it is the final installment in the series, since the *Lux Radio Theatre*, for which it was a summer replacement, would be returning the following week. However, he returns at the break to declare that a new series of broadcasts, the *Mercury Theatre on the Air*, would begin the following week on a different day and time. The shift from Monday night at 9:00 to Sunday night at 8:00 would have been necessary in any case, given Mercury's upcoming theatrical commitments, most notably preparing and staging *Danton's Death*. Unfortunately, that time slot put them up against the very popular *Chase and Sanborn Hour* on NBC, featuring ventriloquist Edgar Bergen and his dummy Charlie

McCarthy, a program match-up that would provide an interesting backdrop to Mercury's broadcast of *War of the Worlds* on 30 October.

The Man Who Was Thursday is a complex and surreal story. It is centered on anarchist intrigue and laced with philosophizing. Welles, as Gabriel Sime, carries the brunt of the narrative. Sound effects are minimal, the musical score (Alexander Semmler) does not seem to know what it wants to do, and patience is required to follow the course of events. For whatever reasons, perhaps a rising tension in their relationship or Welles wanting to affirm the upper hand, he shooed Houseman away from writing this adaptation and insisted on doing it himself. He procrastinated as usual, and with only a day until air time, not a word had been written. Houseman had to be brought back in, and with scissors and paste (literally), the two of them labored to make the book into a radio drama. Creating a script on such short notice left the actual performance fifteen minutes short. The first step in stretching the time was to have Dan Seymour note again how this was the last episode in the current Mercury series and that a new one would begin the following Sunday. He adds that the first offering will be *Vincent Van Gogh*, based on his letters. (Days later Welles would do another switcheroo and substitute *Julius Caesar*.) The cast is then introduced . . . slowly, after which poor Seymour is forced to repeat the previous information.

While this delay was going on, Welles had dispatched Houseman to the studio's library to fetch him an armful of classics. Orson then took the microphone and in the remaining time read passages from some of his favorite novels.[20] He interspersed the readings with a comment or two, noting that it would stories of this caliber that the audience could expect. The spontaneous brilliance involved made the extended sign-off seamless and engaging.

On 2 September, *Julius Caesar* renewed the series under its new rubric, *The Mercury Theatre on the Air*, in the new Sunday night time slot. It was a case of Welles drawing from Mercury's debut and most successful stage production, *Caesar*. In announcing the transition from *First Person Singular* to *Mercury Theatre on the Air*, Dan Seymour mentions the favorable reviews previous programs have garnered. One in particular struck me, an unnamed critic's observation that there was "nothing in the productions the ear could not see."

For the benefit of those listeners not familiar with Mercury's stage version of *Julius Caesar* done the year before, Welles mentions it in his opening comments. He also cites the relevance the story has to contemporary events in Europe. Marc Blitzstein is again present as musical director. Martin Gabel (Cassius), George Coulouris (Antonius), Joseph Holland (Caesar), and Welles (Brutus) all reprise their stage roles in this scaled-down production. To give the broadcast a newslike aura, CBS radio announcer H. V. Kaltenborn served as narrator, supplementing his reportage by reading passages from Plutarch's *Lives of Noble Grecians and Romans*. Kaltenborn's was a well-known news voice, authoritative and believable. However, he sounds a bit hyper in the production—as if he were on stage trying to outdo the actors.

As unconventional Shakespeare the radio play is laudable; the various elements are clever enough to be interesting, even though they are not always successful. As prime-time drama the production is somewhat less compelling. Shakespeare is always a tough go on radio, even with all the Wellesian bells and whistles. Despite his innovations, the performance seems somewhat lethargic and the scenes hard to envision. The tone of the production did, however, make me yearn to experience the stage version, with its stark modernism and cinematic lighting.

The dark mood that surrounded *Julius Caesar* continued the following week with *Jane Eyre*. This Gothic melodrama was by all accounts, including Welles's, a first-rate production. Unfortunately, the original disks have been severely damaged, making a fair assessment impossible. According to Bret Wood, when Welles reprised the role of Rochester in the 1944 film version directed by Robert Stevenson, he used the disks in preparation.[21] How much this influenced Stevenson's direction is uncertain. The film, however, does have a Wellesian look reminiscent of *Citizen Kane*; and it has Agnes Moorehead and Bernard Herrmann, who were both involved in *Kane* as well as the *Jane Eyre* broadcast.

Mercury's next radio offering would be *Sherlock Holmes*. This allowed Welles to reprise a character who was the subject of what might have been his very first radio broadcast: the little known production of *Sherlock Holmes* over the small station at the Todd School seven or eight years earlier. This time the textual source was not Sir Arthur Conan Doyle but the William Gillette play, which Orson had seen performed as a child. It distilled the essence of the Baker street sleuth from several of the novels. With the failure of Mercury's attempt to stage Gillette's *Too Much Johnson*, this radio version of another of his plays served as homage to the popular playwright/actor who had died the previous year. The result is a great listen. All the Holmes clichés are present. Watson (Ray Collins) gives us a historical overview of Holmes the man and the legend, as the two of them emerge from semiretirement to take up one last case. The dialogue is crisp and humorous throughout. Welles, although convincing and enthusiastic as Holmes, is not quite up to the standard that would be set by Basil Rathbone the following year when he began starring in a run of Sherlock Holmes films. Rathbone also played the character in several superb productions for BBC radio.

With *Too Much Johnson* having proved to be too much for Mercury, the company's stage energies now turned to *Danton's Death*. The radio broadcasts began to feel the pull of this other commitment. On 2 October Mercury presented a very pedestrian version of *Oliver Twist*; only hours before, Welles had done an episode of *The Shadow:* "The Black Abbot," on the Mutual Network. For Houseman and Welles, keeping the standards of their radio dramas high was a luxury they had to afford, even if it meant hiring an additional writer. The new scribe, Howard Koch, would turn out to be a godsend.

Houseman had deemed Koch eminently qualified to work for Mercury. He described him as a young man who was "pleasant, well informed, serious, and literate," to which he added, "destitute and desperate."[22] The latter qualities, it should be noted, were not forced upon Koch but the result of career choice. He had been a lawyer but left the profession to pursue his writing ambitions. One modest success preceded his stint with Mercury, a play called *The Lonely Man*. It was produced by the Federal Theater Project in Chicago and featured a young John Huston, who played a reincarnated and disillusioned Abraham Lincoln.[23] As it turned out Welles and Mercury were fortunate to secure Koch's services for a mutually rewarding tenure that would last six months. Under Houseman's tutelage Koch had completed his first radio play for Mercury, *Hell on Ice* (9 October), before he even met Welles. It dealt with the disastrous De Long expedition to the North Pole in 1880, and in it we can hear an anticipation of the apocalyptic tone that would make his work several weeks later on *War of the Worlds* so chilling.

The script for *Hell on Ice* was adapted from Commander Edward Ellsberg's chronicle of the voyage, which made use of the diaries of Captain De Long and Chief Officer Melville. These memoirs are used to provide contrasting first person accounts in a relentlessly paced script. Prospects of polar glory turn into a protracted nightmare as De Long's ship, the *Jeanette*, becomes trapped in drifting ice. Escape must wait until the summer thaw. It never comes and another year is spent enduring bitter cold, reduced rations, and boredom. Malnutrition and psychotic episodes result. When the thaw finally comes, it is only partial, and the ship is crushed by shifting ice. The crew abandons the vessel and takes to the ice, dragging lifeboats southwest in search of open sea. When they find it a storm separates them, sinking one of the boats. De Long's boat reaches land first (the Lena River delta in Siberia), but his overland trek leads to death from starvation and exposure. He perishes with diary in hand, which provides a chronicle of events to the bitter end. Melville eventually discovers his captain's remains and erects a cross on 6 April 1882.

The interplay in this broadcast between first person narratives, dramatic scenarios, and sound effects is well nigh perfect. For almost an hour we are transported back in time to a frozen hell. The production values and emotional power even surpass what would be achieved with *War of the Worlds*. The next day Welles, who was understandably impressed with the writing, summoned Koch for a first meeting. Dispensing with pleasantries, he picked up the script and read a particularly poetic line. He asked Koch if the line was a quote from the source, or Koch's own. The writer acknowledged his authorship. Welles evidenced no response, but Koch rightly interpreted this as signifying official acceptance.[24] His salary went from fifty dollars a week to sixty-five, and then eventually to seventy-five by the time of *War of the Worlds*.

During this period Welles, busy with the logistics of staging *Danton's Death*, gave his radio program short shrift. With little time available for script revision, he must have been relieved to know that Koch could handle assignments competently as fast as they were served up. On 16 October, Koch's adaptation of Booth Tarkington's *Seventeen* was broadcast. Tarkington, although passé by the late 1930s, remained a Welles favorite. Enamored by his fin-de-siècle descriptions of the Midwest in transition, Welles would go on to broadcast *Clarence* (27 November 1938) and *The Magnificent Ambersons* (29 October 1939); the latter story would also be rendered into one of his most memorable motion pictures.

Seventeen contrasted markedly with the wrenching polar tragedy broadcast the previous week. It is nostalgic fluff grounded in soft core melodrama. Light violins and a player piano regurgitate *Let Me Call You Sweetheart* ad infinitum, as seventeen-year-old William Sylvanus Baxter discovers love and life. Welles plays him as an insufferable adolescent, whining and pining through each scene. Before Will's uncle, played by Mercury stalwart Ray Collins, says, "That boy has more idiocy in his face than anyone I have ever seen," we suspect as much. The girls he encounters are shrill scatterbrains, and a too obvious example of adult actors trying to effect teenage roles.

In his concluding sign-off, Welles describes the production as "good old-fashioned theater sentiment." Saccharine would be more apropos. Perhaps he was trying to recapture the spirit of period farce that characterized his *Horse Eats Hat* stage production two years previous. Bret Wood has noted that Welles's portrayal of Will Baxter can be seen as a harbinger of the way he would both play George Amberson Minafer in the radio production of *The Magnificent Ambersons* and direct Tim Holt in the movie version. To a degree. Certainly the diffident and spoiled persona would resurface, but "Georgie" Minafer would exude far more resolve and confidence.

Following *Seventeen*, Koch was assigned Jules Verne's *Around the World in Eighty Days*, a novel that blends high adventure with a comedy of manners.

Welles introduces the story by mentioning the then record for global circulation, which was held by Howard Hughes at three days, nineteen hours, seven minutes. He then slips into the character of Phileas Fogg. In a highly inflected English tenor he wagers he can circle the world in eighty days traveling west to east. Fogg is a kind of Gallic conception of an archetypal Englishman: confident, punctual to the point of obsession, and emotionless at the surface. Accompanied by his trusty French servant, Passpartout (Edgar Barrier), the two set off, but they are followed by a detective (Ray Collins) who mistakenly assumes Fogg is a noted criminal.

The script, sound effects, and Bernard Herrmann's music make the excursion a delight. From balloon, to steamer, to train, a soundscape of movement envelops the story. The syncopation often suggests a clock, implying that no matter who happens to be chasing them at the moment, time is their ultimate pursuer. En route they rescue the lovely Princess Ouda (Arlene Francis) from a funeral pyre in India where she was consigned to be immolated with her deceased husband. The reserved Fogg, although falling passionately in love with her, cannot indicate these feelings until the voyage is almost over, and only after she proposes to him!

In the finale, Fogg, after having spent his fortune trying to win the wager, believes he has failed by fifteen minutes . . . only to find out that he gained a day because of the logistics of crossing the international dateline west to east. Welles tries to explain the theory behind this in his improvised closing commentary but admits to not understanding the principles involved and to his own failings in the area of punctuality. However, it is worth noting that although tardiness plagued his work in theater and film, it was virtually absent from his radio commitments. To not show up on time would be disastrous, possibly jeopardizing his series and future work in the medium. In theatre and film he regularly managed to stretch his deadlines, but not without problems ensuing.

The successful rendering of *Around the World in 80 Days* on radio probably instilled in Welles the idea to someday adapt the novel to the stage, which he did in 1946. By all accounts the production was lavish, but done on a shoestring. It differed from the radio version by emphasizing scenes for which effective stage sets could be created, the exotic interiors for example, while minimizing the protracted traveling sequences that would make the 1956 film by Mike Todd (who had pulled out of a partnership with Welles when the stage version was being planned) so exhilarating.

Both *Seventeen* and *Around the World in 80 Days* were stories that could be transposed to radio in a fairly straightforward manner. Creative selection and condensation sufficed. Not so with Koch's assignment the following week,

War of the Worlds. The outrageous conjuring entailed in doing it in a news bulletin format was a daunting task of radio adaptation; a less than successful script might not only be boring, but ridiculous as well. As Koch labored over each page, they were typed by his secretary, Ann Froelich, who sensing the impossibility of the project said, "You can't do it! Those old Martians are just a lot of nonsense. It's all too silly! We're going to make fools of ourselves."[25] Maybe. But they would be joined by over a million others.

PART TWO

MERCURY DOES MARS: THE PANIC BROADCAST

CHAPTER FOUR

Genesis

> And the Lord said, I will destroy man whom I have created from the face of the earth.
>
> —Genesis 6:7

In the second half of the twentieth century the possibility of life on other worlds was not just entertained, it was seriously explored. Beginning with Project SETI (search for extraterrestrial intelligence), through Voyager and subsequent probes, we have tried to reach out, however tentatively, and make contact. The darker side of what might result has been dramatized in motion pictures such as *The Arrival* (1996), *Independence Day* (1996), and *Signs* (2003).

Until recently our concept of what space aliens might be like, whether friendly or malicious, has usually had them originating from outside the solar system. The idea of Martians, such as those depicted in the literary, radio, and film versions of *War of the Worlds*, was eventually overridden by the hard-nosed results of unmanned solar system exploration. Mars became too mundane a place—a mere local rock pile—to harbor alternative intelligence. More compelling and distant vistas seemed better suited to the task. In *Close Encounters of the Third Kind* (1977) Steven Spielberg suggested them to moviegoers. Today, Gene Rodenberry's various *Star Trek* incarnations continue to provide us with imaginative glimpses of what worlds beyond the solar system might be like. However, in the late 1990s, with the discovery of the "so-called" Martian meteorite, followed by the close approach of Mars in 2003 and the subsequent unmanned probes, serious speculation again began to address the possibility of life on the Red Planet, if not now extant, perhaps once upon a time. More unfettered imaginations have conjured underground civilizations eying us with curiosity or menace. One imagines the venerable Wells (H. G.) responding with "Oh my, how intriguing"; and Orson the Terrible snapping, "Been there, done that."

Yes, he was and did. The *War of the Worlds* radio drama on Sunday, 30 October 1938, is probably the most infamous broadcast in history. The ensuing panic devoured a million-plus people. It resulted in part from a belief that any kind of live on-the-spot newscast, especially one faked so convincingly, must be true, and in part from an invasion fear prompted by those Darth Vader–like Axis forces, whose machinations were the subject of regular news bulletins. Mars became the catalyst when, a week before the next scheduled *Mercury* broadcast, Welles and Houseman decided that H. G. Wells's science fiction classic was a viable radio project, provided the story was made contemporary and radio news reports given a prominent role.

Although by 1938, scientists were becoming increasingly skeptical regarding the possibility of life of any kind on Mars, for the lay public the jury was still out. The idea, although centuries old, was by the time of the Panic Broadcast regularly and affirmatively assessed in popular science literature, a situation similar to contemporary discussions about the probability of intelligent life outside the solar system. The key difference of course being the proximity of Mars—a veritable overnight flight, rather than umpteen light years distant.

If this otherworldly speculation, which provided a basis for widespread culture shock in 1938, can be seen as having a beginning, a likely point of origin is the Renaissance. A new cosmography argued that other planets in our solar system could be occupied by sentient beings, and that the fixed stars are suns, replete with inhabited planets. Although this idea, known as the "plurality of worlds," deprived human life of its unique position, thus threatening some aspects of religious orthodoxy, it was also a view that *did not* depend on acceptance of the controversial sun-centered theory of the solar system espoused by Copernicus and later Galileo. Thus it had adherents even within the church. Why, some churchmen asked, following what was called the "principle of plenitude," would not God impart life to other worlds, as he has done to virtually every nook and cranny on Earth?[1]

When Galileo first turned his telescope to Mars in 1610, he subscribed to at least part of the new cosmography: that the plurality of worlds is an aspect of our solar system. His glimpse of Mars as an uneven spherical disk, however, failed to yield hard evidence for the contention. Half a century later the case improved when Christiaan Huygens surmised that the dark markings on Mars were bodies of water. Then in 1666, Giovanni Cassini calculated the rotation of the planet at an Earthlike twenty-four hours. By the late eighteenth century, when the noted astronomer Sir William Herschel observed the waxing and waning of Martian polar caps, he assumed oceans, lakes, and life.

Herschel's views probably inspired a nineteenth-century precursor to Welles's Martian hoax. In August 1835, the *New York Sun* ran a series of articles that became known as the "Moon hoax." The paper had Sir John Herschel, William's son, commanding a new super telescope in Cape Town, South Africa. With it he was alleged to have seen intelligent Moon men communicating with the context of a benign theocratic civilization. The public bought it. So did notable academics. This bit of journalistic legerdemain seems to have gone unmentioned in the 1938 holier-than-thou press tirade directed against Welles's broadcast, and the medium of radio, for fraudulent reportage.

Thoughts of extraterrestrial life flared again in the nineteenth century when Giovanni Schiaparelli discussed the streaks on Mars called *canali*; the English translation should be "channels," but subsequent commentators could not resist referring to them as "canals." The *canali* were first named by Father Secchi in 1869, who did not assume they were manmade.[2] Schiaparelli did not assume they were not. He eventually went on to name various surface features on Mars using a schema based on circum-Mediterranean geography—one dry world used to label another. Anyone with a telescope turned it on the Red Planet in search of the enigmatic *canali*. Some saw them, others did not. One who did was Percival Lowell.

This scion of Boston high society—his younger sister was the poet Amy Lowell—set up his own observatory and launched a continuous Mars watch. In popular books, such as *Mars* (1895), *Mars and Its Canals* (1906), and *Mars as an Abode of Life* (1910), as well as in numerous articles, he argued that the planet is a drying, dying world, whose inhabitants had built a vast network of irrigation canals. Knowing that such canals would have to be at least thirty miles wide to be picked up in the best telescopes, he posited that what observers see are the dark irrigated crop lands that border them.

Few scientists accepted Lowell's contentions. The evidence seemed inconclusive; also, what he saw through his telescope did not always coincide with what other observers had seen through theirs. However, to the general public and many educated lay persons the whole idea was fascinating and seemed plausible. One newspaper ran a full-page story with the headline "Martians Build Immense Canals in Two Years." No, this did not appear in the yellow press or any other precursor of contemporary tabloids, but in the 27 August 1911 issue of the venerable *New York Times*. The article, replete with Lowell's drawings, reported, did not question, the notion that Martian engineers might still be at work. Such momentous excavation also had a terrestrial counterpart that may have been on reader's minds because of extensive *Times* coverage: the Panama Canal was well underway and only three years from completion.

Lowell's influence on science fiction ultimately exceeded his legacy to orthodox astronomy. H. G. Wells's *War of the Worlds* drew sustenance from his work, as did the eleven Martian novels of Edgar Rice Burroughs, Ray Bradbury's *Martian Chronicles*, and ultimately, Orson Welles's Panic Broadcast. When Welles, as the voice of astronomer Richard Pierson, tells the interviewing reporter that the streaks on Mars are "not canals, I assure you," the escalating news bulletins about possible activity on the planet suggest that the ghost of Lowell might have the last word.

If these historical preludes on the theme of extraterrestrial life can be seen as helping create a context for the shocking events of 30 October 1938, then they were followed by a complementary overture during the birth of broadcasting following World War I. The seemingly miraculous way the radio used electromagnetic waves to span great distances led some to think of the process in cosmic terms. Might it not be possible, it was argued, for someone beyond Earth to pick up our transmissions, and vice versa? In her history of early American broadcasting, Susan Douglas notes how in 1919 Marconi believed that several of his wireless stations were picking up signals that might be emanating from beyond our planet.[3] When Nikola Tesla, another wizard of electrical invention, insisted the signals were from Mars, Marconi did not dismiss the possibility. Established periodicals, such as the *Scientific American*, were cool to the idea. Less orthodox journals, such as *Illustrated World*, voiced enthusiasm over the possibility. This popular magazine, which occupied a niche between science fact and science fiction, urged that the scientific community make a concerted effort to attempt radio contact with whoever might be out there. Few researchers planned to take up the challenge, but the public was fascinated by the consequences of what might happen if they did and succeeded. Those advocating communication with Mars believed that such an exchange could be a learning experience for earthlings, a way perhaps of helping us heal the scars of World War I and of bettering the human lot. By 1938, however, with Europe on the brink of another debacle, the possibility of alien contact took on more sinister connotations.

Welles's idea of capitalizing on the escalating tension in Europe by dramatizing an interplanetary conflict was created during discussions with Houseman approximately ten days before the actual broadcast. Houseman conveyed the project idea to the newest member of the Mercury staff, writer Howard Koch, who was less than thrilled and suggested changing the project. He claimed that it would require an entire rewrite of the story to shift the location of the Martian invasion from England to the United States.[4] Welles would not hear of abandonment.

Koch's plea that Welles and Houseman reconsider *War of the Worlds* was also countered by the fact that they had already vetoed an alternative choice for the upcoming broadcast, R. D. Blackmore's *Lorna Doone*. Houseman had started to work on a version of it earlier that summer but thought that the story was just too boring to be worth doing. When a hasty reevaluation yielded the idea of doing a work of science fiction, *War of the Worlds* won out over another apocalyptic saga, M. P. Shiel's *Purple Cloud*, and Arthur Conan Doyle's *The Lost World*.[5] In response to Koch balking at the assignment, Houseman was told by Welles to say that it was Orson's favorite project, although Houseman suspected that Welles had never read it. For Koch then, like New Jersey in his radio script, there would be no escaping the Martians. *War of the Worlds* would go on to become his second most famous piece of dramatic writing. The hand that penned, or rather penciled on yellow notepaper, this memorable radio drama also co-scripted what would become one of the most memorable motion pictures.

Arriving in Hollywood a year later, "from outer space" as he put it, Koch signed with Warner Brothers as a result of a recommendation from John Huston.[6] He was assigned to write *Sea Hawk* (1940), *The Letter* (1940), *Shining Victory* (1941), and with Huston, *Sergeant York* (1941). Then came an intriguing project with uncertain potential, *Casablanca* (1942). Like *War of the Worlds*, it was a story previously written (in the case of *Casablanca* an unproduced play rendered into a partial screenplay), which seemed impossible to adapt for the medium in question. As he labored, first on the *War of the Worlds* radio play and then later on the *Casablanca* film script, Koch wondered each time whether the project would lead to his writerly undoing. He emerged more than unscathed—a multifaceted writer who exemplified Nietzsche's adage that if the challenge does not kill you it will make you strong; and in the case of the *Casablanca* script, earn you an Academy Award.

With the weight of having to adapt *War of the Worlds* heavy on his mind, Koch used his off day, Monday, to drive upstate and visit family. On the way back he decided to get a map and draft the pattern of invasion the Martians would follow. When he stopped at a gas station to purchase it he was on Route 9W in northern New Jersey, so he secured a map of that state to begin outlining the sequence of events. Arriving home he spread it, closed his eyes and, in pin-the-tail-on-the-donkey fashion, dropped the first Martian cylinder on the small town of Grovers Mill.[7] One thing led to another. Princeton University was nearby, hence an observatory and the character of Richard Pierson, "noted astronomer," who would witness the first attack and narrate the last part of the story.

If all this sounds exciting after the fact, it was quite mundane at the time and filled with a fear that the Martians might turn out to be turkeys. Working fifteen-hour shifts while trying to allay trepidation, Koch wrote and rewrote. Houseman, unable to contact Welles at this time, encouraged Koch and made further suggestions.[8] By Thursday a draft was ready for preliminary rehearsal. Associate producer Paul Stewart (later the butler in *Citizen Kane*) conducted the proceedings. The run-through, with most of the cast and a few sound effects, provided no inkling of what was to come. An acetate recording was made, which Houseman brought to Welles's room at the St. Regis Hotel shortly after midnight. Not impressed, they worked on the script until dawn, believing that the best chance of salvage lay in accentuating the newscast and eyewitness format, especially by adding more recognizable locations.

The Saturday rehearsal was again conducted by Paul Stewart sans Welles. New and compelling sound effects were added: the laserlike heat ray, an artillery barrage, and several harbor sounds that accompany survivors putting out to sea to escape a poison gas attack. Doubts still lingered. When Welles phoned CBS from the theater that evening, he was told by a sound technician—most probably John Dietz—that the show had little promise.[9] Then at noon the next day the maestro finally put in an appearance to conduct a run-through. According to Mercury assistant Richard Barr's fly-on-the-wall account, Welles was in tempestuous form.[10] He berated the script and intimated that the show might be an embarrassment for all concerned. Could this have been a strategy to exhort his troops to deliver their utmost? Did he somehow know that this material, which seemed so implausible on the page and in preliminary rehearsals, could be incendiary over the airwaves if delivered in just the right way?

My own feeling is that by the time of the hectic final rehearsal just prior to the broadcast, the arrival of Bernard Herrmann and his orchestra helped set a tone that allowed the script to come alive. Perhaps at that point, Welles sensed that if he gave it his best shot and timed everything right, many in the audience would be amused and a few gullible listeners shocked. Just before 8:00 P.M. he downed his second container of pineapple juice, adjusted the earphones, and, with a wave of his hand, cued the Mercury theme.

There is a revealing photograph taken just after the broadcast began. In the foreground the actors, Ray Collins, Frank Readick, and the others, are clustered around a microphone holding their scripts. On stage left Bernard Herrmann fronts the CBS orchestra. Welles stands on the podium in the background, arms raised as he conducts the actors and the conductor. His eyes burn with creative intensity. He resembles two flamboyant musical maestros of his era, Toscanini and Stokowski . . . nay . . . one from an earlier time . . . Beethoven.

CHAPTER FIVE

Exodus

Also take your flocks and your herds, as ye have said, and be gone.

—Exodus 12:32

In Woody Allen's masterful evocation of an era, *Radio Days* (1987), he has a character react incredulously to the idea of someone listening to a ventriloquist on the radio. But it happened. In 1938, at 8:00 P.M. on Sunday nights, Edgar Bergen (father of Candice) and his wooden alter ego, Charlie McCarthy, hosted NBC's *Chase and Sanborn Hour*. What an exquisite irony of the Golden Age of Radio it is, that this bit of illusionism was broadcast at the same time the *Mercury Theatre on the Air* was giving the Martians their say on CBS. Edgar and Charlie were more popular than the comparatively highbrow offerings Welles served up. They easily won the ratings battle on 30 October 1938. But to no avail. It was those listeners who tuned in to the Panic Broadcast, "by chance or design," to quote a phrase from the opening lines of the program, who made history.

It began innocently enough. The by now familiar strains of Tchaikovsky's First Piano Concerto backgrounded the announcement that Orson Welles and the *Mercury Theatre on the Air* would present their rendering of H. G. Wells's *War of the Worlds*. Dan Seymour then introduced Welles as "the director and star of these broadcasts." To regular listeners things must have seemed quite normal; another Sunday, another Welles radio play. *War of the Worlds* had been announced at the end of the previous week's program, *Around the World in 80 Days*, and in newspaper listings.

Much has been made over the years about the Martian hoax being a Halloween broadcast, in part because Welles ends the show by declaring the whole thing to have been a trick-or-treat prank. The occasion was actually Halloween eve, which hardly has the segue power of, say, Christmas Eve, in evoking a sense of the holiday to follow. We do know that most who panicked, especially in the exodus from New Jersey, were not *Mercury*'s regular listeners. It was Bergen and his dummy, or to be more precise, dummies (since his act included a dream team of wooden heads), who had the largest slice of the ratings—at least at the outset of their show. That audience share (typically, 34.7 percent versus 3.6 percent for Mercury as estimated by the Crossley survey) was theirs to lose.[1] They could usually hold it through the opening banter; Charlie's insults to Edgar were and still are hilarious. However, since this *was* a variety show, if the subsequent act was a dud, well, "what else is on."

Channel surfing is not solely a late twentieth-century phenomenon. Many console radios of the 1930s had large, easy to grasp dials that were a pleasure to twirl. Round and round they went when, following Edgar and Charlie, Nelson Eddy blandly crooned "Neapolitan Love Song." Approximately 12 percent landed on CBS and the receiving end of news bulletins from Grovers Mill, New Jersey, where something untoward was happening with a cylinder believed to be of Martian origin. Sufficiently riveted, many late listeners phoned their friends, who in turn called other friends, and so on. Estimates suggest that listenership peaked at between six and twelve million.[2] This must have been one of the largest single audiences Welles would enjoy until he started doing television talk shows forty years later.

Even *Mercury* regulars who tuned in from the beginning must have sensed that this was no ordinary broadcast. Rather than introducing the drama in his semiformal but relaxed style, Welles's voice was unusually ominous. He delivered the following prologue in the manner of an incantation:

> We know now that in the early years of the twentieth century this world was being watched closely by intelligences greater than Man's and yet as mortal as his own. We know now that as human beings busied themselves about their various concerns they were scrutinized and studied, perhaps almost as narrowly as a man with a microscope might scrutinize the transient creatures that multiply in a drop of water. With infinite complacence people went to and fro over the earth about their little affairs, serene in the assurance of their dominion over this small spinning fragment of solar driftwood which by chance or design man has inherited out of the dark mystery of Time and Space. Yet across an immense ethereal gulf, minds that are to our minds as ours are to the beasts in the jungle, intellects vast, cool and unsympathetic regarded this earth with envious eyes and slowly and surely drew their plans against us. In the thirty-ninth year of the twentieth century came the great disillusionment.

It was near the end of October. Business was better. The war scare was over. More men were back at work. Sales were picking up. On this particular evening, October 30, the Crossley service estimated thirty-two million people were listening in on radios.

This oracular pronouncement follows quite closely the opening lengthy paragraph in H. G. Wells's novel. The second paragraph, however, is all Koch, or Welles, or Houseman. It effectively puts the narrative in a dynamic present by implying that what follows is not past tense, a story previously written and now being recounted, but one that occurs during the telling.

Soon after both the literary and radio versions of *War of the Worlds* pronounce that malevolent Martians have designs on us, there is a marked divergence of story. H. G. goes on to discourse about Mars—some of this information is later incorporated into the radio play when Welles is interviewed as Professor Richard Pierson, "famous astronomer"—whereas the radio version quickly shifts to a music format punctuated by news bulletins. The remainder of the two versions of the story contain a number of parallels: the physical description of the Martians and their destructive apparatus, the concluding first person chronicle, and the unforeseen way the Martians meet their demise.

The differences in the Wells and Welles narratives are not just the result of changing the location of the story from England to the United States and adapting it to radio; they necessarily follow from a marked disjuncture in time. H. G. penned the original as a serial for *Pearson's Magazine* in 1897, a decade still dominated by equine transport and gaslight. Yet part of the fun of the story, which often reads like pulp fiction, lies in those moments when the narrator offers some prescient reflections on what the future might hold in terms of technology and social life. One intriguing area of common ground between his and Orson's versions was the public's fear of German military expansion. Although the Fatherland at the turn of the century did not have a Fürher, it did have a Kaiser, whose aggressive and competitive attitude toward Britain occasionally induced war anxiety. It has also been pointed out by Wells, and Welles scholar Harry M. Geduld, that part of H. G.'s agenda in writing *War of the Worlds* was to suggest a Judgment Day scenario for British imperialism.[3] When H. G. discussed with his brother Frank the sorrowful extermination of Tasmanian natives by British colonists, Frank presented him with an intriguing "what if" scenario. Suppose technologically superior beings from another planet came to earth and did the same to us? This thought inspired the story and the dedication of the novel to Frank.

In the novel, events begin to unfold when, with the preliminary discourse about Mars dispensed with, we meet our protagonist-narrator in the English countryside adjacent to London. The radio drama opens with a brief weather update, after which we are taken to the Meridian Room of the Park Plaza Hotel in New York City, where Ramon Raquello leads his orchestra in a program of dance music. The first song, "La Cumparasita," is soon interrupted by a special bulletin from the fictitious Intercontinental Radio News, reporting a series of hydrogen gas explosions on the planet Mars that appear to be headed toward Earth. The information is delivered without urgency, by the voice and in the style of the previous weather bulletin. We then return to the orchestra and the next announced song, "Stardust" (!).

Ramon Raquello is of course Bernard Herrmann who, unable to get a dance band for the occasion, used symphony musicians. The two opening songs were suggested by Paul Stewart.[4] In rehearsal, Herrmann and his musicians had difficulty infusing the appropriate rhythm into the tunes, so Stewart gave them an impromptu lesson. Still, the musical numbers in the broadcast sound quite stiff. After the first two, I suspect that aficionados of Latin or swing music might have twirled their dials in search of Edgar and Charlie. At this point in his career, Herrmann was not adept at arranging and conducting jazz.[5] Yet, he appreciated the music and was a great admirer of Ellington and Gershwin. Through the years, however, beginning with his first movie assignment, *Citizen Kane* (1941), he would gradually and with increased proficiency explore jazz sonorities. In his last film, Martin Scorsese's *Taxi Driver* (1976), he created a masterful modern jazz score.

The orchestra's rendering of "Stardust" is soon interrupted by more Mars stuff. This time it is an interview with astronomer Richard Pierson (Welles) conducted by Carl Phillips (Frank Readick). It takes place in Princeton Observatory. The setting is vividly described and Welles is totally convincing as he answers basic questions in an appropriately conservative scientific manner. These include facts about Mars and the possibility of intelligent life there. He is then asked to account for the recent gas outbursts. His response, "Mr. Phillips, I cannot account for it," was according to Howard Koch a decisive moment in the broadcast. Referring to Welles's voice as "an incomparable dramatic instrument," he notes how in the delivery of this line, it "was filled with portentous meaning."[6]

The tension builds. Before the interview concludes, Pierson is handed a message that Phillips in turn reads on the air. It reports seismic disturbances within twenty miles of Princeton. The astronomer denies a link with the gas explosions on Mars and suggests the cause is "probably a meteorite." After a brief piano interlude comes news of more gas explosions, augmented by a report that a flaming object has fallen to Earth near Grovers Mill, New Jersey. Phillips announces that a mobile unit is being dispatched there, and, as we wait with bated breath, another musical interlude is offered: Bobby Millette and his orchestra playing at the Hotel Martinet in Brooklyn. Millette gets even less air time than Raquello. In half a minute we are transported to the Wilmuth farm in Grovers Mill and Carl Phillips who, accompanied by Professor Pierson, claims to have made the eleven-mile trip there in ten minutes. In actual broadcast time it is considerably less, but the effective pacing of various segments in the drama make it easy for the listener to suspend disbelief.

At this point Phillips launches into what he aptly calls "a word picture of the scene before my eyes." He describes the flaming object, a cylinder, and the general pandemonium surrounding it, while eliciting comments from the professor. The style is loose and realistic, what could be called radio vérité. It effectively captures the aura of an on-the-spot news report, which people were becoming used to as a result of updates from the turmoil in Europe and the increased use of mobile units to cover domestic crises in progress, such as fires. The scenario at the Wilmuth farm also effectively employs a staple of radio drama, the establishment of context through specific verbal and nonverbal means. The compelling verbal information derives from the quality of the writing and the delivery of the actors, especially Frank Readick. He has Carl Phillips speaking with a breathless urgency that, although at times a bit too fast, is riveting—perhaps one reason why many fearful listeners could not turn their dials to another station to verify events.

Nonverbally, the setting is vivified through the sine qua non of radio drama, sound effects. A good measure of the credit here, although due to the input of Welles, Houseman, and Stewart, must be shared by CBS, the most innovative network in this area, especially John Dietz, who engineered the broadcast.[7]

Although latecomers tuned in throughout the program, the sequence from the Wilmuth farm, coming as it does about thirteen minutes in, was the point at which Edgar and Charlie lost the estimated 12 percent of their audience. Some of these listeners must have arrived during the interview between Phillips and Farmer Wilmuth. Describing what he saw and heard during the crash, Wilmuth is somewhat leisurely in his delivery. Phillips attempts to hurry him in getting to a climactic revelation. It never comes, but the farmer wants to keep on talking anyhow and Phillips has to insist several times (by thanking him) that he stop. This awkward exchange seems so spontaneous that anyone tuning in during it could hardly have suspected it was part of a carefully scripted drama.

Phillips's continuing description of the hubbub surrounding the cylinder is punctuated by a humming and scraping sound. Pierson attributes it to the unequal cooling of the surface but expresses doubt that the object is a meteorite. This is verified when the top screws off and the reporter's quivering voice draws us into an unfolding nightmare:

> Ladies and gentlemen, this is the most terrifying thing I have ever witnessed. . . . Wait a minute! Someone's *crawling out of the hollow top*. Some one or . . . something. I can see peering out of that black hole two luminous disks . . . are they eyes? It might be a face. It might be. . . . [SHOUT OF AWE FROM THE CROWD]
>
> Good heavens, something's wriggling out of the shadow like a grey snake. Now it's another one, and another. They look like tentacles to me. There, I can see the thing's body. It's large as a bear and it glistens like wet leather. But that face. It . . . It's indescribable. I can hardly force myself to keep looking at it. The eyes are black and gleam like a serpent. The mouth is V-shaped with saliva dripping from its rimless lips that seem to quiver and pulsate. The monster or whatever it is can hardly move. It seems weighed down by . . . possibly gravity or something. The thing's raising up. The crowd falls back. They've seen enough. This is the most extraordinary experience. I can't find words. . . . I'm pulling this microphone with me as I talk. I'll have to stop the description until I've taken a new position. Hold on, will you please, I'll be back in a minute. [FADE INTO PIANO]

This unnerving description draws heavily from the original novel. As a radio drama sequence it defies convention, since the announced pause to reposition the microphone suggests, again, a live news report. Also, the tone and some of the phrases must have reminded many in the audience of radio reporter Herbert Morrison's heart-stopping description of the flaming crash of the *Hindenberg* zeppelin in Lakehurst, New Jersey (!) on 6 May of the previous year. Although this is often cited as a live broadcast, it was in fact a recording made by Morrison, who set up his apparatus to chronicle the historic arrival of the airship. When tragedy struck, leading to the death of thirty-five people in a fiery explosion, Morrison, choking with emotion, stayed at his microphone to describe the inferno. His moving account, broadcast the next day and often thereafter, has become a defining moment in the history of radio. The parallels with Carl Phillips's reaction to the Martian cylinder was no coincidence. During the Sunday rehearsals, Welles had Readick listen to the Morrison recording several times.[8]

When Phillips resumes his account he is separated from the professor, who has circled around to the other side of the cylinder. Good thing for him, because at that moment the Martians unleash their laserlike heat ray. The beam immolates people, buildings, and landscape. Phillips nervously describes the carnage, and the weapon as it points in his direction, then . . .

dead air ... complete silence. Welles made the six seconds he cued the pause seem like an eternity, both for those behind the microphone as well as the audience. It is perhaps the most terrifying moment in the broadcast. Looking back, this would have been a prudent moment, coming sixteen minutes in, to take a station break and announce that the program was a dramatization. Not surprisingly, it was at about this juncture that executive producer Davidson Taylor made the first of several such attempts. According to Welles's assistant, William Alland, Taylor was waved off each time by Welles, who did not relent until the forty-two-minute mark.[9] By that time the panicked hordes were already in flight.

When transmission returns after the dead air segment, the announcement only exacerbates tension by declaring that due to "circumstances beyond our control" we have lost the signal from Grovers Mill. There is no urgency in the announcement and it is followed by a bulletin suggesting the gas explosions on Mars are probably volcanic in origin. Cut to a piano interlude. The Martian heat ray also succeeded in lighting up switchboards at police stations and at CBS. The police immediately made inquiries to the radio station and were curtly told the program was a drama. A squad car was sent to investigate, but the officer in charge was not allowed to enter the studio and potentially disrupt a broadcast in progress. More police arrived, but they were in an understandable quandary as to what to actually do. The death of Phillips and subsequent dead air sequence was also perhaps the single moment in the program most responsible for launching the exodus from New Jersey, which clogged highways leading to New York and Pennsylvania.

After the piano interlude, which Houseman believed effectively exacerbated uncertainty and tension,[10] the announcer acknowledges the mayhem that has occurred at Grovers Mill. General Montgomery Smith of the state militia (the New Jersey National Guard in the original script) then informs listeners that martial law has been declared in several counties in the vicinity of the attack. We next hear an eyewitness description of the tragedy from Professor Pierson, who escaped Martian wrath by taking refuge in a nearby farmhouse. In a telephone linkup, he uses formal academic language to verify what we have already surmised.

The professor's ominous report is followed by the voice of Harry MacDonald, vice president in charge of operations. Operations of what is never made clear, but we can probably assume it is the network itself, since he declares that the entire broadcast facility will be turned over to the state militia. The reason given seems so humorous after the fact that we can easily imagine Welles and his actors trying to restrain their laughter. MacDonald declares that the transference of the medium to the military is being made because of a belief "that radio has a definite responsibility to serve in the public interest at all times." Thus radio itself would not only be an ear on events to come but an active player in the story it was initially sent out to report.

With coverage of the crisis now in the hands of the military, the next voice we hear is Captain Lansing of the signal corps of the militia. In bold and reassuring tones, "A quick thrust and it'll all be over," he describes the formidable array of military personnel and weaponry deployed around the cylinder. In seconds, however, the captain is toast, transmission is cut, and we return to the voice of the studio announcer who summarizes events to date. He confirms the Martian invasion and chronicles the widespread destruction it has caused to New Jersey and eastern Pennsylvania. Any listener reflecting on this update should have realized, unless they tuned in late, that such widespread chaos could not have occurred in the ten minutes since the first Martian jack-in-the-box opened in Grovers Mill. Yet many still believed. Others, who were only confused and uncertain, had another Wellesian shock awaiting them.

The "secretary of the interior" comes on the air and addresses the nation regarding the gravity of the situation. In somber tones the unnamed politician urges us to consolidate our faith and show courage in the face of an adversary who threatens "human supremacy on earth." If the words alone were not frightening enough, the actor, Kenneth Delmar, gives a near perfect imitation of the voice of President Roosevelt doing one of his address-the-nation talks known as "fireside chats."[11]

When an announcer's voice returns, we learn that more cylinders have landed and the military is preparing a counterstrike. A direct radio link is established with the 22nd Field Artillery. We hear the commands of the officer calculating the trajectory of the weapon, followed by its explosive report. In retaliating, the Martians do not use their heat ray; instead, as in the novel, they begin dispensing black clouds of poison gas. The artillerymen put on gas masks and continue their barrage. But Martian gas is potent stuff. It penetrates the masks, and we soon hear the coughing soldiers gradually overcome. Fear of this new airborne threat apparently led a number of listeners, who stayed put to defend hearth and home, to seal their windows and doors with wet cloth.[12]

The next voice we hear is that of Lieutenant Voght commanding a squadron of army fighter-bombers out of Langham Field (Langley Field in the original script), Virginia. With the drone of the planes in the background, he provides us with an aerial view of war-ravaged New Jersey. Apparently the Martians, after wreaking havoc on the Garden State, are now Big Apple bound. Voght counts six of their terrestrially mobile tripod machines, including one disabled by the earlier artillery attack. As they advance they leave a cloudy wake of black poisonous gas.

The lieutenant and his squadron prepare to strike. We hear the range of their target being called off in yards, along with the high-pitched whine of his plane's engine in an attack dive. The scenario is very cinematic. Welles puts radio where, in previous aerial combat movies such as *Hell's Angels* (1930), we usually find the camera. He does this with an uncompromising realism. For example, when Voght's plane is crippled by the Martian heat ray and crashes, it is not with the thunderous explosion we would expect in a dramatization, but with an explosive silence—as would occur in the case of a severed transmission. Several seconds later the worst is confirmed when we are privy to an exchange of radio operators. We learn that the entire squadron was zapped, but they did manage to destroy one Martian tripod. Credit for this kill probably goes to the redoubtable Voght, whose last words after his plane was disabled by the heat ray were, "No chance to drop bombs. Only one thing left . . . drop on them plane and all."

These overheard radio exchanges are highly effective in giving us a sense of being there. However, it is not the first time the technique was used in a radio dramatization. Harry Geduld makes a convincing case for this aspect of *War of the Worlds* being influenced by Welles's old mainstay, *The March of Time*.[13] Earlier that year, on 28 January, the program documented a disastrous flood in the Midwest. Some of the information was imparted to listeners through the use of recreated conversations among ham radio operators.

Following Voght's plane crash, subsequent messages by the military take us to the next major scene, an announcer speaking from the roof of the Broadcasting Building (the Columbia Broadcasting Building in the original script) in New York. We hear bells ringing in the background. They toll for New Yorkers, warning them to evacuate the city as the Martian menace approaches. The harbor is full of boats and the streets jammed with fleeing residents. The Martian tripod machines, dispensing thick black poison gas, stride into Manhattan. (The devastation and panic described in the broadcast eerily foreshadow the real drama that would be played out on those same streets sixty-three years later, on 11 September 2001.)

We are soon told that Martian cylinders are falling all over the country. People begin dropping by the thousands. The announcer's quivering voice describes the horror and the deadly gas cloud as it drifts toward his position. He then gasps, chokes, and drops to the floor. But radio lives, since the microphone is still on. For twenty haunting seconds we hear a fugue of ship horns, sirens, and factory whistles, gradually fading to ten seconds of silence. Then a lone ham radio operator finally breaks through the pall and our hearts sink further. The message is a plaintive and repeated "Calling CQ" (the general call to any receiving station), followed by "Isn't there anyone on the air?" No response. The end has come . . . and so does a station break. Finally! The subsequent announcement that the program is a dramatization was met with a combination of relief and outrage by those listeners still by their radios who assumed they had been hearing the real thing.

The auditory moments of terror and destruction portrayed just prior to the break may have been influenced by what Welles heard the previous Thursday. At 10:00 P.M., just prior to his midnight script-revising session with Houseman, he arrived at his St. Regis Hotel suite and turned on the radio. CBS was broadcasting Irving Reis's *Columbia Workshop*, this week featuring the verse play *Air Raid*, by Archibald MacLeish. The narrator, borrowed for the occasion, was Mercury's own Ray Collins. Like *Mercury Theatre on the Air*, the *Columbia Workshop* was a sustaining program.

Air Raid is set in a fictitious European town at the crossroads of a burgeoning military action. Today the play seems to be a clear harbinger of events that would transpire in September 1939. Although such a dark possibility was on MacLeish's mind, a major influence on his fear of the horror that might come was a horror that had already occurred: the Spanish Civil War, in particular the unprovoked bombing of civilians in the city of Guernica. When he saw a newspaper reproduction of Picasso's famous painting *Guernica*, which depicted the tragedy, MacLeish was inspired—"I heard it," he would later remark.[14]

Beginning with a documentary-style introduction, *Air Raid* soon goes on location for live reportage and commentary. Like *War of the Worlds*, events are ushered in with a weather update. We are then taken to a rooftop overlooking the town, where the voice of Ray Collins describes the scene. We then hear, in radio vérité style, the everyday sounds of the place, laughter, gossip, and talk about the possibility of war. When the announcer's voice returns, the drama swings back and forth between his commentary and the sounds of the town and its people. We hear a boy conversing with his sick mother. He is worried about the danger a possible war might pose to children. The mother reassures him. She was there before when war came—an obvious reference to World War I—and the soldiers only passed through and were friendly.

A plane is heard. The announcer describes its hawklike pattern of circling. Then, the hubbub of the town returns, accompanied by women singing up and down a scale. This musical segment would become a defining motif throughout the drama. The plane heads away and we hear a siren rising and falling in the distance. It suggests the singing women's voices. The sounds fade and the announcer editorializes about the danger the people might face, even though they believe the threat has passed. His prophecy is fulfilled immediately. A shrill whistle leads to a loud repetition of "Air raid!" and "The bombers!"

There is confusion but no panic. A policeman urges people to take cover. He is interrupted by an old woman who, in a lengthy speech, tries to convince him that the planes are coming to attack only military personnel and politicians, not the townspeople, and especially not women and children. He is unconvinced, and jeered at for his pessimism by a gathering crowd. The sound of the singing scale returns, accompanied by soft explosions in the distance. The blasts proliferate and move closer, along with the drone of numerous planes. There is consternation, but the old woman insists, "Ah, they'll go over. There's nothing to fear: they'll go over." The announcer then describes the plethora of bombers as they cruise by, circle, bank, climb directly above the town, and then dive. Concerned women run out into the open, waving their skirts to show they are female. To no avail. A thunderous avalanche of machine-gun fire pours out of the aircraft, strafing the town amid the screams of those who thought such a horror impossible. As the terrifying cacophony fades away, we hear again the musical scale motif, now sung as an agonized dirge. It breaks on the last note as the sound of the aircraft recedes into silence.

The emotional power of *Air Raid* is extraordinary. Nevertheless, MacLeish's verse play of the previous year, *Fall of the City*, had drawn criticism for bringing to the modern medium of radio a dramatic form with too many archaic overtones. His eloquent response, "The ear is half a poet,"[15] must have doubtlessly appealed to Welles, who had narrated the drama and in 1935 played the lead in MacLeish's theatrical verse play *Panic*. *Time* magazine was also in accord with the literary form and manner of presentation of *Air Raid*, giving the broadcast a highly favorable review in the 31 October 1938 issue. Other publications that reviewed radio programs were equally disposed. Clearly, MacLeish's work inspired aspects of *War of the Worlds*: his *Fall of the City* for its apocalyptic tone and eyewitness-to-history narration, and *Air Raid* for dramatizing the plight of ordinary citizens in the face of a surprise attack. *War of the Worlds*, in capturing part of the terrifying aura of *Air Raid*, nevertheless fell short of the near perfect production values evidenced in the earlier drama. But as Welles biographer Frank Brady wryly notes, MacLeish's broadcast was seven months in the making, while Orson did his in just under seven days.[16]

When *War of the Worlds* returns after the station break and the announcement that it is a dramatization, the format is completely changed. Since Martians have destroyed most of civilization, including radio stations, the story is continued by Professor Pierson reading from his diary. His presentation recalls the original title of *Mercury Theatre on the Air*, *First Person Singular*, and the manner in which Welles often provided narration for large parts of his dramas.

To liven up the reading it is done in the present tense, with one recreated conversation. The sequence is as uninspiring as the first three-quarters of the program is riveting. The pacing is lethargic and the pauses interminable. Why? My guess, and it would be consistent with what went on behind the scenes with the production of a number of other Welles broadcasts, is that they were running ahead of schedule and had to slow down to avoid an embarrassing gap at the end that would require filler. Somewhat surprisingly, Houseman, who was in the studio at the time, would later comment that he thought this segment was highly effective.[17] My own sense is that during it, listeners who had tuned in from the beginning of the program, aware of its fictional nature, and who were aware of the ending of the novel, might have been tempted to surf to NBC and the finale of Edgar Bergen's program.

In his protracted narration, Pierson tells us that he has been hiding in an empty house near Grovers Mill, terrified at the prospect of being the last living person on earth. He emerges from his refuge, confused and disheveled: "Am I Richard Pierson? What day is it? Do days exist without calendars? Does time pass when there are no human hands left to wind the clocks? . . ." Rambling on in this manner he searches for something to eat while trying to avoid being eaten, since we are now informed that the preferred cuisine of Martians is *Homo sapiens*. Traveling north, he describes the blackened and devastated New Jersey landscape. Pierson also discovers lush enclaves of greenery in the region. He enters one. A chestnut tree provides sustenance while a beech tree harbors a friendly fellow traveler. Face to face with a quizzical red squirrel, he celebrates the encounter: "I believe at that moment the animal and I shared the same emotion . . . the joy of finding another living being."

Pressing on, our postapocalypse professor enters a deserted but undemolished Newark, New Jersey. From out of a doorway emerges a knife-wielding artilleryman. In a threatening way he inquires as to the professor's identity. When questions are turned the other way, the somewhat shell-shocked soldier pours forth observations and opinions. We learn that the Martians have taken New York and are bent on global conquest. Wherever they go they devour humans at will, sometimes domesticating them for later consumption. This gruesome scenario is more extensively described in the novel, where Martians roam the countryside plucking people like fruit and tossing them into large metal baskets.

The artilleryman's plan to evade becoming a Martian main course is to let, even help, the slimy creatures capture anonymous hordes of people, "who haven't any stuff to 'em." By sacrificing the weak, the strong would then be in a position to escape and live underground in subway and railway tunnels. They could then observe the Martians and make sporadic raids for food and equipment. Eventually the day might come when these ruthless survivalists would be able to seize several tripod machines and turn the heat ray on its creators, thereby taking over the world. The good professor is less than impressed with this plan and soon bids the artilleryman adieu.

The whole sequence is drawn out and unconvincing, although quite faithful to a similar exchange in the novel. In H. G.'s original, it is a fascinating page turner, a chance to reconnoiter the damage already done and reflect on possible futures. Better pacing might have helped the radio version, or it could simply have been a case of something working well in one medium but not another. Welles was usually astute when transposing from print to radio. However, with the preparations for *Danton's Death* consuming his time, along with a concern that *War of the Worlds* at least get off to an impressive start, he perhaps ran out of the time necessary to render this latter section convincing.

Entering New York through the Holland Tunnel, Pierson treks from lower Manhattan to midtown. A devastated cityscape surrounds him. Civilization has been stopped dead in its tracks: "I noticed models of 1939 cars in show rooms facing empty streets." Moments later he realizes the end has also come for the invaders. Central Park is strewn with abandoned Martian machines. The reptilian bodies of their makers, who once wanted to feed on earthlings, are now being fed upon by ravenous birds and dogs. After having been largely immune to the military might thrown against them, they eventually succumbed in a most unexpected way.

> Later when their bodies were examined in laboratories, it was found that they were killed by the putrefactive and disease bacteria against which their systems were unprepared . . . slain after all man's defenses had failed, by the humblest thing that God in his wisdom put on this earth.

Waxing philosophical, the professor gives us a soliloquy steeped in the moral lessons that might be derived from the invasion. Although civilization is now on the mend, he hints that we should remain vigilant, lest the Martians return. This point is elaborated at greater length in the novel, but tempered by the assumption that Venus might be their preferred next stop. And, just as the drama began with phrases from the first paragraph of the novel, so it ends by paraphrasing excerpts from the last. The final sentence in the radio play, which is spoken against an orchestral crescendo, is almost verbatim H. G.:

> Strange it now seems to sit in my peaceful study at Princeton writing down the last chapter of the record begun at a deserted farm in Grovers Mill. Strange to see from my window the university spires dim and blue through an April haze. Strange to watch children playing in the streets. Strange to see young people

strolling on the green, where the new spring grass heals the last black scars of a bruised earth. Strange to watch the sightseers enter the museum where the dissembled parts of a Martian machine are kept on public view. Strange when I recall the time when I first saw it, bright and clean-cut, hard and silent, under the dawn of that last great day. [MUSIC]

In these closing minutes following the dialogue with the artilleryman, the drama picks up considerably. Welles puts enormous emotional conviction into his lines. Then, seconds after the orchestral finale, he reminds us that the whole thing was only Mercury's way of playing trick-or-treat.

This is Orson Welles, ladies and gentlemen, out of character to assure you that the *War of the Worlds* has no further significance than the holiday offering it was intended to be. The Mercury Theatre's own radio version of dressing up in a sheet and jumping out of a bush and saying Boo! Starting now, we couldn't soap all your windows and steal all your garden gates, by tomorrow night . . . so we did the next best thing [in the broadcast he says "best next thing"]. We annihilated the world before your very ears, and utterly destroyed the Columbia Broadcasting System [he actually says, "the CBS"]. You will be relieved, I hope to learn that we didn't mean it, and that both institutions are still open for business. So good-bye everybody, and remember, please, for the next day or so, the terrible lesson you learned tonight. That grinning, glowing, globular invader of your living room is an inhabitant of the pumpkin patch, and if your doorbell rings and nobody's there, that was no Martian . . . it's Hallowe'en. [MUSIC]

What was Welles thinking when, after delivering these lines, the Mercury theme closed out the show and Dan Seymour announced next week's program, three unspecified short stories? He must have felt relief to have so smoothly pulled off what only days before had seemed to be an unwieldy story idea. He must have also suspected that the drama probably threw a few people into a momentary tizzy. But he was probably as unprepared as the residents of Grovers Mill were for the bombshell that awaited him when he exited the studio.

CHAPTER SIX

Revelation

> Write of the things which thou hast seen, and the things which are, and the things which shall be hereafter.
>
> —Revelation 1:19

Without apology, I begin this chapter as I did the last, with a reference to Woody Allen's *Radio Days*. In a hilarious scene, he has a would-be Lothario deceptively arranging to run out of gas while driving his date to a secluded spot on a fall evening, circa 1938. As the man makes passionate advances, he turns on the radio for musical support. Big mistake. An urgent voice declares, "We interrupt this broadcast" . . . and follows with news of a Martian invasion. The man flees in terror, stranding his date. She is outraged, and instructs her family that if he calls again to tell him that "I married a Martian."

In this vignette a courtship that at least hinted at the possibility it might lead to marriage was ended by a hoax broadcast. The incident seems farfetched, yet the reality of what actually happened to many people that night still generates incredulity. Never, before or since, have so many lives been disrupted by a media event emanating from the imagination rather than from the world at large. The incident reveals a lot about the times in which it occurred and the medium causing the occurrence.

Although the initial panic began several minutes into the broadcast, let us consider first the panic that later enveloped the perpetrators. As the final theme played, John Houseman was called to the phone in the control room to speak with the mayor of a small midwestern city. His Honor was irate. He screamed for Welles's hide in response to the situation the program was creating: unruly men forming into mobs and looting while the meek huddled in churches and prayed for deliverance. Houseman did his best to placate the man.[1] When he got off the phone, he found the studio inundated by police and the press. He and Welles were then dragged to a back office and held for questioning while several other Mercury staff members managed to hide in a women's washroom. Other CBS employees were not so passive. Concerned with protecting the network (which as it turned out was liable, not Welles), they hid or destroyed material pertaining to the broadcast, mainly scripts and acetate recordings.

Houseman and Welles were soon fed to voracious reporters. Both men have described the experience as unnerving and almost terrifying, since at that point the damage caused seemed like a worst case scenario. Numerous deaths were implied, most allegedly occurring on the highways in the evacuation stampede. And did Houseman and Welles know about all the suicides, one reporter asked?[2] Fortunately for everyone at Mercury, it would eventually be revealed that no deaths could be attributed directly to the program. However, in the postbroadcast confusion it seemed as if the New Jersey Turnpike had claimed as many victims as the Martian heat ray.

The press scrum ended without any arrests and much still to be learned. Welles and Houseman left the studio surreptitiously via a back door and made their way to the Mercury Theatre to join the rehearsal of *Danton's Death*. Welles was of course late, a common occurrence. Mercury assistant Richard Barr tried to tell the actors that this time there was a legitimate excuse: Welles had just terrified the nation.[3] Disbelief followed, although the presence of reporters must have given the staff an inkling that this would be no ordinary evening's rehearsal. In any case, proof for Barr's claim was only a few blocks away. The cast, along with Welles who had just arrived, traipsed over to Times Square to see verification for the maestro's con job on America in the moving lights of the famous illuminated news billboard.

On the morrow, as details and consequences of the broadcast burned up wire services and filled newspaper front pages, Welles was called back to CBS for a press conference. He read the following prepared statement, which was reprinted in newspapers nationwide.

> Despite my deep regret over any misapprehension which our broadcast last night created among some listeners, I am even the more bewildered over this misunderstanding in the light of an analysis of the broadcast itself. It seems to me that there are four factors which should have in any event maintained the illusion of fiction in the broadcast. The first was that the broadcast was per-

formed as if occurring in the future and as if it were then related by a survivor of a past occurrence. The date of the fanciful invasion of this planet by Martians was clearly given as 1939 and was so announced at the outset of the broadcast. The second element was the fact that the broadcast took place in our regular weekly Mercury Theatre period and had been so announced in all the papers. For seventeen consecutive weeks we have been broadcasting radio drama. Sixteen of these seventeen broadcasts have been fiction and have been presented as such. Only one in the series was a true story, the broadcast of "Hell on Ice" by Commander Ellsberg, and was identified as a true story within the framework of radio drama. The third element was the fact that at the very outset of the broadcast and twice during its enactment listeners were told that this was a play, that it was an adaptation of an old novel by H. G. Wells. Furthermore, at the conclusion a detailed statement to this effect was made. The fourth factor seems to me to have been the most pertinent of all. That is the familiarity of the fable, within the American idiom of Mars and Martians. For many decades "The Man from Mars" has been almost a synonym for fantasy . . . this fantasy, as such, has been used in radio programs many times. In these broadcasts, conflict between citizens of Mars and other planets has been a familiarly accepted fairy-tale. The same make-believe is familiar to newspaper readers through a comic strip that uses the same device.[4]

Yes, he did announce that it was a play at the outset and conclusion, but those "twice during" declarations came within seconds of each other during a station break at the forty-two-minute mark; however, it should be noted that 60 percent of affiliated stations carrying the program made more frequent announcements once they sensed its unusual nature.[5] His last point probably refers to Buck Rogers on radio and Flash Gordon battling the Martians in the comics and in the 1938 movie serial featuring Olympic swimming champion Buster Crabbe. The series was pure fantasy, a wacky and wonderful portrait of Martian civilization that seems indebted to Fritz Lang's *Metropolis* (1926). Escapist fare to be sure, but it no doubt led some to reflect on the possibility of intelligent life on Mars; coincidentally, the Martians depicted in the serial attack our planet with a laserlike beam similar to the heat ray in *War of the Worlds*. Not surprisingly, in the aftermath of the Panic Broadcast, the *Flash Gordon* serial was reedited and released as a motion picture.

The press conference was filmed, and in it Welles gives one of his greatest acting performances—he must have sensed that his future in radio and overall career might be on the line. Unshaven, glassy-eyed, and feigning sincerity, he looked more like a victim of the Martian invasion than its perpetrator. When questioned, he denied any malicious intent and said he was more worried about the broadcast sounding boring or silly than in it scaring people. He also tried to downplay his creative role by saying that he had used standard radio techniques. Luckily for him nobody mentioned the dead air sequences, microphone testing, or any of the other remarkable devices used to invoke realism, which diverged considerably from what had been used in conventional radio dramas.

Howard Koch was present at the interview and suspected a Wellesian ruse.[6] He saw verification of it when the proceedings ended. Welles and Houseman exited simultaneously from different doors, turned toward each other, and without saying a word, exchanged congratulatory gestures—a rare moment of warmth in their extraordinarily productive but tempestuous partnership.

Koch had not been at the broadcast. Exhausted from writing against impossible deadlines, he listened to it in his apartment and then went immediately into a deep sleep from which Houseman's anxious phone calls could not rouse him. The next day, his off day, he sensed something was amiss when, heading to the barber, he heard excited passersby speak the words "invasion" and "panic." Suspecting Hitler as the cause, he was surprised to find out it was his own words when the barber showed him a newspaper headline.[7]

The extent of Welles's nefarious intentions has always been a matter for speculation. Koch was never certain just how far the shock waves were supposed to carry. Not so William Alland, an assistant to Welles at Mercury who would later play the role of the reporter, Thomson, in *Citizen Kane*. In an interview in the television documentary, *The Battle over Citizen Kane* (PBS 1996), he claims that Welles was fixated on shocking any and all available listeners. In later years Welles had no reason not to be candid. Yes, he told Peter Bogdanovich, the effect achieved was the one hoped for, but the extent of it "was flabbergasting," a total surprise, especially given the typically small *Mercury* audience.[8] Neither Welles nor anyone else involved could have anticipated the chain reaction of listeners phoning friends, who then tuned in and phoned other friends. When Alexander Woollcott sent him the following telegram Welles gleefully posted it on his office door: "This only goes to prove, my beamish boy, that the intelligent people were all listening to a dummy, and all the dummies were listening to you."[9]

Back in England, H. G. Wells was probably unaware of the dummy, Edgar Bergen, or even *Mercury Theatre on the Air*. But he was cognizant of a panic that had occurred in America and its connection to his work. He also knew that this could only have been possible through major alterations to the original story. This led the seventy-two-year-old writer to vent his spleen. Fearing damage to his reputation, he insisted that CBS publicly retract their use of the novel as the basis for the radio play.[10]

His case was weak, but CBS did offer apologies and some additional remuneration as a peace offering. It had been his New York agent, Jacques Chambrun, who sold the rights to Mercury, with no clause stating how faithful to the novel the radio version had to be. Fortunately for H. G., all blame for the panic was directed at Welles and CBS, while the novel received praise for its ingenuity, along with increased sales. Sales were also brisk for his latest effort, *Apropos of Dolores*, released on 27 October. Some critics even thought the broadcast was timed to create publicity for the new novel.[11]

It is surprising that H. G. and his agent were not more prudent in licensing *War of the Worlds*, given past history. As David Y. Hughes has pointed out, the story was tampered with shortly after it was first serialized in *Pearson's Magazine* in 1897.[12] That year and the next, Wells had allowed the *New York Evening Journal* and the *Boston Post* to reprint the authorized American version which had just appeared in *Cosmopolitan* magazine. The story's location in the newspaper renderings was changed from London, to New York and Boston, respectively. The new versions also suffered the embellishments of the yellow press: alterations for the sake of sensationalism and lurid illustrations. H. G. was understandably outraged and made his feelings known in an open letter to *The Critic*, but legally he had no case. There is no evidence indicating that anyone at Mercury was familiar with these earlier Americanized versions.

In the days following the Panic Broadcast, the venerable Wells was relieved to see that it did not tarnish his reputation. He would subsequently follow Orson's artistic conquests with interest. On 28 October 1940, while on an American tour, he met his younger namesake when their schedules overlapped in San Antonio, Texas. That evening, a conversation between them was broadcast on KTSA. H. G., playing the old tiger, opens with an amiable tribute to the young lion:

> I've had a series of the most delightful experiences since I came to America, but the best thing that has happened to me so far has been meeting my little namesake here, Orson. I find him most delightful. He carries my name with an extra "e" which I hope he will soon drop.[13] I've known his work since before he made his sensational Halloween spree—are you sure there was such a panic in America?

The two then discuss the Panic Broadcast without being very specific, although we are informed by Welles that Hitler made reference to it to show how gullible Americans are. The exchange is somewhat halting, a situation worsened by the exuberant announcer's attempt to move it along. Perhaps Welles was intimidated by H. G.'s status as "the world's most famous man of letters," according to the announcer. Nevertheless, Orson goes on to praise a lecture delivered earlier in the day by H. G. The elder Wells in turn helps him plug the nearly completed *Citizen Kane*. Orson talks about it in humble terms as an attempt at creative storytelling. H. G. predicts that it will have "lots of jolly good new noises in it." This would certainly turn out to be the case, both figuratively, since it would become a pathbreaking film, and literally, in terms of the innovations in sound it brought to cinema. Almost a year later H. G. actually saw the film and sent Orson a warm congratulatory telegram. If the elder Wells recognized the film as a send-up of press baron William Randolph Hearst, I wonder if he got some gratification by remembering that it was Hearst's *New York Evening Journal* that had bastardized the serial version of *War of the Worlds* over forty years earlier.

By poetic quirk of fate these two namesakes, whose paths crossed so briefly and intriguingly in life, became in death archival neighbors in the American Midwest: H. G.'s *War of the Worlds* manuscripts and proofs are at the University of Illinois, while Welles's correspondences, scripts, and radio recordings, including the original acetate disks of *War of the Worlds*, are at Indiana University.

To what degree H. G. was aware of the extent of the chaos caused by the Panic Broadcast in the days following its occurrence is not certain. In North America everyone knew it was considerable. However, to this day the exact size of the audience remains a matter of speculation. At the time, the American Institute of Public Opinion (AIPO) found that 12 percent of those polled heard the broadcast. This was a Gallup poll based on the voting public. It yielded nine million listeners, mostly adult males. If we factor in children over ten and the disenfranchised, Southern blacks for example, who were not registered to vote, estimates of up to twelve million have been suggested.[14]

Somehow these figures seem unduly high, given the radio listening habits of the time. My sense is that, owing to funding delays, since the AIPO poll was done six weeks after the broadcast, more people claimed to be earwitnesses to the historic moment than would have been the case had it been done the day after. Many of them, in addition to reading about the program, might have talked to relatives or friends who heard it, and then, over time, began to believe that they too were part of the audience. I have interviewed several people who claimed to have heard the broadcast, including a close relative. Even allowing for lapses of memory, their perception of it in terms of time, place, and content was so skewed that I was left with considerable doubt. A more realistic figure of four million was posited by the Hooper research group. This private commercial pollster did not survey as wide a sample as did the AIPO in making their projections, but their specialty was in monitoring radio program audiences, and they did the research in the days following the broadcast.

The AIPO poll also indicates that 1.7 million people took the broadcast to be the real thing. Proportionately this was 28 percent of those surveyed. But in this instance, the relative numbers might be less than was actually the case. There remains the possibility that embarrassment over having been duped eventually led such listeners to deny that they had been taken in by the program. Many in the audience did concede that they tuned in late, 61 percent in the AIPO poll and 42 percent in a special CBS survey. In the AIPO tally, 11 percent of those who tuned in from the beginning thought they were listening to a bona fide news report, as did 35 percent who tuned in late. The CBS figures are 20 percent and 63 percent respectively.[15]

What is remarkable here is that thousands who had tuned in to the program from the outset, many of them regular *Mercury* listeners, still thought it was being interrupted by real news reports. Two factors contributed. On one hand, Welles so convincingly made the segue from fiction to faked fact that he overrode part of the audience's normal frame of reference. The second reason should be familiar to contemporary television viewers. Often we put on a specific program at the appointed time and then go about other activities, until something interesting or unusual prompts us to pay attention to the broadcast.

War of the Worlds was heard coast to coast. A surprisingly high number of listeners in the South and West were frightened by it. The southern reaction can be attributed to a poorer, less educated population. Reaction in the West—higher for example than in New England—still begs explanation; fear of Japanese aggression might have been a factor. In the Middle Atlantic states, fear on the part of listeners was close to the national average. However, proximity there to the scene of the alleged Martian mischief led those who were anxious, especially in New Jersey, to do something about it. Some headed for the hills, literally. Roads to the Orange Mountains, which to most non-flatlanders are at best medium-sized hills, became congested.

Even before Welles would unhinge them, residents of central New Jersey, especially in the city of Newark, may have sensed that all was not right with the world that evening. Between 6:15 and 6:30 P.M., there were power fluctuations. Lights were affected, as was radio reception. Calls to the Public Service Gas and Electric Company found those who were supposed to be in the know just as baffled as customers.[16]

Telephone lines became much busier after 8:00 P.M. Switchboards to police precincts, newspaper offices, and CBS were at or near overload. So were private lines in general as people phoned friends and relatives to warn them, or to say good-bye. One telephone company employee, no doubt taking seriously an earlier mandate to be polite under all circumstances, calmly responded to a frantic caller demanding to know if it was the end of the world, with "I'm sorry we don't have that information here." By 8:45 P.M. the Associated Press sent a wire to affiliated papers informing them that the reported deaths from a meteorite in New Jersey are "the result of a studio dramatization."[17] At 9:00 P.M. the ever popular Walter Winchell came on the air for NBC. He announced that there was no cause for alarm, "America has not fallen." This was a cryptic statement for those unaware of the Panic Broadcast, and he no doubt delivered it in his usual frenetic style. CBS, concerned with damage control, kept interrupting its regularly scheduled programs at half-hour intervals to announce that the earlier broadcast of *War of the Worlds* was only a dramatization.

Postbroadcast assessments indicate that some listeners took every moment of the program seriously. Some began laughing at the outset and never stopped. Others took it seriously until they perceived incongruities, such as the time compression, or the very idea that these invaders were Martians and not Germans. And some even believed the Martians *were* Germans, either in some new militaristic guise, or because the announcer was making an interpretive mistake—a deduction that probably resulted from associating the Martians' use of poison gas with similar attacks by the Kaiser's army in World War I.

Also relevant to the panic was CBS's self-proclaimed status as "the news network." They interrupted their programming for news updates far more frequently than other networks. By 1938 CBS had correspondents such as Edward R. Murrow and William Shirer reporting regularly from Europe; earlier in the year they had covered the Nazi takeover of Vienna and the Munich crisis. Only two months before the Panic Broadcast, on 29 August, *Mercury's* presentation of *The Count of Monte Cristo* was prefaced by a brief bulletin reporting the German threat to Czechoslovakia. If any network had a finger on the pulse of dangerous late-breaking events, everyone knew that network would be CBS. People also thought that, just as newspapers could "scoop" a major story, so could broadcast networks, something that rarely happens today save with hard-to-access distant stories, such as CNN in the case of the Gulf War. Therefore, when some concerned listeners tuned to NBC for verification of the Martian attack and heard Edgar Bergen dialoguing with his dummy, they concluded that the network was just not as astute as CBS.

Actions taken in response to the assumed invasion varied. In Providence, Rhode Island, several distraught citizens phoned the electric company urging them to effect a blackout so the city might be spared a Martian attack. In one

New York suburb a woman hugged her radio, crucifix in hand, and contemplated sealing the room with cement to avoid being gassed. She wanted to go on the roof to see how close the Martians were but could not leave her radio.[18] In the rural Midwest, a woman and her family knelt in prayer while her husband went out in the yard and stared at Mars. In several communities religious officials phoned police to query why so many people were rushing into churches. At one evening service, parishioners were informed of the peril but stayed until the proceedings concluded, then bolted. In an Indianapolis church, a woman ran in and interrupted the service with "New York has just been destroyed. You might as well go home to die. I heard it on the radio." The congregation left immediately. In Pittsburgh a man came home and found his wife with a bottle of poison in her hand. "I'd rather die this way than that," she said. The man calmed her down and began making phone inquiries.[19]

In a New York theater, playgoers left immediately when someone rushed in with news of the invasion. In West Manhattan a man claimed to have spotted smoke rising from decimated parts of New Jersey. Uptown in Harlem, a group of people went to the police station asking where they should go to be evacuated.[20] One of their members claimed to have heard the president advising citizens over the radio. This was not so farfetched: Kenneth Delmar, playing the secretary of the interior, had done a great FDR imitation. Police throughout the city were eventually sent the following message: "Broadcast just completed was dramatization of a play. No cause for alarm. Repeat, no cause for alarm."[21]

Bedlam reigned in New Jersey. In one Newark apartment, residents fled in various states of undress; in another they exited with wet towels over their faces in anticipation of a gas attack. Highways were chaotic. One New Brunswick man, after joining the road exodus, realized he had left his dog tied up in the yard. He headed back through the traffic to retrieve the animal.[22] At ground zero, in Grovers Mill, there was more purposive action than panic. The small fire brigade went looking for the fires the Martian heat ray was supposed to have touched off, while a posse of farmers grabbed shotguns and prepared to face the dastardly invaders. A topless windmill was mistaken for one of the Martian tripod machines and riddled with several rounds. The local police gradually restored calm, but it did not last. The next day curiosity seekers and reporters mounted a real invasion. The Wilson farm in Grovers Mill was assumed to be the one mentioned in the radio play; the actual site mentioned in the broadcast, the Wilmuth farm, was therefore conveniently displaced by the name Wilson in subsequent media coverage. The day also saw several professors from Princeton, perhaps unaware of all facets of what had occurred the previous evening, combing the area for meteorite fragments.[23]

The diverse reactions to the program—who was affected and why—were gathered and sorted. Patterns emerged, but they were laced with exceptions. In general the more educated a person, the less susceptible they were to the hoax; however, many college students and graduates were believers while numerous minimally schooled persons discerned a ruse from the outset. Strict religious convictions also seemed to increase susceptibility. Perhaps a belief in angels made the leap to accepting the existence of Martians a short one. And then there were stories of children, familiar with Welles's voice and trickery as the Shadow, reassuring their parents that Armageddon was not at hand.

Lawsuits inevitably followed. But it was CBS that was under the gun, not Welles. Whether it was a stroke of brilliance or just sound contract negotiations, his lawyer, Arnold Weissberger, had arranged it so that the network would be held responsible for anything untoward caused by a Welles broadcast. Orson's only accountability was for personal libel and literary plagiarism.[24] Close to a million dollars in damages were claimed against CBS. Each case was settled out of court. It is conceivable, however, that CBS could have won every case, especially since the program was announced as a dramatization in newspaper radio listings and in the opening credits. From the network's point of view, the money lost in the settlements might have been well spent, since it minimized subsequent negative publicity. Not surprisingly, listenership to *Mercury Theatre on the Air* went up 100 percent the following week. The Campbell Soup Company took note and would soon offer the series the sponsorship they had vetoed after the *Treasure Island* broadcast.

Many of the foregoing incidents were chronicled in the press for days, and in some cases weeks, after. It seemed as if madness had been let loose upon the world. The finger of culpability variously pointed at Welles, CBS, the American public, and radio itself. In some cases Welles was seen as a Svengali or Rasputin-like artiste who had used his dramatic legerdemain to bewitch a nation. In less personal indictments, CBS was called to account for failing to monitor its programming more closely; most papers regarded as totally justified the upcoming FCC (Federal Communications Commission) investigation of the broadcast.

Not surprisingly, it was in the sober pages of the *New York Times* where the naiveté of the public became a primary issue. This was especially apparent in the 1 November edition, which reprinted parts of the script. When reproduced on the page, the words hardly seem a recipe to induce panic. The *Times* also printed a letter from H. G. Wells's New York agent, Jacques

Chambrun. He was worried about aspersions being cast on H. G. and demanded a retraction from CBS for the unfaithful adaptation. Most *Times* readers, however, were aware that a radio version of any novel requires wholesale changes, so were probably blasé regarding his concern. It is not insignificant that the *Times* had been an astute follower of the fortunes of the Mercury Theatre, occasionally serving as a voice for the announcements of Welles and Houseman. On 1 November they allowed Orson the last word. In Puckish fashion—imagine the glint in his eyes—he claimed to have received many telegrams from listeners telling him how much they enjoyed the show.

A good deal of editorializing emerged in the days that followed. Most of the commentary, although conceding that people should not have been so taken in, put the blame on radio. There was a hidden agenda here—a rivalry between the two media that went back at least a dozen years.[25] As the new kid on the block, radio had challenged the monopoly of the press in presenting news. This was exacerbated during the Depression, when radio listenership grew at the expense of newspaper circulation, and advertising revenue followed suit. Even motion pictures felt the squeeze, since with a one-time purchase, radio guaranteed continuous entertainment.

Newspapers eventually and grudgingly came to accept radio as a viable entertainment medium. But they argued that the medium's entertainment conventions were being extended to the way it presented news, leading to superficiality and emotionalism; the tabloids understandably refrained from this accusation. One way newspapers protested the situation, although it was not done consistently or universally, was to refrain from printing radio schedules. In a more direct action they either denied radio access to wire service news, or placed strict limits on the amount of such news that could be broadcast. CBS, always the innovator, responded in 1933 by forming its own news division. When the network later presented the Welles drama using a news format, it was a moment for critique the press could not let pass.

The public, long weary of a press tradition of internecine rivalry, gravitated to radio. It had a higher credibility quotient. No one exploited this better than President Franklin Delano Roosevelt who, in addition to his fireside chats, often used radio to make general announcements. The anti–New Deal Republican newspaper chains lined up against him, but to no avail. He was reelected by a landslide in 1936. In later years his campaigns would be bolstered by the eloquent voice of an ardent supporter, Welles. There is even a pro-Roosevelt slant in *Citizen Kane*, which imaginatively deconstructs one of FDR's most unyielding antagonists, William Randolph Hearst.

Not all press commentary, however, blamed radio for the *War of the Worlds* panic. A few papers followed the lead of the *New York Times* in expressing concern over a populace unable to separate fact from fiction. Better education was called for. The exact path to further enlightenment was not defined, but the implication was that it should include a greater reliance on print-based media and diminished time accessing the airwaves. To further protect people from themselves, greater regulation on the part of the FCC was called for—not the kind of moralistic censorship that was invoked in 1934 under pressure from the Catholic Legion of Decency, but specific imperatives that would prevent any future media shaman from inciting mass delusion.

"Mass delusion" is the term that noted journalist Dorothy Thompson used in her editorial on the Panic Broadcast in the 2 November *New York Tribune*. Of all the commentaries written about the event hers was the most influential.[26] By no means was it the only one that defended the broadcast; nevertheless, she cut through the various debates like a scythe, and in so doing helped get Welles off the hook.

Thompson argued that Welles's broadcast was the "story of the century." It exposed how susceptible mass society is to "theatrical demagoguery," and how powerful and dangerous a medium radio can be. The incident also dramatized for her how the suspension of reason that allowed Hitler, Mussolini, and Stalin to impose their ideologies was not as removed from America as many believed. Other lessons include never allowing any political body to have a monopoly over radio, and recognizing deficiencies in the education system, especially in the area of reason and logic. She was also convinced that part of the problem resided with the popularization of science, which imparted just enough knowledge to allow gullibility, but not enough to engender healthy skepticism. In her view, Welles "ought to be given a Congressional medal and a national prize for having made the most amazing and important of contributions to the social sciences," and his historic hour on the air was "an act of unconscious genius performed by the very innocence of intelligence." Such accolades doubtlessly helped stem part of the hostile tide. How well Orson actually knew the popular journalist personally is not certain, but for the record, they were neighbors in the small community of Sneden's Landing just north of the city.

Although a small handful of other journalists were of similar opinion, none stated the case as forcefully or eloquently. In the other bastion of the printed news media, magazines, *Time* (7 November) refrained from using the broadcast as a basis for social commentary, dealing instead with its effectiveness as dramatic art. The verdict was positive. The *Time* review had the catchiest title of any piece written about the broadcast: "Boo!"

With the popular press spilling so much ink over the incident, it was inevitable that academe would follow suit. Almost a year prior to the broadcast the organization destined to put it under a microscope was founded. A grant from the Rockefeller Foundation to Princeton University helped create the Princeton Office of Radio Research. The director was Paul Lazarsfeld, an Austrian Jewish émigré and social psychologist, whose expertise in quantitative methods was tempered by a humanist leaning. He was teamed with two associate directors, psychologist Hadley Cantril and CBS researcher Frank Stanton, a Ph.D. in psychology who would eventually become network president. The project was formed in response to the increasing influence of radio on public life. Although the agenda was fluid, the primary leaning was toward studying the nature of radio programming, the type of audience it attracted, and their reactions to the medium. Polls were used, as well as questionnaires and demographic data. Lazarsfeld was particularly interested in contrasting the radio audience with those who relied more on print media. In 1940 he published *Radio and the Printed Page*, one of the most significant publications to emerge from the research group, which by 1939 had moved to Columbia University in New York City to be closer to the radio action. This media think tank was highly influential in establishing the empirical study of mass communication as an academic field in the United States. The catch phrase often attributed to it is "who says what to whom with what effect."

In the aftermath of the Martian visit, Cantril organized a study of its impact. The result was a revealing book, *The Invasion from Mars: A Study in the Psychology of Panic* (1940). With help from researchers Hazel Gaudet and Herta Herzog, and the cooperation of Welles and Howard Koch, Cantril examined numerous aspects of the broadcast. If we use the communications catch phrase mentioned above to describe his project, the "who says what" part is covered by a reprint of the radio play along with a brief discussion of the circumstances surrounding its production; "to whom" is dealt with by using demographic data on the broadcast's audience; and "with what effect" is gleaned from a ten-page interview questionnaire given to 135 people, supplemented by press data. The book has become an important case study for both media scholars and Welles researchers.

One significant name mentioned by Cantril, yet omitted in press accounts of the broadcast, is Howard Koch. The way this occurred irked Welles. He was sent a set of the galley proofs of the book and asked to write a blurb for the jacket to help promote it. Assuming the galleys were close to what was actually published, he would have seen Koch's name mentioned twice. The first citation is in the preface: "Howard Koch has kindly permitted us to publish for the first time his brilliant adaptation of the *War of the Worlds*"; and then in the opening paragraph of chapter 1, we get, "Orson Welles with his innocent little group of actors took his place before the microphone in a New York studio of the Columbia Broadcasting System. He carried with him Howard Koch's freely adapted version of H. G. Wells's imaginative novel, *War of the Worlds*."

Welles was furious. He believed that this acknowledgment overrated the contribution of a seventy-five-dollar-a-week writer and slighted his own. A war of the words ensued over authorship of the broadcast. It would eerily foreshadow the much larger "auteurship" debate over the script for *Citizen Kane* regarding the relative contributions of Welles and Herman Mankiewicz, which still prompts controversy. In fact Orson and "Mank" were working on that self-same project when the Cantril correspondence began. Cantril, unused to dealing with celebrity egos (although academic ones can be just as insufferable), must have been taken aback by the response.

Welles claimed that attribution of the script to Koch was a serious error. Koch, he argued, was only part of a team. The roster cited includes Houseman (now an enemy, although *Kane* would lead them into a brief but uneasy alliance), who is referred to as "my partner and chief collaborator"; Paul Stewart, "who did a great deal"; John Dietz, the sound man; Davidson Taylor, whom he credited with helping to give the broadcast a news format; and Bernard Herrmann, whose music was said to have directly influenced the script. As for Koch, "he was helpful in the second part of the script and did some work on the first," which Welles insists "was necessary to revise."[27]

In trying to convince Cantril to downplay Koch's role, Welles used a two-pronged argument that in hindsight appears self-serving and contradictory. On one hand he states that given the collaborative nature of the broadcast, he is not asking to be considered the principal writer, only that it be credited to the collective. However, the motivation for his seeking redress soon surfaces: "I do feel that you have unwittingly implied a slur on my position as the creator and responsible artist of my broadcasts." Perhaps he would have been more accommodating two years earlier. In the intervening period the broadcast had become legendary and Orson's name was usually the only one mentioned in conjunction with it. Hollywood was his milieu now and *War of the Worlds* had helped write the ticket. He also knew that Tinseltown harbored enemies. But Cantril's book was no cause for alarm. Welles's detractors were not searching for controversy in his past radio life, only hoping he would fail in his present filmic one.

Cantril must have been perturbed by the response, and maybe a bit exhilarated—academics rarely get to interact with media celebrities and Welles was as big as many movie and television stars are today. His response, "wiser than Solomon," according to Simon Callow,[28] also seems as balanced an acknowledgment as was possible at the time: "Script idea and development by Orson Welles, assisted by John Houseman and the Mercury Theatre staff. Written by Howard Koch, under the direction of Mr. Welles." Succinct and accurate, it was offered as an entry in the introduction in lieu of a bizarre suggestion by Welles that an errata slip be inserted in the book if last-minute changes could not be made. The slip would state that his reputation was slighted by an unfair attribution of artistic responsibility.

Welles immediately fired off a telegram vetoing Cantril's compromise. He again insisted that "Howard Koch did not write *War of the Worlds*."[29] Cantril continued the exchange. He probably was aware that Welles could not be persuaded but wanted to make his position clear. He cited an affidavit from Ann Froelich. She had worked for Houseman and Koch, typed the script, and claimed that Koch was the principal writer and copyright holder. Welles overheated. Houseman had become an enemy, Froelich was still working for Koch, and Cantril was privileging the say-so of former employees over their boss. Again he denied Koch, reiterated that his own reputation would be damaged, and made an idle threat: "I know that you will understand that I cannot permit this to occur."[30]

His fears were unfounded. The book was published as Cantril intended. Never a best seller, it was and still is highly regarded. And no one responded to it by questioning Welles's role in the most written about broadcast in history (prior to JFK and O. J.). Welles seems not to have made any further comment on the publication. That he secured and read a copy is likely. While going through his personal papers at Indiana University's Lilly Library, I came across a copy of the book's jacket and promotional flyer. Koch's name appears on both and is boldly circled in red pencil, presumably in Welles's hand.

As copyright holder Koch decided to have his say in 1970. In *The Panic Broadcast: Portrait of an Event*, he discusses the circumstances of the program and its aftermath. The script is reprinted. Koch also has a few things to say about Mars, radio, and television. As a pièce de résistance he visits Grovers Mill thirty-one years later, which he notes with irony is probably the only place in the world made famous by a historical event that never took place. The book provides an intriguing and humorous postmortem of the imaginary invasion, and the real one in the aftermath, made up of curiosity seekers and tourists. Koch also indicates that he was the primary writer and implies that what took place as the script went back and forth to the studio were minor revisions. He then makes reference to the original novel: "I could use practically nothing but the author's idea of a Martian invasion and his description of their appearance and their machines." In 1996 Harry Geduld challenged both contentions.[31]

His arguments are convincing. However, it must also be noted that Koch never begrudged Welles's "auteurship" of the broadcast itself. In 1988 (Koch died in 1995), at the Museum of Broadcasting's tribute to Welles on the fiftieth anniversary of the Panic Broadcast, Koch gave him full credit for its success.[32] Coincidentally, perhaps not, that same year the original *War of the Worlds* script was sold at auction for $135,000 to an individual who has opted to remain anonymous. As regards giving H. G. Wells his due, here Geduld rightly finds Koch wanting. A list of direct transferences from the novel to the radio script is presented, along with a mention of several scenes in the novel that might have been included in the radio play but were not.

Koch later became embroiled in another writing credit controversy. In 1973 he published *Casablanca: Script and Legend*, with part of the text appearing in a *New York* magazine article (30 April 1973). He argued that the original play, *Everybody Comes to Rick's*, which he mistakenly refers to as *Everybody Goes to Rick's*, had Rick and the exotic locale, but little else on which to base a movie. The authors of the unproduced play, Murray Burnett and Joan Allison, felt slighted. Burnett sued Koch and *New York* magazine, and lost. He then sued Overlook Press, which had published the aforementioned book. After losing this litigation, he went after Warner Bros. for the rights to the characters in the story, and lost yet again.[33]

As time went by Koch waxed apologetic and admitted to never having read the play until after the controversy. What he had seen at Warner's was an early partial screen adaptation of it by Julius and Philip Epstein, which he claimed to have completed by rounding out the characters and imparting continuity. The situation was more complex. In a thorough study of the making of *Casablanca*, Aljean Harmetz has clarified much surrounding the film's history, especially since the making of it has become almost as mythical as the movie itself.[34] In all, seven writers labored on *Casablanca*. The work of the first two was never used, and the contribution of the last two provided only touch-up. The Epsteins and Koch, as primary writers, justly copped the Oscar. Despite Koch's early denials, they did work on the script at the same time, but not in a face-to-face collaborative context. By the mid-1980s he came to accept this.

Koch was a remarkable man and a talented writer. His autobiography, *As Time Goes By*, is a candid and perceptive look at a life lived at the center of the creative vortices of radio and motion pictures. But in these media the center was, and still is in the case of film, rarely visible. The writer is a phantom, occasionally glimpsed in a credit, rarely acknowledged in public, but always heard in the dialogue. I would like to think that when Koch published the scripts of *War of the World* and *Casablanca*, it was not to steal credit from others, but as a paean to the entire tradition of radio and screenwriters who have long struggled, often with minimal recognition, to make story come alive. It should also be noted that despite Welles's argument with Cantril, he never begrudged Koch personally. Nevertheless, he must have been miffed by Houseman's account of the broadcast, published in *Harper's* (December 1948) and later summarized in the first volume of his autobiography, *Run-Through* (1972). In it he gives substantial credit to Koch for being the principal writer, but he also acknowledges that it was Welles's genius that made the program so extraordinary. He was less generous over the script for *Citizen Kane*, ceding more to Herman Mankiewicz than Welles, and several later Welles commentators, would accept.

Often referred to as the Orson Welles broadcast, *War of the Worlds* is replayed regularly on Halloween. It has long been available on LP records and can now found in CD format. In 1975 CBS aired a remarkable television movie, *The Night That Panicked America*, which deals with how the broadcast was produced, and the way a diverse group of people were affected by it. Welles himself has commented on the Panic Broadcast in an unusual documentary he made in 1974, *F for Fake*. The film is ostensibly about art forgery, art, lies, truth, and the fallibility of experts (implying film critics). Welles also chronicles his own life history as a conjurer in various media. Discussion of the infamous broadcast includes a commentary by Paul Stewart and hilarious clips of extraterrestrial mayhem drawn from 1950s science fiction films. Appearing on camera Welles assesses the impact of the program on his career. He mentions that the idea was later tried in South America. In fact, the concept of a fake news drama had also been attempted over a decade prior to *Mercury*'s effort, and then later in modified form on television in 1984. These efforts are worth a brief look.

On 26 January 1926, England was undergoing labor unrest and was on the eve of a general strike. The regular newscaster for the BBC, Father Ronald Knox, decided to give his listeners something to ponder. He created an unruly mob wreaking havoc on Parliament and lynching a government minister. The broadcast ended with the destruction of the radio station. Frantic citizens phoned police and the media, but the size of the radio audience at the time was relatively small and an extended panic did not ensue.[35] In other cases, South America was less fortunate.

On 12 November 1944, Radio Santiago in Chile broadcast their own Wellesian-inspired version of *War of the Worlds*, set locally. There was considerable panic and one death from a heart attack.[36] The fact that no action was taken against the perpetrators may have led to a reprise of the idea for such a program by station HCQRX in Quito, Ecuador, on 14 February 1949. Panic was widespread. Even the police and military thought the threat was real and went after the Martians. Sensing the chaos, the station repeatedly declared that the broadcast had been a hoax, only to be besieged by an angry mob. The building was set on fire and numerous employees prevented from leaving. Fifteen perished. The art and drama directors managed to escape but were soon arrested.[37]

By the television era the dangers of disguising a fictional story as news were obvious, but as a dramatic device the technique was too good to abandon altogether. In 1984 NBC, the most innovative of the major networks—whereas in the 1930s it had been CBS—decided to try a modified version of the format in the made-for-television movie, *Special Bulletin*. Shot on videotape, the movie enacted in real time the story of a group of domestic terrorists who seize a nuclear weapons depot in Charleston, South Carolina—note the use of real place names, as in 1938. To get an airing for their views in favor of disarmament, they threaten to suicidally detonate one of the bombs. They court the media. Television networks are played off against one another and the government, as part of the strategy. When the president promises one thing—a compromise—and the Pentagon delivers another, a commando raid, the terrorists respond. Broadcast coverage on location goes blank, and then, as in the infamous radio play, we are transferred back to network central. There is confusion, but in a few moments what happened in Charleston is revealed through the feed of an affiliate in a town twenty miles away. As the mushroom cloud rises, it becomes clear that the result has been one of the most exciting and well-written television dramas of the decade.

NBC knew, from the 1938 Panic Broadcast, that there would be risks involved in doing *Special Bulletin*. During the previous week, in print ads and in on-air promotional announcements, they mentioned that it would be done in a simulated newscast style. The drama was also interrupted at frequent intervals to announce that the events being portrayed in it were fictitious. Still, a handful of people panicked, at least momentarily; and there were those who complained because they found the story distasteful or even treasonous, since it featured a botched military assault reminiscent of the one that occurred during the Iran hostage crisis. The movie's only real failing, however, was that it drew a small audience and little in the way of subsequent commentary.[38]

Whether or not Welles saw *Special Bulletin* is uncertain. It aired a year before his death, at a time when he was doing the television talk-show circuit. When asked about *War of the Worlds*, he would usually end his reminiscence with something along the lines of "Well, you know they tried it in South America and were put in jail, but my punishment was a Hollywood contract."[39] True, but before that momentous passage there were still other radio worlds to conquer.

PART THREE

THE SOUND IN THE FURY

CHAPTER SEVEN

Campbell Playhouse

> Indeed, as in the novel, it isn't only the dialogue, the descriptive clarity, the behavior of the characters, but the style imparted to the language which creates meaning.
>
> —André Bazin

A week after the mayhem caused by *War of the Worlds*, the languid strains of Tchaikovsky announced *Mercury Theatre on the Air* to a greatly expanded audience. Some were probably disappointed. Instead of the usual format involving a single literary classic, Howard Koch had adapted two shorter works, Joseph Conrad's novella, *Heart of Darkness*, and Clarence Day's turn-of-the-century memoir, *Life with Father*. Originally, three works were slated for adaptation, but O. Henry's *The Gift of the Magi* was eventually dropped so as not to overload the hour. Nevertheless it was overloaded. There was simply not enough time to do justice to the two divergent stories. Without mentioning the previous program's controversy, Welles introduces *Heart of Darkness* by referring to it as a "deliberate masterpiece." The production values of the broadcast are not exceptional and the pacing is slow. He would do a better, but still less than inspiring interpretation of the story on the 13 March 1945 broadcast of *This Is My Best*. *Heart of Darkness*, it should be noted, was originally scheduled to be his debut film for RKO, but owing to projected cost overruns and logistical difficulties, it was wisely abandoned in favor of *Citizen Kane*.

Life with Father fared better, but it still seems dated, even for 1938. The wonder of it all was that despite the events of the previous week Welles was able to summon his resources and stay the course of such a humorous story—acting as both narrator and Father—with élan. He was doubtlessly intrigued by Father's difficulty with new electric technologies, especially the telephone. The scenes pertaining to it are remarkably similar to those dealing with the automobile in Booth Tarkington's *The Magnificent Ambersons*. The glimpse both authors provide of an earlier America in transition was, by the late 1930s, of little interest. In the case of Clarence Day, Hollywood's timing would prove better than Orson's. *Life with Father* was made into a movie in 1947. It proved a great success, a soothing reminiscence to a nation ravaged by two world wars of the naiveté that had preceded these harsh benchmarks of twentieth-century life.

Much of Welles's attention at this time was directed toward making his theatrical interpretation of George Büchner's *Danton's Death* a success. The cause would be lost for several reasons. In his postmortem, Houseman feels that the play lacked structure and texture. To be an effective Wellesian vehicle at least one of these elements should be present—he points out that *Caesar* had the former, *Faustus*, the latter.[1] Technical glitches also plagued the production. The obscurity of the play might have also alienated the average theatergoer; and, because of the parallels that could be drawn between the duo of Danton and Robespierre, and Trotsky and Stalin, the production did not go down well with the militant left who composed a large part of Mercury's audience. Yet, many critics liked the play. Unfortunately, while negative criticism can be disastrous for a production, positive reviews do little good unless there is a favorable buzz from the initial public who has seen it. *Danton's Death* yielded no buzz. It opened on 5 November and closed after twenty-one performances on the 26th.

Welles lamented Mercury's faltering fortunes publicly by linking it to a decline in the American theater overall. There may have been some truth to the latter part of the assertion—movies were sucking up Broadway talent like a black hole and then spewing it onto a firmament seen by millions. However, the Mercury had talent from the very beginning and was constantly adding to its list. Furthermore, it had found a niche. Welles simply assumed that the niche could be broadened. Unfortunately, *Danton's Death* showed the risks inherent in a theatrical company playing against type. Three months later he would try again with *Five Kings* and the venture would collapse.

Throughout its run, Mercury attracted mostly favorable press. The eminent drama critic Harold Clurman once described the company as "rebellious" and "sensational," having "originality" and "zip," but added that it was also "safe" and "not controversial."[2] Clurman's appreciation may bear a tinge of jealous rivalry, since for a time he was involved with the likes of Lee Strasberg and Stella Adler in that emporium of method acting, The Group Theater. Nevertheless, he was probably right.

From the beginning, theater never offered Welles any guarantees. In a humorous aphorism of the time, person X asks person Y about theatrical person Z: "Is that how he earns his living?" The response is, "No, that's how he loses it." In Welles's case, many of the financial losses he incurred on stage were covered through his work in front of the microphone. Always at the ready, radio was both a consistent provider and a means of artistic expression, although it was not his first choice as the medium through which he would be known to posterity. Nevertheless, it offered easy access to an audience that theater, and later film, yielded grudgingly. The *Mercury Theatre* broadcasts also allowed him to take frequent risks. A failed program one week could be quickly forgotten by a success the next. One such chance was taken on 13 November. Departing from its normal fare of presenting renowned literary works, Mercury broadcast *A Passenger to Bali*, based on the novella by unheralded twenty-seven-year-old Ellis St. Joseph.

The story is a variation of the *Flying Dutchman* saga; lest there be any doubt, it opens with Bernard Herrmann playing snippets from Wagner's overture. Welles gives one of the most extreme and successful character portrayals he would bring to radio. He plays the allegedly Dutch, allegedly Reverend, Ralph Walkes, who boards a Bali-bound steamer in Shanghai. When Balinese authorities deny him entry, he proceeds to make himself at home on the ship, much to the chagrin of the captain (Everett Sloane). With a suitcase of gin, an enormous appetite, and implied physical size, Walkes exerts a Svengali-like effect on the crew that undermines the captain's authority. When Shanghai refuses to take him back, the skipper contemplates killing him. Walkes is totally aware of the situation and taunts him. The murder never becomes necessary, at least directly. A huge storm—the sound effects are impressive—leads to a shipwreck, whereby the captain denies the reverend access to the lifeboats, forcing him to remain on the abandoned vessel.

Excellent performances by Welles and Sloane are bolstered by a keen-edged script in which every word is telling. Although sources attribute the writing to Koch, in Welles's concluding sign-off he credits the adaptation to the original author, St. Joseph. The intriguing story idea would be reprised in a 1961 British film, *Ferry to Hong Kong*, starring Welles and Curt Jürgens. In this instance, it is Welles who plays the straight-laced captain, with Jürgens as the inebriated mystery man whom neither Hong Kong nor Macao will accept. Nevertheless, he redeems himself with heroics during a storm and wins the heart of a young woman (Sylvia Syms).

The three weeks following *A Passenger to Bali* saw Mercury broadcast three entertaining but unexceptional literary adaptations, *The Pickwick Papers* by Charles Dickens on 20 November, *Clarence* on 27 November—their second Booth Tarkington story—and Thornton Wilder's *The Bridge of San Luis Rey* on 4 December. The latter featured some spectacular auditory conjuring for the climactic destruction of the bridge. Welles worked for hours with sound effects man Bill Brown. The collapsing bridge was done with an inner tube slapping vines and leaves against a wall, to which Welles added a sequence of one actor's scream segueing into another's. It did not come off exactly as he wanted but still sounds effective.[3] This broadcast would be significant as the last one the *Mercury Theatre* aired under its own name. At the end of the show listeners are informed that the program now had a sponsor— hereafter it would be known as *The Campbell Playhouse*—and a new time slot, Friday night at 9:00 P.M.

Campbell had first entertained thoughts of sponsorship following *Mercury's* second broadcast, *Treasure Island*. They refrained from a commitment at the time probably because the ratings potential and profile of the show did not seem high enough. Following *War of the Worlds*, and Welles's theatrical success and omnipresence in the media, they reconsidered. But before making him an offer, Campbell wisely waited several weeks following the Panic Broadcast to make sure his career would not be tainted by the controversy. Just prior to Thanksgiving a deal was struck. Negotiations gave new meaning to the term *power lunch*. Welles and Houseman were given a tour of the plant in Camden, New Jersey.[4] They strolled past racks of dead livestock and huge cauldrons of bubbling soup. (Did this prompt Welles to recall the witch's scene in *Macbeth?* Note how he would shoot it in his 1948 film.) Finally, they entered the executive dining room to consume the product they had just seen processed.

Without doubt *Campbell Playhouse* sought to access the audience who tuned in faithfully to radio's number one show, Cecil B. De Mille's *Lux Radio Theatre*, which utilized a live studio audience. Never fond of the Lux format, Welles would, nevertheless, be allowed to retain his no studio audience policy. In sponsoring *Mercury*, Campbell decided to drop Louella Parsons's *Hollywood Hotel*, which had previously occupied the Friday night time slot. The program had started in 1934 as an attempt at rapprochement between the film and radio industries.[5] Hearst columnist Parsons used her considerable influence, and powers of intimidation, to get movie stars to appear on the show gratis to promote their films. Interviews and film clips were interspersed with musical numbers. By late 1938 the show had lost its novelty, and obviously its soup-selling capacity. On 9 December it was replaced by the *Campbell Playhouse* debut broadcast of Daphne du Maurier's *Rebecca*.

The new program offered Welles more money, $1,500 a week, a production budget well in excess of the shoestring on which *Mercury* had operated, and the kind of consistent publicity that only sponsorship could buy. But artistic compromise was necessary. Commercials, sometimes involving Welles, would appear at the beginning, twice during, and once at the end of each performance. They would often adopt a storytelling format that pitched the virtues of this or that variety of soup—chicken and tomato being the most popular. Humorous at first, they become tedious in subsequent programs and cut into the amount of time that previous *Mercury* broadcasts had devoted to the radio play.

The stories too would change. Popular romances—one program a month would feature a best seller—would prevail over the classics. The 4 March 1939 issue of *Publishers Weekly* commented on the format, noting that it called for $1,000 to be paid for the broadcast rights for each book selected—which could be a novel, biography, history, or adventure story. The author would receive a silver memento for having been so adapted. The positive effect on sales was hard to determine; it was certainly not of the magnitude we find in contemporary market responses to Oprah Book Club selections, for example. Some books, such as *Rebecca*, were already doing well. Nevertheless, publishers were pleased with the idea overall and cooperated willingly.

To increase audience interest a movie or theatrical star was usually featured in each broadcast, although the nucleus of *Mercury* regulars remained on call. The guest star format was one Welles was comfortable with as an idea. However, in reality there were stars he wanted and could not get because of an agent or studio impasse, and those he did not want but had thrust upon him because of their audience appeal and availability. One star he wanted, and got, was the "first lady of the American theater," Helen Hayes. She turned out to be the most frequent visitor to the show. Her magnificent voice is like a female analog to his. The dramas in which they co-star are excursions into radio Valhalla. This new format was not dictated by Campbell per se, but by the agency that represented them, Ward Wheelock. Welles would come to chafe under their demands, which were fueled by numbers, surveys, and other forms of audience research that he found anathema. The writing would be done, as it was with the *Mercury* broadcasts, by Houseman and Koch, with the assistance of Paul Stewart and the occasional outside collaborator. Welles would in turn impart his changes to the script during the final rehearsal.

All parties were in agreement regarding the choice of *Rebecca* for the *Campbell Playhouse* debut. It was a runaway best seller in 1938. The screen rights had already been sold to David O. Selznick, who would enlist Alfred

Hitchcock to direct it. It was Hitchcock's first Hollywood assignment and earned the Oscar as best picture of 1940. In going after the radio rights, Campbell, or rather Ward Wheelock, appreciated the story's audience appeal, while Welles liked its Gothic dramaturgy. He also respected the author's pedigree, since her grandfather was British novelist George du Maurier (1834–1896) and Daphne had already written several highly touted novels. The resulting broadcast became the third and last of Welles's great radio debuts: the first being *Les Misérables* for Mutual, his initial effort with total creative control of the program; and the second was *Dracula* on *First Person Singular*, the series that first put the Mercury company on the air.

Campbell Playhouse opened with a fanfare, figuratively and literally. Blaring brass ushered in a new and more lush orchestration of the by now familiar Tchaikovsky theme. There were other changes as well. Announcer Dan Seymour was gone, off to Hollywood and obscurity as a bit player—he appears in *Casablanca*. The new voice of Edwin C. Hill, more mature and authoritative but somehow less knowing, now called Welles to the microphone with a litany of accolades.

Welles is introduced as "the great white hope of the American stage"—did they think Joe Louis was going to try his luck on Broadway?—and as someone who "writes his own radio scripts"—hardly the case—"and directs them and makes them live and breath with the worth of his genius"—the truth at last. His history of successful stage ventures is cited and said to surpass Noel Coward's "from here to Kalamazoo." Past radio successes are also mentioned, especially his capacity to tell stories in a realistic and exciting way. *War of the Worlds* is used as an example, although when Welles negotiated the contract at the Campbell factory he was forced to swear on a warehouse full of tomato vegetable that he would do nothing like it again. Building to a crescendo, Hill touts Orson's gifts, "his genius . . . ambition . . . and amazing character acting."

Nonplussed but enthusiastic, the hero of the hour steps up to the mike. He acknowledges the opportunity and promises to present good stories, whether they derive from the stage, novels, or motion pictures. Note the absence of any mention of material written explicitly for radio. It was a rarity at this time, except in formulaic series such as *The Shadow*, and the experimental dramas of Irving Reis and Norman Corwin. Even *Mercury Theatre on the Air* had eschewed attempting an original radio play. Toward the end of the Golden Age of Radio they began to appear in increasing numbers. Perhaps the most notable was Lucille Fletcher's (wife of Bernard Herrmann) *Sorry, Wrong Number* (1943), which starred Welles's former Mercury colleague and radio veteran, Agnes Moorehead. In 1948, it became a rare example of a story that originated on radio being later made into a film; in the screen version Barbara Stanwyck replaced "Aggie."

Welles goes on to say that neither he nor his sponsor think the radio audience has the mentality of an eight-year-old—perhaps this was a jab at social psychologists who had demeaned the medium—and that there would be no curtain or studio audience—in other words, this is not *Lux Theatre*. He affirms that the only illusion *Campbell Playhouse* will create is "the illusion of a story." At this point the announcer, sounding like a shill, interjects by querying, "But the star too is important Mr. Welles, is that not so?" Orson's status is implied in the question; however, lest the egoism of the moment overwhelm, the remark is used as a segue to introduce Margaret Sullavan, the first of a series of distinguished guests who would grace the program during its eighteen-month run. The novel to be adapted, *Rebecca*, is then given high praise. Welles adds that the author herself has flattered him by granting radio rights to Mercury and will be listening to the broadcast via shortwave telephone hookup. If true—rumor has it that she was down the hall in another studio—it would have been a very expensive call given long-distance rates in 1938.

The drama finally opens with Benny Herrmann's orchestra evoking a wistful romantic mood. His score throughout seems preferable to the syrupy one composed by Franz Waxman for Hitchcock's 1940 film. Margaret Sullavan's breathy but resonant voice—she has a tendency to almost sing the final vowel of each line of her dialogue—provides the first person narration. She takes us back to the beginning, to her courtship in Monte Carlo by the widowed and wealthy Maxim de Winter. Welles plays him as a gruff, confident, and lonely man, harboring just enough compassion to render his relationship with the unnamed girl plausible. The de Winter character, in all his incarnations, novel, radio, and film, comes across as a variation of Rochester in *Jane Eyre*. In fact there are several similarities in these two Gothic romances written almost a century apart, most obviously, the concluding immolation of the palatial home, Manderley in *Rebecca*, which frees the two lead characters to seek a new life untainted by the ghosts that dwelt there. In the early scenes we also encounter Mrs. Van Hopper, a talkative snob who has hired the unnamed girl as a companion. Agnes Moorehead plays the role, although one would think her talents would have been better served as the diabolical Mrs. Danvers. Nevertheless, Mildred Natwick gives an appropriately chilling performance as the treacherous housekeeper.

As the story begins to assert itself so does the new order sponsoring it. Earnest Chapple is introduced (he would become the show's regular announcer) and he pitches Campbell's chicken soup with a reasonably entertaining anecdote.

Several minutes later, as Mrs. Danvers is about to push our heroine out the window, Mr. Hill interrupts the story by pushing another Campbell saga before our ears—one wonders if the program was ever referred to as a "soup opera." This one is about the human side of business and how much the company cares. When the story resumes, the murder attempt, which was planned to look like a suicide, is interrupted by the thunderous blast of a ship's distress rocket.

The intricate plot resolves with de Winter, although guilty of the murder of his evil first wife Rebecca, not being indicted when the judge concludes her death was accidental. His new bride, knowing the circumstances that led him to it, forgives him, and when the estate, Manderley, goes up in flames, they are given a clean slate. As we ponder the ethics of the ending, Mr. Chapple returns to again remind us of the virtues of Campbell's chicken soup. Then, enter Welles with Miss Sullavan. She says that the character she played is one of her favorites in narrative fiction, and informs us that she too, likes the aforementioned soup. Welles then gets flirtsy . . . says he would like to get to know her better . . . laments that after this first meeting she will be passing out of his life . . . but quickly lets us know this interest is professional and concerns the Mercury Theatre's future. She would work with him again on the *Campbell Playhouse* but not in any of his stage productions.

Enter Miss du Maurier. Allegedly speaking from London at 3:00 A.M., she tells us how delighted she was to hear the voices of her characters. When asked by Miss Sullavan if there really is a Manderley, the author responds with protracted directions to what was probably her mansion in the West Country. When asked the name of the heroine in the story, she bids the cast adieu without answering. Within seconds a telegram from Miss du Maurier to Miss Sullavan is handed to Welles. It states that the name of the girl is . . . "Mrs. Max de Winter." One suspects that the author was in fact nearby, as some contend, and part of another Wellesian ruse. The following week's production is then announced, along with the cast of Rebecca. Finally, Orson signs off by declaring himself, "obediently yours," a closing signature that he would retain in the years to come. It suggests the jester or trickster, who, while pleading that he is only our humble servant, nevertheless beguiles and controls.

Rebecca was a well-received debut. Despite, or because of, the hype and the soup sponsorship, the public sensed that the series would present entertaining programs in the months to come, stories with perhaps more of an edge than the *Lux Theatre*. It also seemed to represent a taming of Welles. Although few denied his talent, many were annoyed by his arty pretensions. Flogging soup would be a mild comeuppance, a way of forcing him to face a mass audience in a commercial medium. Ironically, he had been an advertising pitchman early in his broadcasting career with My-T-Fine Chocolate Pudding; and he would be one at the end, when Paul Masson Wines used him in their television ads, then dropped him because his overweight image was not tracking with their yuppie market.

The success of the show attracted attention. David O. Selznick was so impressed with the results that he obtained a transcript of *Rebecca* and sent it to Hitchcock as a primer on how adaptations from literature should be done.[6] Hitchcock, who early in his Hollywood career had to work with Selznick on several films, was never enamored by the collaboration.[7] The film *Rebecca* wound up owing almost as much to Selznick's machinations as it does to Hitchcock's imagination.

Somewhat constrained by the weight of sponsorship, Welles was nonetheless exhilarated by the recognition it brought, and the showmanship it brought out in him. The week following *Rebecca* he did a very soapy *Call It a Day*, from the novel by Dorothy Gladys Smith. He then geared up for what promised to be a real tour de force, *A Christmas Carol*, with Lionel Barrymore in the role of Scrooge. Campbell had broadcast a version of the story as a Christmas special for the past four years and was now excited, as was CBS, over the prospect of this classic being given the Wellesian touch. For his part, Welles researched the story assiduously. Among his papers we find detailed notes and miscellaneous articles on the novel and subsequent theatrical stagings of it, including the first American performance, along with copies of the introductions to previous Campbell broadcasts of the story.

Some of this material was incorporated into his bravura introduction to the show, along with regrets that Lionel Barrymore, owing to illness, would not appear—he had missed the first one in 1934 for the same reasons. The role of Scrooge, however, being a quintessential character part, was an easy stretch for Welles. In both his introduction and staging, he emphasized the ghost story aspect of the drama—after all, the Panic Broadcast had made him a maestro of the otherworldly on radio. Benny Herrmann's music is suitably eerie (*Kane*-like in places) and the spirit voices that wail during the time travel sequences are chilling. It was a first-rate production, but the one a year later with Barrymore would be even better.

Hemingway's *Farewell to Arms* would close out the year. Katherine Hepburn was the guest and gave her usual solid performance, but at that point in her career was not as popular as she would be in later decades. A Wheelock agency survey would list this broadcast, and her performance, as among the least favorable in the series.

The new year opened with Elmer L. Rice's *Counselor-at-Law*, an overly talky—yes, such a thing is possible on radio when the dialogue is loose—account of a young lawyer's professional and personal angst. On 13 January, *Campbell Playhouse* recalled the original *Mercury Theatre on the Air*, albeit with commercials, when they broadcast *Mutiny on the Bounty*. In adapting the Charles Nordhoff and James Norman Hall account, Howard Koch, as he had done with *Hell on Ice* and probably in part with *A Passenger to Bali*, demonstrated a flair for scripting maritime narrative. Welles, of course, was born to play Captain Bligh; and with Joseph Cotten in the role of Fletcher Christian, the pairing was perfect. The two would later face off on celluloid to great effect in *Kane*, *Journey into Fear* (1942), and *The Third Man* (1949).

The following week Welles, as was his wont, followed tragedy with farce and broadcast Barry Benefield's *Chicken Wagon Family*. The title says it all. Although he had considerable gifts as a humorist—witness his stint on the *Tonight Show*—light comedies such as this failed to inspire his best work. The humor often seems forced. More challenging comedic portrayals, such as Falstaff, and as producer Sidney Brandt in *I Lost My Girlish Laughter* the following week, were more his métier. Koch adapted this radio play from the novel written by Jane Allen, a pseudonym for someone who was probably a Hollywood script writer or columnist. (David Thomson claims that former Selznick secretary Silvia Lardner may have had a hand in it, therefore any resemblance between Brandt and Selznick is wholly intentional.) Although *Girlish Laughter* is one of the best *Campbell Playhouse* productions, later surveys would rank it as the least successful. The reason might have been that, as the radio equivalent of screwball comedy, it was exploring a genre, which if skewed in certain directions, could backfire and turn a mass audience sour. For example, in movies the previous year, Kate Hepburn and Cary Grant had co-starred in *Bringing up Baby* and *Holiday*, deservedly ranked today as classics of the screwball genre. At the time, however, both films were box office disasters. Perhaps there were limits to what audiences would tolerate when certain social conventions and institutions were lampooned. If so, this might explain why *Girlish Laughter*, which satirized how Tinseltown created its product, was so disliked.

In the radio play, Hollywood is glimpsed through the machinations of producer Brandt, who buys the rights to a play written by John Tussler. Tussler is in fact played by the noted dramatist George S. Kaufman, whose writing far surpasses his abilities as an actor. The overall dialogue, however, is scintillating, and driven to a manic tempo by the background sound effects. The parody is merciless, and it foreshadows in spirit what Robert Altman would do in *The Player* (1992). Brandt, informed by hearsay, buys the screen rights to a play he has not read by a writer he has never heard of, and then cedes to the man's request for double the offered price. He then hires, with no screen test, a European actress based on her looks and star potential. (A veiled reference to Hedy Lamarr?) She turns out to be temperamental and incapable of following simple stage directions. The script, of course, has to undergo revision after revision, including a title change to make it into a marketable film. This dismays the original writer, who protests to no avail through a series of telegrams. They are countered with Brandt's response that "this business is full of heartaches but I've got to show profits."

Several aspects of *Girlish Laughter* are especially intriguing, given Welles's eventual move to Hollywood later that year. The play's cynical view of the studio system as artless and market driven is the way many in the industry would suspect Welles thought about them when he arrived there in the summer of 1939. Second, the movie portrayed in the radio play is screened before a test audience and then changed to make it more market friendly, a situation that would recur in 1942 with Welles's near masterpiece, *The Magnificent Ambersons* (although this might have been done simply to reduce the running time). Finally, there is an attempt by Brandt to wrest screenwriting credit from playwright Tussler, and then to restore it. A similar, although not identical incident between Welles and Herman Mankiewicz would precipitate a controversy over *Citizen Kane* that continues to the present day. The weakest part of the broadcast is its conclusion. In a gimmick probably inspired by having Daphne du Maurier on the phone at the end of *Rebecca*, Jane Allen does the same here. Speaking from an adjacent studio, she reveals that she is a Random House author using a pen name. Welles pleads with her to reveal her identity, but to no avail.

The following week was more notable for its guest star than for anything unusual about the production. Welles recruited Helen Hayes to play opposite him in Sinclair Lewis's *Arrowsmith*, reprising the role she had played in the 1931 film. It is the story of a country doctor, Martin Arrowsmith, who goes into research and makes a great discovery, only to find out that he might not have been the first. Rather than building a case for priority, he takes his research to the Caribbean to fight a growing plague. The costs are high, his devoted wife dies, but the reward is an arrested epidemic and the Nobel prize. The role of Leora Arrowsmith is primarily supporting, and although Miss Hayes's lines are few, her warm resonant voice brings extraordinary plausibility to her character. In the chitchat wrap-up following the final soup sell (tomato), she admits to having thoroughly enjoyed the experience and welcomes the opportunity to return. The truth of her statement would be borne out by subsequent visits, seven in all.

Continuing with the pattern of following one genre with another, the noble, albeit fictional biography (Welles always insisted on pronouncing it "beeography") of *Arrowsmith* was succeeded in the next broadcast on 3 February by the romantic adventure of William Archer's play, *The Green Goddess*. Madeleine Carroll, who rose to stardom in several Hitchcock pictures, most notably *The 39 Steps* (1935), is featured. The story is a variation of the romantic triangle theme, perhaps *quadrangle* would be more apropos in this case. A plane crashes in the Himalayas and the survivors are taken to the kingdom of Rukh, ruled by a Western-educated rajah (Welles). In the story, Lucilla Crespin (Miss Carroll) is married to an insensitive military officer but in love with a devoted doctor; she is also being courted by the rajah, who will not let his guests leave. A planned rebellion against the British leads to the death of Lucilla's husband, a fate in store for the rest of them if she does not consent to marry her captor. All turns out well, however, when a rescue is effected, the rebellion quashed, and the lovers united. In a humorous epilogue they meet the rajah at a party some years later. He is very cordial and informs them that he escaped the British reprisal and is now living in a villa in Monte Carlo.

Welles reveled in this kind of character part. Portraying an exotic ethnic with a British education allowed him to play some of his best dialect cards—he would reprise the role that summer in a twenty-minute condensation of the play for an RKO vaudeville tour. Miss Carroll played the heroine with zest and conviction. In the concluding banter she mentions what some listeners may have already gleaned from their newspapers. In a Scripps-Howard poll Welles was picked as the outstanding new radio star of the past year. For him to earn such an accolade there must have been some forgiveness on the part of voters regarding the Panic Broadcast. Indeed, as the event receded in time, it was perceived more as an aberration in mass society than the result of a diabolical scheme hatched by Welles.

Although the Scripps-Howard acknowledgment may have made Welles feel like part of radio's hallowed pantheon, at this point in his career there was another world he wanted to rule even more: theater. He sought the throne through the auspices of *Five Kings*. It was his most ambitious production to date; and, in a case of reach exceeding grasp, the one that would finally lead to the ungluing of Mercury as a theatrical company. True to form, Welles preceded this ambitious drama with a successful comedy, Thomas Dekker's *The Shoemaker's Holiday*, which ran from January to April. Part social satire, part ribald comedy, Shoemaker was minus Welles as actor but featured Joseph Cotten, George Coulouris, and Vincent Price.

Five Kings was conceived as a two-night extravaganza. It combined parts of Shakespeare's *Richard II*, *Henry IV*, and *Henry V* in the first evening, with almost the entirety of *Henry VI* and *Richard III* in the second. The story encompassed the rise and fall of monarchs, great battles, and Falstaff, the part Welles was born to play. When British émigré Maurice Evans, whom Welles disdained as overrated, had the audacity to play Falstaff on Broadway as well as other parts Orson thought were his property, he was livid; when great reviews showered Evans, Boy Wonder became apoplectic.[8] With *Five Kings* he would show them all who was the true master of theatrical performance and conception in America.

That he could not pull it off should not obscure the ingenuity of the project and the moments of acting brilliance he displayed. Ditto for Burgess Meredith as Prince Hal who, according to Houseman, "brought a warmth and energy that I have never seen equaled in the part—even by Laurence Olivier."[9] At the center of the production, literally, was a thirty-foot revolving stage—a "lazy Susan," Houseman called it. When actors moved from one scene to another the transitions were cinematic rather than theatrical. Unfortunately, constant problems with the electric motor made these movielike moments appear to be running at the wrong speed.

The majority of funding for the venture was fronted by the somewhat conservative (artistically) Theatre Guild, which now sought to associate itself with young and vibrant talent. They also provided a solid base of subscribers in the cities where *Five Kings* was slated to open. When it premiered in Boston on 27 February, the production was both filled with glitches and overly long, but reviewers appreciated the effort. Technical and human problems continued in Philadelphia, where the press was less kind. The Theatre Guild pulled the plug. Welles pleaded for the play's continuance and tried to find alternative funding but was unsuccessful. Anyone with knowledge regarding the production invariably knew about his history of absenteeism from rehearsals (heresy for a director), tardiness when he did appear, and binges of debauchery and womanizing. His theatrical credibility, if not his genius, was now suspect.

Throughout this ordeal the Friday night soup broadcasts went on in consistent fashion. Several merit comment for either their guest stars or subject matter. On 17 March Welles teamed up with the rising young British star of stage and film, Laurence Olivier. In *Beau Geste*, by Percival Christopher Wren, they would become two-thirds of a Foreign Legion brother act. The novel had also been made into a successful silent film in 1926 starring Ronald Colman; a sound version, with Gary Cooper, was in production when Welles did the radio play. The broadcast closely follows the story line used in both films. Noah Beery reprises the role he played in 1926, Sergeant Lejaune, with a gravely voiced intensity that makes it one of the best villain performances in radio drama. The action sequences employ large-scale sound effects yet are full of subtle touches. For example, when the division of Legionnaires stops to survey the fort before deciding whether it is safe to enter, the unsyncopated shuffling of the horses' hooves evokes an immediate mental image of the scene; and in the later battle, amid the cacophony of gunfire, we can always distinguish the shots that come from the Arabs on the hill and those fired by the men in the fort.

Surprisingly, of all the performances in *Beau Geste*, Olivier's seems weakest, although it is more than adequate. There are times when he sounds hesitant, and times when he rushes his lines, flubbing the opening of several. Lack of both rehearsal time and radio experience may have contributed to the impression that he was doing a reading in character rather than giving a performance. In later years Welles would see Olivier as a kind of rival in terms of bringing Shakespeare to the screen. Nevertheless, the two would work together again in 1960 with Orson directing Larry in a London production of Eugene Ionesco's *Rhinoceros*, a very un-Wellesian play. True to his penchant for concluding gimmickry, at the end of *Beau Geste*, Welles trots out a former Legionnaire. In a disarming commentary the man notes the various points where life in the Legion was both similar to and different from the drama we have just heard.

Lighter fare followed on 31 March: an adaptation by Howard Teichman of the Ben Hecht/Charles MacArthur play, *Twentieth Century*. It was another venture into the wacky world of screwball, notable because it might have started Welles thinking that his Hollywood time was at hand. The story concerns a successful theatrical producer, Oscar Jaffe (Welles), who makes a big star out of a young actress, Lily Garland (Elissa Landi). Despite the romance between them, she heads for Hollywood and is just as triumphant there. Without her, the producer's theatrical ventures begin to fail. Mention is made of an ambitious but disastrous staging of *Joan of Arc*, which employed a revolving stage—a not so subtle reference to the same device in *Five Kings*. Eventually, desperate impresario woos back ambitious prima donna with a fake suicide attempt and the promise (false) of the part of a lifetime. This entertaining radio production was preceded by a 1934 film of the play with John Barrymore and Carole Lombard, and later followed by a 1957 television broadcast in which Welles reprised his role of Oscar Jaffe, with Betty Grable as Lily Garland.

The idea of broadcasting a self-referential theater piece continued in a different vein on 31 March with *Show Boat*. Margaret Sullavan returned as a guest and Helen Morgan reenacted the role she played in the 1936 movie version. Even more notable was the radio acting debut of the author, Edna Ferber. As was the case with playwright George S. Kaufman's debut several weeks earlier, she would have been well advised to keep her day job. The story is pure period romance, with eccentric characters, love, heartbreak, and the metaphor of life as a stage, signified by the show within the radio play, which is being enacted aboard the *Cotton Blossom* as she plies the Mississippi.

More socially telling is the depiction of racism, especially when Julia Dozier (Miss Morgan), whose mother is black, is let go because the law forbids performers of mixed blood. Ironically, in his sign-off Welles mentions that the following Monday *Amos 'n' Andy* will be coming to CBS and that he is a great fan of the program. It was a controversial show, especially among blacks; white liberals were also sometimes divided in their opinion. Yet, many on both sides of the color line thought that by giving black humor (even when done by sympathetic whites such as Freeman Godsen and Charles Correll, who created the show) mass media exposure, the cause of race relations would be furthered. Welles must have thought along these lines or he would not have endorsed the show regardless of any network pressure to do so. Time and again he inserted antiracist sentiments in his work, and in 1941 he directed a stage version of Richard Wright's *Native Son*.

By this time *Five Kings* was in its death throes. Nothing remained to do with it in the coming weeks but to dismantle the sets and put everything into storage, an expensive proposition. However, the idea behind the play would arise again and be the subject of one of the most masterful and unheralded of Welles's films, *Chimes at Midnight* (1966). As went *Five Kings*, so would go opportunities to do Broadway on his own terms. Almost, it seems, out of frustration over this closure, he took theatrical performance to radio with a vengeance on 21 April with a version of Noel Coward's *Private Lives*. Scintillating in both production and performance, it even surpasses the fine 1931 film version.

Such cross-media comparisons between radio and film, which I have been inflicting on the reader at regular intervals, are awkward at best. Nevertheless, they are useful if we are to understand this pre-television period. It was a time when the evocative power of radio put the auditory in popular culture more on a par with the visual than is the case in our current image-laden era.

In *Private Lives*, Welles plays Elyot Chase opposite Gertrude Lawrence, who recreates her much-heralded stage role as Elyot's ex-wife, Amanda, now married to Victor Prynne (Robert Spreaight). Elyot is currently wedded to Sybil and honeymooning at the same hotel where he once honeymooned with Amanda. When Amanda and Victor, also on their honeymoon, wind up in adjacent suites, mayhem is unleashed. Elyot and Amanda rekindle their romance, only to revive the kind of squabbling that led to their breakup in the first place. When their spouses discover the situation and add their opinions, the dialogue swirls. Occasionally caught in the crossfire is the hapless hotel clerk played by Edgar Barrier, who revives the French accent he employed as Passepartout in *Around the World in 80 Days* the previous October. In the postperformance conversation, Miss Lawrence reminisces about a school play she was in with Noel Coward.

Private Lives was hardly the kind of innovative literary adaptation that had become Welles's radio trademark. Several weeks earlier, on 7 April, more true to form, he had rebroadcast a shortened version of his successful 1937 rendering of *Les Misérables*. Walter Huston played Jean Valjean this time, with Welles as Inspector Javert. *Private Lives*, in any case, as theater transposed almost verbatim to radio, was the strongest theatrical-type broadcast *Campbell Playhouse* had done to date. Perhaps surprisingly, the weakest would air three weeks later on 12 May: Thornton Wilder's *Our Town*. The play, which had won a Pulitzer Prize the previous year, was being performed all over the country, although the movie version was still a year away. Wilder had also been a key figure in Welles's life, having pushed Welles from Chicago to New York with a list of contacts. Nevertheless, the production lacks oomph. Orson, in the key role of the stage manager/narrator, is unusually bland and overly talkative. Perhaps this character, who can be very effective in a theatrical version of the play, simply does not transfer well to radio.

It is also possible that Welles's attention was elsewhere. At about this time a correspondence began with RKO's new president, George Schaefer, regarding the possibility of Welles joining the studio; negotiations would continue face to face that summer. In any case, *Campbell Playhouse* had to wrap up its season. The final three offerings constituted a Wellesian variety pack. On 19 May he did Porter Emerson Brown's *The Bad Man* with Ida Lupino, a comedy in which Welles plays a Mexican bandito smitten with a honeymooning Miss Lupino.

The following week took a turn for the pedagogical with *The Things We Have: An American Cavalcade* (not to be confused in name with the program *American Cavalcade*). This drama is notable in that it is an original Welles conception, rather than an adaptation, and one for which he did most of the writing. It opens with an immigrant boy coming to America and asking about the new land. From various people we then get a series of flashback history lessons. Strong emphasis is placed on what freedom has meant, from the Boston Tea Party to the 1930s. Most listeners would take little offense with the narrative, but conservatives must have cringed during the segment where he goes on about how we stole the land from the Indians and violated our own principles with slavery—with the attendant implication that blacks are still not free. Welles's knowledge of John Brown, which he had earlier incorporated into his play, *Marching Song*, informs this part of the program. The Civil War sequence that follows in turn draws from the Mercury broadcast of *Abraham Lincoln* the previous August.

The Things We Have is ultimately an entertaining history lesson with little performative drama. In contrast, the subsequent and final broadcast of the season, Laurence Houseman's *Victoria Regina*, gives us a story in which any history lesson takes a back seat to a brilliantly performed character study. Welles, affecting a light German accent, plays Albert, and Helen Hayes's lyrical voice makes us feel Victoria's presence. With Albert's death, her emotional tone changes markedly, and from that point on we can hear Miss Hayes age Queen Victoria through incremental modulations in her voice. This is arguably the best of the many pairings of these two exceptional actors. Miss Hayes most certainly brought to her performance the experience of having successfully performed the role on stage.

Campbell Playhouse then went on what we would now call summer hiatus, although Welles did not. He performed his twenty-minute *Green Goddess* sketch on the RKO vaudeville circuit. By 1939, this form of popular entertainment was anachronistic. Nevertheless, he admired it for the entertainment diversity and era it represented. The tour played to sparse audiences, and by his own account they diminished even further during his performances. Perhaps Welles's impressions of the rajah, as he would be played by John Barrymore or Charles Laughton, were lost on audiences who were not film literate or knowledgeable regarding theater. Still, he enjoyed the experience and used it to explore the character, never doing His Highness the same way twice. Unfortunately the show barely paid the rent and made no dent in the mounting debt of *Five Kings*. The bills and repeat notices from one costume company alone comprise a large portion of Mercury's correspondence file for 1939.

Hollywood loomed as a way both into a new medium and out of the financial consequences of his former theatrical one. Welles told biographer Barbara Leaming that he only intended to go there temporarily and then to come back to the New York stage.[10] Perhaps. This might have been the scenario following a plum acting assignment. But he seemed to want more, especially a chance to direct. If so, he must have known that learning the ropes before he even started to work on a picture would have taken time.

Several studios had been courting him, mostly for quirky character parts such as Victor Hugo's Hunchback or Robert Louis Stevenson's doctor with the split persona. At first George Schaefer at RKO also wanted Welles only as an actor but in the end wanted him so badly that he was willing to throw into the deal directing, writing, and producing. On 20 July Welles arrived in

Hollywood to talk turkey. He claims he was very cavalier with Schaefer and hardly expected the studio head to meet his terms. Much to his surprise, most of the concessions were offered up willingly. On 21 August a sixty-three-page contract was signed. It was a two-picture deal giving him almost total creative control. The primary strings attached were script approval and editing, which were to remain the purview of the studio.

Much has been written regarding this contract; how Hollywood hated him for it, and how he lashed back by making a great movie, which only made things worse. What Tinseltown gained from Welles's charismatic presence, radio lost, but not completely. He still had his *Campbell Playhouse* contract to fulfill, since he had started negotiating with RKO in the midst of it. By July, Ward Wheelock, and anyone else reading newspaper entertainment sections, assumed he had signed a movie contract, although the actual signing was still a month away. In any case, Wheelock was not a happy agency head. On 28 July he sent a stern memo to Welles reminding him of his obligations to Campbell—four single-spaced slaps on the wrist.[11]

The communiqué mentions that Welles's earlier request for two or three shows to originate on the West Coast was granted grudgingly, but to move the entire production there (as Orson must have suggested earlier) was out of the question. The reason for this had been clear from the outset. *Campbell's* big rival was *Lux*, which originated in Hollywood. Broadway sophistication, not Tinseltown glitz, was the soup theater's drawing card, and they had no intention of changing it to suit the movie aspirations of their star. The letter does indicate that Welles had earlier informed Wheelock that he wanted to make a picture. Wheelock's consternation, however, is over the possibility of Welles signing a major movie contract that would keep him in Hollywood for the entire broadcast season. Wheelock, fearing that this would indeed be the case, asks him how the radio programs will get done.

The answer turned out to be through the diligence of John Houseman and Paul Stewart, and the expediency of TWA. The two Mercury stalwarts would keep agency hounds at bay, get scripts written, and conduct preliminary rehearsals. Then, on a redoubtable DC-3, Welles would come to New York on the overnight Thursday flight and go straight to the studio to listen to a recording of the rehearsal. A daylong run-through would fine-tune the performance, and at the new 8:00 P.M. Friday time slot, the show would air; with a repeat performance two hours later for Pacific to Central time zone listeners. Between these two broadcasts, and on the way to Newark airport the following day, Welles and Houseman would discuss the next week's program. That he never missed a show, or was even late under this regime, is amazing. If Wheelock was not pleased with it, TWA would be. They gave him a small

Arriving at the airport after another transcontinental flight. Courtesy of Lilly Library, Indiana University.

brass plaque that still resides among his papers in Indiana University's Lilly Library. It is inscribed, "For traveling more miles in 1939 than anyone else."[12] (Unfortunately, at that time in the history of air travel, such patronage did not lead to frequent flyer points.)

Wheelock knew that with Hollywood now on Welles's plate, the radio shows would have to be carefully monitored if they were going to be successful. He appointed Diana Bourbon as executive liaison between the sponsor, network, and all things Wellesian. She was a formidable watchdog with razor-sharp business savvy and a good sense of what the entertainment industry is all about. The correspondence between her and Welles is fascinating. He constantly tries to sweet-talk her by opening with "Dearest Diana," and closing with "Much Love." Aware of his penchant for sarcasm, she invariably stands her ground, praising his artistic ability while questioning his judgment. Occasionally, she would deliver a biting insult. When Welles and

Houseman passed on the option of doing *Goodbye Mr. Chips*, which quickly became a hit film, she vented her frustration by referring to them as "you two lice."[13] It is doubtful that any male could have reined him in so formidably. Although Welles may have been more tyrannical toward women than men, when they resisted his bullying he could perhaps be even more deferential.

Repeatedly, Welles had to be reminded he was doing a commercial broadcast, and that what he thought was best might not be in the best interests of the ratings and sponsor. Wheelock conducted a series of surveys of the first season as a basis for planning the second. Miss Bourbon sent copies to Orson along with some subtle and some pointed comments.[14]

The top five programs were *Rebecca*, *Victoria Regina*, *Mutiny on the Bounty*, *Arrowsmith*, and *A Christmas Carol*. The list is understandable. These were straightforward and accessible stories featuring solid performances by notable guest stars. The worst five were *I Lost My Girlish Laughter*, *Call It a Day*, *Burlesque*, *Chicken Wagon Family*, and *Show Boat*. These were either lame comedies or limp soapers. The exception is *Girlish Laughter*, a biting satire of Hollywood behind the scenes, which was probably too cynical for those surveyed—most likely employees of Ward Wheelock. The best-liked guest stars were Helen Hayes, Margaret Sullavan, and Walter Huston, with the least liked being Beatrice Lillie, Edna Ferber, and Mary Astor.

Welles himself was rated favorably by two-thirds of the respondents and negatively by the remainder. The dissenters accused him of talking too much and too fast, overacting, and being too serious. The music and sound effects garnered mostly positive responses. One of the surveys asks for suggestions on how to improve the series. The respondents called for the deletion of Welles's introductions and narration, a reduction in the number of interviews, fewer highbrow stories, and more comedies and musicals. Several commentators said the program should be more like *Lux*. Fortunately for Welles this was a direction in which Wheelock did not want to go. *Campbell*, for its part, was not spared. The survey suggested the soup pitches be shorter and get to the point more quickly.

This information, at least the part about stories and stars, provided Wheelock with guidelines for the coming season. They secured literary properties that they thought would make good broadcasts. Sometimes Welles would want to do a story that they said was "unavailable." In other words, if the rights cost more than $1,000, a special permission from the agency was needed, and if they were less than enthusiastic about the story, Welles's choice would be denied. Being in Hollywood most of the time did not put him in a good position to argue. He did retain veto power of a sort when it came to the guest stars, and when he and Wheelock were both enthusiastic about an actor, the purse strings would loosen considerably. Helen Hayes was signed for two programs in the first half of the season (she would eventually make four appearances) and two in the second half—at $5,000 per program.

Miss Hayes not only had great audience appeal, she was able to draw out the best from Welles's abilities as a radio actor. This led to the wise decision to cast her in *Peter Ibbetson*, the season opener on 10 September 1939. Based on the George du Maurier novel and subsequent John Nathaniel Raphael play, it is a powerful romantic melodrama; stranger and more haunting, according to Welles in his introduction, than *Rebecca*, which was penned by George's granddaughter, Daphne. Welles then reintroduces the Mercury regulars and Bernard Herrmann, promising listeners a first-rate season. The enthusiasm in his voice clearly belies the struggle to maintain artistic control. By this time he had more than one foot in Hollywood, and the Wheelock agency was regularly besieging him with suggestions about story selection and guest stars.

Peter Ibbetson had earlier (1935) been made into a film with Gary Cooper and Ann Harding. However, this fantasy romance seems more suited to the suspension of disbelief radio allowed. The story concerns an orphaned French boy, Peter, whose loneliness is assuaged by the companionship of a young girl, Mary. They are eventually separated, with Peter going to London to be raised by his uncle. Twelve years later, by chance, they meet in Paris and gradually discover that they knew one another in childhood. In the intervening years both shared the same dream of their youthful sojourns in her garden. But a conventional romance is not to be. She is now the Duchess of Towers and trapped in an unhappy marriage.

Peter returns to London, only to find out the uncle who had raised him is really his father and an unscrupulous thief. A fight ensues and Peter kills him in self-defense. No matter, he is sentenced to death. The duchess intervenes and persuades the lord secretary to commute the sentence to life. She then sends Peter a note telling him that his life has just begun and that when he goes to sleep he will know why. For the next twenty-five years they dream of each other in the garden of their youth, enraptured by bliss and innocence. These sequences are exquisitely done. The voices, although faint and ethereal, are clearly audible, with Herrmann's subtle chords adding nuance to the otherworldly mood. When Mary becomes terminally ill she sends an old woman (Agnes Moorehead) to deliver a written message to Peter: "Soon again. The Fairy Princess." When Mary dies, she visits his dream world one last time to tell him that he will soon join her. And so it comes to pass. The old woman narrates this part of the story. She tells how she nurtured Peter until his death, and when it came and he was finally united forever with his beloved, there was splendor in his dead face.

In his sign-off, Welles, aware that the program was an emotional tour de force, champions the cause of radio drama. It is not, he insists, something rolled up in celluloid and stored in cans (yet, how he now yearned to roll that celluloid!) but a kind of theater that employs a nationwide auditorium featuring a series of first nights. He is joined by Miss Hayes, who he proudly declares has "adopted us," adding that the *Campbell Playhouse* is the only radio program she will do this season. The inimitable Helen then expresses enthusiasm over her involvement with "radio at its best." However, in her autobiography (which is not lengthy) she makes no mention of her radio work with Welles or her later forays with the medium—she had a short-run anthology series, *The Helen Hayes Theatre*.

The following week Eugene O'Neill's *Ah, Wilderness!* would give Welles a chance to again present a turn-of-the-century coming-of-age story. This was Booth Tarkington turf, and it is possible that *Ah, Wilderness!* was done as a kind of preparatory piece for the 29 October broadcast of *The Magnificent Ambersons*, a work close to Orson's heart. On 24 September, Miss Hayes returned to play Maggie Wylie in J. M. Barrie's *What Every Woman Knows*, reprising a role she played on stage and in the 1934 film. Contemporary audiences might perceive her "Maggie"—the forceful and savvy politician's wife—as Hillary Clintonesque.

The 1 October broadcast of *The Count of Monte Cristo* gives us a rare chance to compare a *Campbell Playhouse* production with one performed earlier by the *Mercury Theatre on the Air*. Although the *Campbell* presentation is tighter, the time utilized during four commercials cuts seriously into the story, especially during the opening segments. One notable sound effect is also missing. In the *Mercury* version, when Dantes is about to be thrown into the sea, the sound of the waves crashing at the base of the prison was achieved by flushing toilets. In the *Campbell* broadcast a wind machine is used. Although the acting in the two versions is on a par, the spontaneity suggested in the *Mercury* broadcast adds realism and makes it preferable to the more finely honed but truncated later version.

Welles must have sensed that any *Campbell* repeat of a *Mercury* broadcast, although long on funding, would be short on the latitude to innovate it would allow him. He did, however, feel that anything done on radio before by someone else could be done better by him, despite the constraints of sponsorship. And so, on 8 October, he mounted an ambitious production of *Algiers*. Fresh in people's minds was the successful 1938 film with Charles Boyer as Pépé le Moko and Hedy Lamarr as Gabrielle; and some may have recalled the *Woodbury Playhouse* radio version broadcast the same year, in which Boyer again appeared. Welles nevertheless felt that his ability to create an effective radio drama soundscape would endow a *Campbell* production with a Casbah to remember. It did, but not in the way he had hoped.

The film had been Miss Lamarr's Hollywood debut. It did not stretch her reputedly limited acting talent, but it did showcase her sensuous European beauty. Welles wanted her for the radio play, and perhaps more. It was not to be. Despite Hedy's interest, MGM nixed the request.[15] They had serious doubts about her acting competence in any situation where she could not be seen; in fact they banned her from radio entirely on the grounds that it was a competing medium. Several years later, during the war, she would get her chance. With star power giving her more say in her assignments, and the studios less possessive over the public appearance of their actors, she played opposite Alan Ladd in *Casablanca* on *Lux Radio Theatre*. For the record, it is a very credible performance. Getting the rights to *Algiers* from Walter Wanger Productions was somewhat easier. A deal had been worked out that August entailing payment of $1,000 and a citation of Wanger Productions, along with the author of the original novel, Detective Ashelbé (Henri La Barthe). In his introduction, Welles mentions that he once lived in the "colorful, sordid, and dangerous Casbah," stretching the truth of what was probably a brief visit with his father. He then notes that his guest star will be Paulette Goddard, who at that time was married to Charlie Chaplin.

The story unfolds as does the movie. Pépé rules the underworld of the Casbah as Pluto does Hades. Bewitched by the ravishing Gabrielle, he loses his perspective, forays into the world of morality and justice, and is killed by police. Through most of the drama the sounds of the Casbah are relentless—music, merchants, and excited conversations create an aural portrait of a place at the crossroads of sinister and fascinating. Unfortunately the mood unravels every time Miss Goddard speaks. She imparts none of the mystery and seductiveness essential to the role, and delivers her lines with an overly rapid and pinched diction. Perhaps Welles sensed he had miscast her. Is that subtle sarcasm in his voice when, in the closing commentary, he notes that "She is exactly why television is inevitable?" His friendship with Chaplin might have been the reason she was invited to appear. Just prior to signing off he plugs the new and as yet unnamed film Charlie was making, which would go on to become *The Great Dictator* (1940).

Following the broadcast, the Wheelock agency, especially its iron lady, Diana Bourbon, were not happy Campbellers. *Algiers* was deemed the worst program to date. Miss Bourbon lashed out, not only at Welles, but also at announcer Ernest Chapple. In a letter to him, a copy of which was forwarded to Welles, she outlined her grievances: the show had been introduced as an "Orson Welles" rather than a *Campbell Playhouse* production; the sound effects were inauthentic and overdone; and the concluding mention of the Chaplin film was inappropriate free publicity. Surprisingly, she makes no mention, nor does Orson in his response, to Miss Goddard's lackluster performance. The letter also patronizes Chapple, accusing him of having been charmed by Orson's "siren song" and warning him to be more vigilant regarding the program's "dangerous" star.[16]

Welles retaliated with an eight-page, single-spaced letter dated 12 October, which begins with "Dearest Diana" and concludes with "My eternal love to you."[17] He denies trying to pull a fast one by having the broadcast referred to as an "Orson Welles Production," but claims he merely wanted to avoid repetition of the usual, "Starring Orson Welles." As to plugging Chaplin in the sign-off, he argues that there was not much that could be said about Miss Goddard per se, and since the Chaplin film was newsworthy, a mention of it was his prerogative as host of the show. He also felt that Chapple was unfairly maligned, and that Wheelock was imposing on the announcer an inappropriate watchdog role, especially since *Algiers* was the first of several shows to originate from Hollywood rather than New York.

He was particularly irked by the criticism of the sound effects, mentioning that the program had originated from a new studio using an unfamiliar orchestra and sound engineer. He also attempted what may have been a bluff. Miss Bourbon is informed that the program was broadcast twice, first to East Coast audiences—the allegedly muddled version—and later for West Coast listeners. This second version, which she did not hear, was according to him a better production and five minutes longer. He need not have been so defensive. The sound effects in the original seem convincing and on a par with, or superior to, what had been attempted in earlier *Campbell* programs. In the remainder of the letter, he defends the overall production, especially the performance of Ray Collins as Slimane, which Miss Bourbon questioned, and insists he has not deviated in any way from the terms of his agreement with Campbell.

The following week marked a return to New York and a less ambitious production, John Galsworthy's *Escape*. The story is part screwball comedy, part thriller. Welles plays Matt Denant, who accidentally kills a policeman while coming to the assistance of a lady of questionable virtue (Wendy Barrie). Sentenced to only five years—her surprise testimony saves him from possible execution—he nonetheless escapes and becomes known as the "Playboy Killer." He goes through a series of zany encounters with various people before a sympathetic priest inspires him to surrender.

A darker story involving crime became the subject of the next program, Frederick Molnár's *Liliom*. Welles plays Liliom, a charming huckster in Miss Muscat's (Agnes Moorehead) carnival. He leaves his job to marry a sweet young girl, Julie (Helen Hayes), whom he abuses mercilessly. Julie also works to support his gambling habit. When her pregnancy threatens to thwart this arrangement, he is furious and conspires with a local thug (Frank Readick) to rob the railway paymaster (Joseph Cotten). The plan is foiled and Liliom fatally shot. The final scene takes place twelve years later and includes some positive reminiscences about Liliom for the benefit of his daughter (who is told he died in South America before she was born), including one from an itinerant beggar (Welles). How audiences might have reacted to *Liliom* is uncertain. Although well done, it is the most downbeat and cruel of all the *Campbell* productions.

If there was one writer, apart from Shakespeare, who held a special place in Welles's literary imagination, it was fellow midwesterner Booth Tarkington (1869–1946). Whether or not his father actually knew Tarkington, as Orson sometimes claimed, the Welles family knew of the people and places he wrote about. On 29 October, Tarkington's *Magnificent Ambersons* (first published in 1918 and awarded a Pulitzer prize) became a *Campbell Playhouse* production. Welles had done Tarkington before, with the *Mercury Theatre on the Air*: *Seventeen* on 16 October 1938, and a month later, on 27 November, *Clarence*. Why he did not do *Ambersons* then (it is, arguably, Tarkington's most completely realized novel) is puzzling and must remain a matter for speculation. Perhaps the lighter material of the two other novels was needed to offset darker productions such as *Hell on Ice* and *War of the Worlds*; or possibly because, unlike *Seventeen* and *Clarence*, *Ambersons* is as much about context as it is about character and might have posed a challenge for which he was not yet ready—staging *Danton's Death* consumed most of his time that fall, therefore most of the *Mercury* broadcasts had been written by Koch and Houseman. To do *Ambersons* justice Welles felt he had to script it himself. The week leading up to the program, Koch, Houseman, and Paul Stewart were told to step back while Welles took time away from learning how movies were made at RKO to write for a medium with which he was far more familiar.

Tarkington was a prolific writer and a superb genre stylist. Critically acclaimed—*Alice Adams* earned him a second Pulitzer—he achieved a popularity in the 1920s that far exceeded that of any other American novelist.[18] He often wrote of the passing of a more genteel and gentle America, nowhere better than in *Ambersons*, where he chronicled the consequences of encroaching industrialization on an idyllic midwestern town and one of its leading families. Several Welles commentators have argued that his fascination with Tarkington suggests a kind of nostalgic longing for the time and place in which his parents grew up. True enough. But there is more to the appeal. Tarkington was an exceptional writer. His characters are multidimensional and he had a keen ethnographic eye for the nuances of daily life. In the 1942 film version of *Ambersons*, although the fascinating opening sequence chronicling the town and its customs employs remarkable images conjured by Welles, the words come straight from the novel; in the radio version, the connection is even more direct.

By the 1930s, however, Tarkington's star was waning. His America seemed more forgettable than nostalgic. A new breed of socially astute novelists had eclipsed him in popularity, among them Theodore Dreiser, Sinclair Lewis, and Sherwood Anderson. This is a major reason why *Ambersons*, the film, failed to interest audiences—not, as Welles would have us believe, because of the studio's postproduction slash and reedit. RKO may have mutilated a film that could have been a masterpiece, but probably nothing anyone could have done with the original story would have made it appealing to wartime audiences. Tarkington's diminished popularity posed less of a problem for the radio play. The well-crafted production and finely drawn characters that Welles provided easily overrode the story's setting in an era to which few people could relate. The script, performance, and significance to Welles's subsequent artistic development also far surpassed what he achieved with his two earlier Booth Tarkington radio adaptations, hence it merits fuller commentary.

The family saga in *Ambersons* begins with a glimpse of how an imaginative inventor, Eugene Morgan (Walter Huston), unsuccessfully courts the lovely Isabel Amberson (Huston's wife, Nan Sunderland). She eventually marries sedate Wilbur Minafer and has a son, George (Welles), who is thoroughly spoiled and becomes the town terror. A number of its citizens predict or hope that one day he will get his "comeuppance," a fate many had wished on Welles, especially after his arrival in Hollywood.

With George grown to manhood, a soirée is held at the Amberson house—Isabel and Wilbur live in her father's home with her brother Fred (Ray Collins). Eugene, after being away for many years, reappears with his daughter Lucy (Marion Barnes). George is smitten and courts Lucy relentlessly. Eventually Wilbur Minafer dies, leaving Isabel free to be courted by Eugene, whom she has always loved. George violently objects and conspires to keep the two apart. Isabel, always the doting mother, has neither the will nor the strength to override the wishes of her son. She dies of an illness without ever seeing Eugene again, and in response Lucy rebuffs George's marriage proposals. His comeuppance soon becomes "three times filled and running over." There is no inheritance and the house is lost to cover family debts. George is forced to do manual labor for the first time in his life. He feels remorse and prays to his mother for forgiveness, but the gods show no mercy. Both his legs are broken when he is struck down by an automobile, a technology he had disdained in front of Lucy and her father, knowing full well that Eugene was involved in the industry. At the nadir of his life George is visited in the hospital by Lucy, who has persuaded her reluctant father to come along. George apologizes to Eugene for the grief he has caused. Eugene is not impressed, until he sees in George part of the woman he had always loved and cedes to what would have been her wish: George is forgiven and the path back to a possible marriage to Lucy reopened.

Comparisons between this radio version and the RKO film are inevitable. The latter, although less consistent, especially in the second half because of studio machinations, has some notable moments, especially the soirée. The camera movement, music, and overlapping dialogue help create one of the great sequences in cinema history. It is also the only Welles feature film in which he did not act—Tim Holt played George.

Several aspects of the film were influenced by the radio play. Welles had a penchant for conceptualizing a film scene from the audio to the visual and, not, as most directors do, vice versa. In the case of Ambersons, he repeatedly used the disks from the radio version as a basis for parts of the film. And again, there was Bernard Herrmann, whose effective multidimensional score for the radio play was later incorporated into the movie; however, as a result of some studio tampering with the music he requested that his name be deleted from the credits.

The film also involved at least two important changes to the story from the radio version, only one of which was Welles's doing. When Orson was out of the country RKO reshot a more saccharine ending. The second change in the film was Welles's inclusion of George's aunt, Fanny Amberson, a spinster whose unrequited love for Eugene Morgan had weighed down her life. Agnes Moorehead plays Fanny with such emotional power that her scenes are almost painful to watch. Not utilizing such a major character in the novel for the radio production is an omission that has puzzled later Welles commentators. It was, however, a wise decision. Perhaps he could have worked her into a one-hour *Mercury Theatre* production, but *Campbell Playhouse*, truncated by soup sell and chitchat to about forty-five minutes of performance time, necessitated limiting the number of characters for whom dramaturgical justice could be done. Partly as a result, *Ambersons* is one of the most balanced and artistically successful presentations in the *Campbell* series.

A week later familial trauma was supplanted by one involving nature. In *The Hurricane*, based on the Charles Nordhoff and James Norman Hall novel, Welles played the insensitive governor of a tropical island and Mary Astor his compassionate wife. When a native named Tarangi (Edgar Barrier?) hits a white man in self-defense he is sentenced by the governor to six months in prison. When he escapes to visit his pregnant wife, he is resentenced to sixteen years, only to escape again. Several years later Tarangi paddles back to the island to warn of the coming of a great hurricane. When it hits (the sound effects and Bernard Herrmann's music are impressive but John Ford's 1937 film version is an "effects" classic), Tarangi not only rescues many fellow tribesmen, he also saves the governor and his wife. In the aftermath the governor listens to his heart and his wife's sentiments, rather than his legal edicts, and pretends not to see Tarangi escape. This action-filled melodrama plays well, and it also serves as an effective forum for Welles's antiracist views.

On 12 November, Agatha Christie's *The Murder of Roger Ackroyd* was adapted for Welles by Herman Mankiewicz. Mank was assigned to do several more radio plays for him, but more significantly he would become Welles's screenwriting partner for *Citizen Kane*. This broadcast also marked the show's permanent relocation to the West Coast. If the presentation was less than successful—a vital clue is omitted leaving the listener somewhat confused—the series would rebound a week later with Robert Hichen's *In the Garden of Allah*. Here Madeleine Carroll helps a wayward monk (Welles) rediscover his faith, and does a better job of it than Marlene Dietrich did for Charles Boyer in the 1936 film.

The next four programs also adapted stories that had earlier been made into motion pictures. In Sinclair Lewis's *Dodsworth*, on 20 November, Welles fails to match the brilliance Walter Huston brought to the lead in the 1936 screen version, but he did have Huston's wife Nan Sunderland as a co-star. James Hilton's *Lost Horizon* fared better. Orson is superb in the dual roles of Father Perreault and the High Lama. The sound effects and music doubtlessly created a vivid Shangri-La in the mind's ear of listeners. The following week, when Helen Hayes returned to do Hugh Walpole's *Vanessa*, she reprised the role she had played in the less than successful 1935 film. And on 17 December, Marie Wilson appeared in Gladys Lehman's blend of comedy and mystery, *There's Always a Woman*, which had been made into an enjoyable film the previous year.

Sadly, *There's Always a Woman* would be the last *Campbell* production that Houseman would have a hand in scripting. In a meeting that week with Welles in Chasen's restaurant in Los Angeles, the discomfort Welles felt over his dependency on Houseman over the previous two years exploded. The reason was ostensibly financial. Orson's failure to finalize a script for RKO had led to a freeze of the salaries of the actors on call. He thought Mercury could pick up the tab, but Houseman informed him that the company's funds had been largely spent—by Orson. Houseman was blamed for the situation. In this confrontation, as opposed to those in the past, he did not retreat before Welles's aggression: "I had wanted my Gotterdämmerung and now I had it."[19]

He challenged Welles's assertions, accused him of lying, and got up to leave. What happened next has led the incident to become known as "the night of the flaming sternos." As Houseman gathered his papers, Welles threw a flaming dish heater at him, and another, and another, briefly setting fire to the curtains. Houseman later sent him a respectful letter of resignation. Orson beseeched him to return, but John was firm. Their radio and theatrical collaborations were ostensibly over. Nevertheless, Houseman did make one concession to Welles for which the world owes him a great debt. He agreed to oversee screenwriter Herman Mankiewicz's germ of an idea for a movie, to be called *American*. It seemed to be Welles's last hope for an RKO project. To get the boozing and erratic Mank to deliver, Jack took him to a retreat near Victorville in the San Bernardino Mountains. Mank wrote, and the pages were delivered to Orson for revision and further input. Houseman also edited the screenplay and did some of the writing. In the midst of the project a name change seemed desirable, the new title being suggested by RKO production head, George Schaefer. Thus did *American* become *Citizen Kane*.

Campbell Playhouse would miss Houseman's input. With continued pressure from Ward Wheelock regarding how things should be done, Welles would have to scramble more than ever to have his conceptions even partially realized. The new year would bring increased frustration, but the old year ended on a high note: a stellar production of *A Christmas Carol* featuring Lionel Barrymore. He had been ill for his slated appearance the previous year. This time around he was in rare form. The date of the Friday night broadcast that year could not have been more apropos, 24 December.

Barrymore's Scrooge manifests more crotchety meanness than Welles would have probably dared give the role. This makes the miser's uplifting redemption even more powerful. Here Barrymore does a remarkable turnaround, especially with the intonation of his voice. The ghostly special effects equal or surpass the previous year's performance, while Bernard Herrmann uses more diverse motifs in his music. This time around Welles only has a bit part, as one of the ghosts, but he does provide effective narration. In the postperformance banter, Barrymore sounds slightly . . . inebriated (?), but not at all during the performance, which would have been consistent with his legend. In the exchange, Welles is exceedingly respectful, almost worshipful. Both wish us holiday greetings as a musical medley of Christmas tunes provides the finale.

One more broadcast remained, 31 December, to officially close the first part of the season. Edna Ferber's light comedy *Come and Get It* is given undistinguished treatment, probably owing to the holiday preoccupations of all concerned.

As per the *Campbell* formula, melodrama again followed farce with William Makepeace Thackeray's *Vanity Fair* launching the New Year season. It was, according to Welles in his introduction, Helen Hayes's choice. If so, it seems uninspired. The story, filmed in 1923 and 1932, and then as *Becky Sharp* in 1935 (the first full-technicolor feature) does not translate well to radio. Miss Hayes plays Becky Sharp and Welles the Marquis of Steyne. The acting is mannered and their usual chemistry absent. The following week, again relying on the maxim that if it works as a movie, why not as a radio play, Sydney Buchman's screenplay (originally a Mary McCarthy story) from the 1936 production of *Theodora Goes Wild* is given *Campbell* treatment. Loretta Young plays Theodora Lynn with Welles as Michael Grant in this comedy about an attractive young novelist from a small town who finds challenge and romance in the New York publishing world.

On 21 January the show broadcast A. J. Cronin's *The Citadel* (which two years earlier had yielded a superb film directed by King Vidor, one of Welles's favorite directors). It tells the story of a devoted but headstrong doctor (Welles) who is tempered by an astute wife (Geraldine Fitzgerald). This is territory the program had visited a year earlier with *Arrowsmith*—in both instances solid, safe productions. Safe can also be used to describe the decision to broadcast an interpretation of *It Happened One Night*, the 1934 film classic that starred Claudette Colbert and Clark Gable. The radio version featured William Powell and Miriam Hopkins in the lead, with Welles playing her father. One suspects the choice of this material, based on a Samuel Hopkins Adams story, came from Ward Wheelock. The subject of the following week's broadcast clearly did not. Helen Hayes returned to play Donna Broome in Clemence Danes's *Broome Stages*, another vehicle of her choosing. By now she was a regular in the commercials as well. When Ernest Chapple asks her to spell tomato soup, it of course comes out

C-A-M-P-B-E-L-L-S.

Broome Stages is about a famous theater family in nineteenth-century England. Welles plays both the patriarch, Harry, and toward the end of the production, Edmund, the son of Donna. The story begins with the family in crisis. A consortium of investors wants to buy the Broome Theatre so they can tear it down and erect an office building. Edmund feels that Donna's presence as an actress can revive the theater and ensure its continued success. She does not feel the call, but acquiesces anyhow. A series of lackluster performances result. Donna eventually becomes involved with a married cousin, Stephen (Eustace Wyatt). When the affair ends she goes to America, marries, and has Edmund. Ten years later, with the death of her father, she returns with her son to co-run the theater with Stephen. A decade passes, after which it is revealed that Edmund is his son. The two men accept the situation amicably and take over the company while Donna retires to the country.

This is unusual melodrama and a curious look at the English theatrical world of the previous century. The dramatic excerpts that begin and end the story, much to Welles's liking no doubt, come from Shakespeare's ever prophetic and symbolic *Macbeth*. Miss Hayes gives an unusual performance as Donna. She plays an actress whose abilities must range from slightly less than adequate, to competent—in the words of an audience member in the story, her performances are "like a machine, bloodless." This remarkable portrayal turned out to be the capstone to Miss Hayes's numerous appearances on the program.

In his introduction to the next broadcast, Welles makes no bones about the fact that he is reprising what he feels is an excellent movie, *Mr. Deeds Goes to Town* (1936). The movie was directed by Frank Capra and features Gary Cooper. It is, to use a term a number of film critics have employed, pure Capracorn. Years later, in conversation with Peter Bogdanovich, Welles would describe Capra as possessing "Enormous skill—but always that sweet *Saturday Evening Post* thing about him."[20] Ironically, just prior to broadcasting *Mr. Deeds*, Welles himself became *Saturday Evening Post* fare. Beginning on 20 January Alva Johnson and Fred Smith wrote a three-part biography of him, "How to Raise a Child: The Disturbing Life—to Date—of Orson Welles." Nothing sweet in this piece. It chronicled both truth and legend regarding his tempestuous talent. Concerned about his reputation at the time, he challenged aspects of the article's accuracy. In later years, with the reputation secure and the legend burgeoning, he claimed it was all true. He was right the first time.

Mr. Deeds is graced with the presence of Gertrude Lawrence, who had done such a superb job in *Private Lives* the previous year. Here she is almost as good, but Welles's performance is flat, a bit too deadpan. Perhaps he was influenced by Cooper's interpretation of Deeds in the film, whereby (and in many other Cooper performances) deadpan becomes very much alive.

Contemplating a miniature for the eventually cancelled Heart of Darkness *film project. Courtesy of Lilly Library, Indiana University.*

Another attempt at recycling the spirit of an incomparable film, and play, came a week later. *Dinner at Eight*, by Edna Ferber and George S. Kaufman, was a 1935 release that featured John and Lionel Barrymore, Jean Harlow, and Marie Dressler. Early in the history of the genre it took screwball to virtuosic heights. Welles's radio play features the same dynamism, somewhat scaled down, and a promising actress whom he believed possessed considerable talent, Lucille Ball. She plays a memorable Kitty Packard—Jean Harlow's role in the film—the socially ambitious but rough-around-the-edges wife of a Texas tycoon (Welles). Orson also wanted to use her in one of his proposed film ideas, *The Smiler with a Knife*, based on the novel by Nicholas Blake (C. Day Lewis), but the studio thought she was not well-enough known and too inexperienced. She did, however, appear as a guest in several episodes of his later radio series, *Orson Welles's Almanac*. They remained good friends and when she became a sitcom star in the 1950s, she invited him to appear on an episode of her show.

At this point it is unclear how much energy Welles was able to put into his radio show. Adapting successful films seemed an easy out. Wheelock did not protest, and probably encouraged it, since the format interested both audiences who had seen the movies and those who had only heard about them. In any case, motion pictures were now very much on Welles's mind. Again and again he tried to come up with a story idea for RKO. In contrast to the aforementioned and then aborted *The Smiler with a Knife*, at least four other possible film projects had already been done by him on radio: *Heart of Darkness, Pickwick Papers, Around the World in 80 Days*, and *War of the Worlds*. Then, on 19 February, a day after the broadcast of *Dinner at Eight*, with RKO executives at the end of their tethers, Herman Mankiewicz was assigned to begin work on the screenplay that would become *Citizen Kane*.

On 25 February, not surprisingly, another movie was made into a radio play, *Only Angels Have Wings*. This story about mail pilots in South America was a romantic action drama filmed in 1939 by one of the most versatile directors to ever work within the studio system, Howard Hawks. Welles's radio version was routine, but it foreshadowed an exciting series about the American air industry and military that he would host during the war, *Ceiling Unlimited*. A historical period piece followed, Kenneth Roberts's *Rabble at Arms*, which deals with the illustrious career of Benedict Arnold during the American Revolution before he was accused of treason. It was succeeded on 10 March by a Pulitzer prize–winning play, George Kelley's *Craig's Wife*, a domestic melodrama featuring Ann Harding, which can best be described as "high soap."

Welles enjoyed the task of adapting popular contemporary material for broadcast. But from the beginning of his career as a radio producer and director, literary classics were his favorite source material. His rendering of *Les Misérables* in the summer of 1937 made radio history, and many of the best programs from *First Person Singular* and *Mercury Theatre on the Air* were based on novels that had withstood the test of time. Campbell and Ward Wheelock let him do this kind of thing on only a few occasions. One came two weeks before the series would end, when he was given permission to present *The Adventures of Huckleberry Finn* on 17 March. Although the story was filmed in 1931 and 1939, neither version influenced the radio play, which would turn out to be a swan song of sorts. It is, arguably, one of the best of the *Campbell* productions; certainly the one that most closely captures the spirit of those halcyon days before sponsorship cramped his radio imagination.

From the outset the innovative nature of the broadcast is evident. Former child star Jackie Cooper plays Huck. In period dialogue, he responds to Welles's narration and queries by affirming his character's proprietary right to tell the story: "That's more than a paragraph or two Mr. Welles.... You just want to read Mr. Twain yourself." This dual narration is interspersed with an enactment of the events. We hear how an abusive father led Huck, with the help of his black friend Jim (Clarence Muse), to run away, fake his death by drowning, and then return in drag to find out what people thought about him. The plan eventually backfires when the death Huck faked is believed to be murder, and, because of racism, Jim rather than the cruel father becomes the prime suspect.

Huck and Jim flee on a raft and drift down the Mississippi in one of the great voyages in literature. They are pursued by men searching for runaway slaves and eventually encounter two eccentrics claiming to be actors (Welles and Walter Catlett). The men stage an impromptu Shakespeare recitation, mixing a *Hamlet* sequence with lines from *Macbeth*, as nineteenth-century traveling thespians were prone to do—often accused of being a ham, here Welles gets to play one! Tom Sawyer (William Alland) makes a brief appearance and promises to "keep mum" on Huck and Jim's whereabouts and the fact that Jim might be an escaped slave. The boys are finally caught and Huck confesses all. When things seem darkest, he hears of his father's death by drowning and the inheritance he will get, plus the news that Jim was made a free man in his former master's will.

The unconventional format of the program works. Alternating the dual narration with episodic dramatizations gives the story a compelling intimacy; one might even be tempted to call the technique postmodern, in that the declared format of the production is part of the performance. Subtle sound effects highlight the story: those relating to the forest and the river almost allow us to smell the Mississippi lowlands. The dialogue is sparkling, especially the philosophizing between Huck and Jim as their raft drifts downriver. Of note is the fact that script adaptation was by Herman Mankiewicz, now on Welles's RKO payroll. The blend of their two talents here clearly anticipates what they would accomplish with *Citizen Kane*.

At this time Welles was spending most of his week in Hollywood working at RKO, and was not, therefore, disposed to appear on other radio programs (the major ones were still New York based). However, in his postperformance comments after *Huckleberry Finn*, he announces that in one half-hour he will be appearing on Jack Benny's show. Benny was on rival NBC, but the reason for the plug had to do with a reciprocal arrangement between the two programs whereby, as Orson notes, Jack would be making his debut as a radio actor the following week in the *Campbell Playhouse* production of the Ring Lardner and George S. Kaufman play, *June Moon*. This kind of crossover occasionally happens on contemporary television, but rarely if ever between shows on rival networks.

Welles's appearance on Benny's show, *The Jell-O Program*, is hilarious. Jack, disappointed that he has never won an Oscar for his comedic performances, wants Welles to coach him for a dramatic role. Orson, as it turns out, is very

Receiving an unusual award from Jack Benny. Most likely on 17 March 1940 as a guest on Benny's "Jell-O-Program." Courtesy of Lilly Library, Indiana University.

busy and hard to get a hold of. Eventually he appears (enthusiastic applause) and is greeted by announcer Phil Harris: "Hi Orson! Still scaring people?" When Orson begins imparting advice to Benny, the comedian declares, "I'm your obedient servant," a reference to Welles's by now famous closing signature. The role for which Orson feels Jack is most suited is Quasimodo in Victor Hugo's *Hunchback of Notre Dame*. Amid constant interruptions—Welles's tailor, a London producer phoning—he has Jack grunting and groaning the part. In the finale, Welles is so impressed with Benny's effort that he invites him to appear in *June Moon* on the *Campbell Playhouse* the following week: "There's a swell part in it for you." Although much of the dialogue between the two men seems adlibbed, perusal of the script, which resides among Welles's papers, reveals that almost every word had been written beforehand.

In *June Moon* Benny plays a song lyricist, Frederick D. Stevens, heading for New York. Welles serves as the narrator and has a small part as a train passenger. There is, however, a series of humorous exchanges between the narrator and Benny's character, a format reminiscent of *Huckleberry Finn* the previous week. The program also featured a live audience, the first in a Welles series. He describes them as "a few hundred of Mr. Benny's fans, who number in the millions, according to Mr. Benny." At times this audience seems unsure when to laugh, but not when Stevens expresses a desire to attend a radio broadcast and notes that the talented Jack Benny might be a good choice, while the cast groans.

Although *June Moon* was atypical *Campbell* fare, it would be followed by a prototypical episode, *Jane Eyre*, to end the series. Welles had performed the story two years earlier with *Mercury Theatre on the Air*. He would later do it on *Lux Radio Theatre*, then again in the 1944 film, and lastly on a broadcast of *Mercury Summer Theatre* in 1946. The *Campbell* version features Madeleine Carroll as Jane. Her first person narration exudes warmth and sincerity. Bernard Herrmann's music explores themes that would resurface in *Citizen Kane*. Welles's performance as Rochester, although not his best, is solid and seems tinged with emotions that might be linked to it being his *Campbell* finale.

For most listeners, an awareness that Friday nights would no longer be the same came from Ernest Chapple's words at the end of the performance. He announces that the series is over, then, on behalf of the sponsor, refers to it as having been "splendid" and thanks Welles for making it possible. With *Auld Lang Syne* playing in the background, Welles thanks the sponsor for an enjoyable opportunity and "a genuine happy experience." It of course had begun that way, but by this point, after endless confrontations with the sponsor, the show had become an artistically limiting obligation. His desire now was to be both behind and in front of a movie camera, not a radio microphone.

He concludes by paying tribute to his Mercury players, all of them having been with him from the summer of 1938 when *First Person Singular* was born: George Coulouris, Ray Collins, Everett Sloane, Edgar Barrier, Agnes Moorehead, and Frank Readick. Unfortunately, the last few seconds of the broadcast sour the tribute. Instead of a quiet fade-out, Chapple returns to inform us, as he has done in most previous broadcasts, that if we have enjoyed the program we should tell our grocers when we order Campbell's chicken soup. If it were not bad enough to taint the mood of farewell with such a plug, he goes on to remind us that there are other shows sponsored by Campbell. Welles probably could not wait to get back the movie studio—but two years later RKO would treat him with even less respect.

CHAPTER EIGHT

Orson at RKO

> All his passions—theatre, magic, circus, radio, painting, literature—suddenly fused into one.
>
> —Peter Bogdanovich

In the first half of the twentieth century radio was our dominant mass medium; in the second half it was television. However, when we look back at that century overall, it is motion pictures that have defined the realm of popular culture. Film has also given us what is arguably the most important and influential work of art of the past one hundred years, *Citizen Kane*.

With *Kane* topping almost every greatest film list, despite recent Spielbergomania, Welles's place in the pantheon of hallowed movie directors is assured. Welles of course made other significant films, and cinematically savvy polls, such as those that appear in the influential British film journal *Sight and Sound*, readily acknowledge this. Unfortunately, the tendency to think of his film career solely in terms of *Kane* has been paralleled by media commentators often discussing his radio legacy the same way. Speaking to this problem, and with understandable frustration, Peter Bogdanovich notes, "So many of his programs were far better, more inventive and beautiful than *The War of the Worlds*, but that's the only one people want to talk about."[1]

Because we think of film primarily as a visual medium, the fact that radio was a significant influence on its history often goes unacknowledged. Yet it was the success of radio in the late twenties that whetted the desire of people to hear movies talk, despite the poor audio and unquestionably weak artistic quality of many early sound films when compared to the last of the silents. And, even before Welles made the leap to celluloid, radio had been a source of movie talent, especially in the area of comedy and music—Bob Hope, Bing Crosby, Jack Benny, and George Burns and Gracie Allen, to name a few.

When Welles entered Hollywood he brought to filmmaking the eye of an innovative theater director and the ear of someone who had used sound in radio to explore the limits of storytelling and character development. Fortunately, the terms of his movie contract with RKO constituted a virtual license to innovate. In fact it was probably the best of all possible studio worlds in which he could extend his talents. The opening logo of their films must have seemed like a clarion call, urging him to bring ideas from his previous medium to this new one: a tower beeping signals into the ether while the words read "An RKO Radio Picture."

The three letters signify Radio Keith Orpheum; the latter two representing a vaudeville theater chain. The studio was launched under the three-letter moniker in 1928, as a result of wheeling and dealing by Joseph P. Kennedy, patriarch of the clan, and David Sarnoff. Sarnoff had emerged as the head of RCA and its new radio network, NBC.[2] He thought the new movie venture could make use of NBC talent and RCA technology. Just as he had, over a decade earlier, seen the entertainment potential of Marconi's wireless by proposing a "Radio Music Box" for every home, he now saw the future of movies as intimately tied to sound. And he had the technology, or rather one of the competing technologies, for putting it on film, a process called Photophone. RKO served as a vehicle for the system to strut its stuff.

From the beginning RKO was a studio in flux. Rather than concentrating on specific genres, widely divergent kinds of films were tried. The studio, therefore, never succeeded in establishing a signature identity along the lines of MGM's gloss and stars, Paramount's European sophistication, or Warner's urban crime dramas. Personnel changes were also frequent, as were trips to the financial brink. Through it all a diverse array of excellent pictures were made. They include a musical, *Swing Time* (1936); a western, *Cimarron* (1931); an action adventure saga, *King Kong* (1933); a screwball comedy, *Bringing Up Baby* (1938); and an urban melodrama, *Kitty Foyle* (1940). Not known for currying a stable of superstars (although they had Fred Astaire and Ginger Rogers), RKO nevertheless had a coterie of brilliant technical people who could create the context for almost any kind of film, as the above list attests. This was a boon to an experimenter like Welles. When he has young Charles Foster Kane deliver the line "I don't know how to run a newspaper, Mr. Thatcher, I just try everything I can think of," it is not a stretch to imagine Orson uttering to himself, "I don't know how to make a film, Mr. Schaefer [RKO's production head], I just try everything I can think of."

Much has been written about the making of *Kane*, from the controversy surrounding the authorship of the script, to the cinematic legerdemain Welles employed using RKO resources. Less has been said regarding the use of radio conventions that characterize the audio portion of the film. Before looking at the ways in which *Kane* truly fulfilled RKO's mandate to be a studio that made "radio pictures," the general context in which Welles was allowed to do what he did (or did so without asking and got away with it) should be considered.

He entered the studio a filmic neophyte, although he had had a camera in his hands before: at Todd; then while making *Hearts of Age*; and later during the filming of the introduction for *Too Much Johnson*. This did not, in any case, prepare him for using the arsenal of resources now available. Whatever uncertainties he had regarding the techniques to be learned, they were masked in a public bravado that provoked Hollywood insiders. Clearly, he was bringing his conjurer's sensibility to the new medium. But to succeed, he had to learn how this new collection of smoke and mirrors worked. Fortunately, he was a quick study, asking a myriad questions. A couple of his tutors were women. Amelia Kent instructed him in the format of screenplays, and Miriam Geiger showed him the camera's repertoire. As he learned what could be done, he contemplated what might be done. Accomplishing it, however, would require help at every level of the production process.

Although few would question Welles's "authorship" of *Kane*, the renowned film critic Pauline Kael has argued that the script is largely the work of Herman Mankiewicz, who deserves major credit for the film's success.[3] This view has not stood up to the many challenges directed at it.[4] In any case, what makes Welles's role in bringing forth *Kane* so impressive is not solely the creative "authorial" vision he brought to it, but the way he also "conducted" a team of extraordinary collaborators—a dream team if you will—getting them to put forth efforts they rarely surpassed in subsequent years. And whether the script was mostly or minimally driven by Welles's ideas, he did take seriously the insights and style of Mankiewicz, who had already worked with him on radio as an uncredited writer for such *Campbell Playhouse* productions as *The Murder of Roger Ackroyd*, *The Garden of Allah*, *Dodsworth*, *Vanity Fair*, and most notably *Huckleberry Finn*. He also had accumulated a modest string of film credits, and noncredits when he was an unbilled writer. His dark vision of the world and searing humor complemented Welles's bent for provocation.

Welles also wanted the music in the film to not merely enhance the story, but to be an integral part of it. Again he turned to radio. What Bernard Herrmann had done with him at CBS surpassed in dramatic ingenuity the scoring, often lush and memorable, that the first generation of sound film composers such as Erich Korngold, Max Steiner, and Franz Waxman were doing. Herrmann, for his part, was reluctant to work in Hollywood. He had been advised by colleagues not to disrupt his "day job" at CBS and his budding concert career. But he also knew that working for Welles would give him enormous latitude in transferring the scoring ideas that worked in radio to celluloid. RKO agreed, although they underestimated his financial worth. Welles became strident. He insisted that "Benny should get what Steiner gets, $10,000."[5] Schaefer reluctantly agreed.

Welles was also the producer and therefore took a proactive role in casting the players in *Kane*. Most had no previous film experience. The exceptions are hardly noteworthy. Dorothy Comingore, who played Susan Alexander, Kane's second wife—"the most important role in the film" Orson told her—had a résumé highlighted by a few walk-ons with the Three Stooges. And Mercury regular George Coulouris had small roles in a couple of pictures while waiting for Orson to begin production.

The dominant background that characterizes the actors Welles assembled for *Kane* is radio. Coulouris (W. P. Thatcher), Everett Sloane (Bernstein), Agnes Moorehead (Mary Kane), William Alland (Thompson, the reporter), Paul Stewart (Raymond, the butler), Ray Collins (Boss Gettys), Richard Barr (Hillman), Erskine Sanford (Herbert Carter), and Joseph Cotten (Jed Leland) were all veterans of *Mercury Theatre on the Air* and *Campbell Playhouse*. Coulouris, Alland, Sanford, and Cotten had also been with Mercury during its theatrical incarnation. Even Ruth Warwick (Emily Norton Kane), although not previously a part of Mercury, had radio experience. In *Kane* they all give superb performances. Of special note is the range of expressiveness in their voices. This was crucial to the film, and either a result of, or a reason why, Welles used few closeups. Therefore, throughout the film it is voice, sound, and music which usually cue us to the emotional state of a character or scene.

Helping Welles achieve and mix these auditory elements was James G. Stewart who, like many sound technicians in film, came from a radio background. Like most of them, he welcomed the challenge of working in pictures but found the creative latitude was more limited than it had been in broadcasting. Stewart quickly appreciated Welles's efforts to stretch the sound possibilities of cinema so it could accommodate techniques that had proved so successful in radio. According to Stewart, "Orson's method, at least with me, was to run a sequence, give me the idea of the effect he wished to achieve and several suggestions as to how it might be done, and then allow me full play in producing it."⁶ The track would then be run with Welles making further suggestions. Given the experimental nature of the picture, what was tried did not often work, so it would be redone and then rerun until Welles was satisfied.

Of the cinematography, much has been written. Gregg Toland, director of photography extraordinaire, showed up virtually on Welles's doorstep—just outside his office patiently waiting for the wunderkind to emerge—to say he wanted to work with him. As a member of Goldwyn Studios' technical stable, Toland had earned an Oscar for *Wuthering Heights* (1939) and critical acclaim for his innovative work in *The Long Voyage Home* (1940) and *The Grapes of Wrath* (1940). He claimed a familiarity with Welles's theatrical productions and expressed a desire to help him achieve whatever new perspectives the young director wanted to bring to the screen. Toland was also known for his experiments with the hardware of his craft: new and faster wide-angle lenses and special coatings to improve their light-gathering capacity. When Goldwyn lent him to RKO they doubtlessly had no idea how his name would eventually appear on the credits—not in the shopping list of dutiful laborers who worked on the film, but on the primary credit that closes it, just below Welles's name, as one of its "auteurs." This was not a first. He had received a similar credit from director John Ford for *The Long Voyage Home*.

As impressive as *Kane* looks, and art director Perry Ferguson's sets along with Toland's cinematography have become cinema legend, the soundtrack is no less impressive. There are few scenes in the film where what we see rather than hear reveals vital information. The major one, of course, occurs at the end, where the words of the reporters indicate confused resignation that the mystery of Rosebud will never be resolved, but viewers then discover the solution when they see the infamous sled consigned to the flames. It is almost as if this moment, one of the most purely cinematic in the film, is one Welles had been building toward throughout the production by using a mixture of sounds and images, until revelation was finally beyond dialogue.

Listening to *Kane*—what a splendid radio play it would have made—is an experience that can be complete unto itself. In several later interviews Welles insisted that the images in his films invariably follow what he hears:

> With me the visual is a solution to what the poetic and musical form dictates. I don't begin with the visual and then find a poetry and music and try to stick it in the picture. The picture has to follow it.... I don't go around like a collector picking up beautiful images and pasting them together.... There is no picture which justifies itself, no matter how beautiful, striking, horrific, tender ... it doesn't mean anything unless it makes poetry possible.⁷

Welles's emphasis on sound, especially dialogue, sometimes creates situations where what we see, for example when Kane and his entourage take over the *Inquirer*, is described verbally by the characters as it would be in a radio drama. Another example occurs when Kane leaves the *Inquirer* building for his honeymoon to France and Jed Leland (Joseph Cotten) suggests that the staff observe the departure. "Let's go to the window," he says, when a simple gesture (enthusiastic or mischievous) might have had more cinematic effect. The film also contains moments of dialogue so trenchant that the only image that can do them justice must come from our imaginations. One such scene has Thompson the reporter (William Alland) interviewing an elderly Bernstein (Everett Sloane) in a stark boardroom with soft thunder in the background. Nothing much to see, and the conversation, speculating on what Rosebud might be, is very matter of fact . . . until Bernstein unleashes a reminiscence:

> One day back in 1896, I was crossing over to Jersey on the ferry. And as we pulled out there was another ferry pulling in, and on it a girl waiting to get off. A white dress she had on; she was carrying a white parasol. I only saw her for one second. She didn't see me at all. But I'll bet a month hasn't gone by since, that I haven't thought of that girl.

This scene, despite the legendary visual moments in the film, remained Welles's favorite. He also willingly acknowledged that it had been written by Mankiewicz. Reminiscing about the reminiscence, he told Peter Bogdanovich that

> If I were in Hell and they gave me a day off and said, "What part of any movie you have ever made do you want to see?" I'd see that scene of Mank's about Bernstein. All the rest could have been better, but that was just right.[8]

Throughout the film, the sound, especially the dialogue, endeavors to reflect the place in which a scene is set. In exterior shots, it is more diffuse and contains subtle bits of ambient noise. In the interior sets, offices and rooms, reverberation is sometimes added to complement the location (a major innovation in the film was also Welles's insistence that the interior sets have ceilings to allow for the low wide-angle camera shots he favored). As a result, we have an especially haunting resonance in the scenes that take place in the cavernous confines of the Thatcher Memorial Library, also in the room with the gigantic hearth in Xanadu, and in the warehouse containing Kane's treasures—the collection described as "the loot of the world" in the "News on the March" segment. In these large spaces the dialogue yields voice overtones that quickly fade. A visual parallel would be the infinite regress we see in Kane's image when he briefly pauses in a Xanadu hallway between opposing mirrors.

In previous motion picture soundtracks we occasionally get this kind of locational fidelity, but rarely if ever in such a wholesale manner. Their primary concern is that the dialogue be heard clearly, even under conditions of poor projection, and that the sound effects be unambiguous and well synchronized. Radio, and not just the Mercury broadcasts, had been more daring. The pioneering work of Irving Reis cannot be overlooked in this regard, or underestimated, especially since Welles had worked with him in several productions. What Reis accomplished with sound in *The Fall of the City*, with Welles playing the role of the reporter/narrator, eventually inspired his Mercury broadcasts, and entered the movies through daring productions such as *Kane*. In radio, the tradition of Reis and Welles continued through the work of the legendary Norman Corwin who, as did his predecessors, used the *Columbia Workshop* as a creative laboratory.

A notable but generally unnoticed feature of the soundtrack of *Kane* is the depth of auditory field Welles utilized. It can be seen as a complement to the much discussed depth of the visual field achieved by Toland's deep focus cinematography. Having everything in focus in a given scene allows viewers to select the part of it they wish to scrutinize. One of the most famous examples occurs in the first flashback, when we are transported back to the snowbound cabin of the young Charlie Kane as his mother is about to sign over custodianship of him to Thatcher. In the foreground we see the two of them commiserating over the arrangement; in the middle ground is the father, perplexed by and questioning the plan; and in the background we see through a window young Charlie playing in the snow, oblivious to the dealings that are about to change his life.

These visuals are so arresting they tend to draw us away from the auditory construction of the scene. If we concentrate, or turn off the picture, we can experience depth of field in the soundscape. In the foreground we hear the negotiators of Charlie's fate insisting on the necessity of their plan; further back in the room the father vainly tries to interject his opinion; and out in the snow, very faintly, comes the sound of the boy at play. His words are largely inaudible, except for "the union forever" which is said at least twice. It is not in the shooting script and might have been improvised on the spot by Welles who, not appearing in the scene, must have given it his total directorial attention.

Throughout the film, whenever a character in dialogue moves up or down stage, the distance is suggested by the volume of the actor's voice, his or her footsteps, or whatever other sounds are taking place in different parts of the room. Notable examples include the reporters walking and talking in the screening room after the "News on the March" segment, and again in the closing scenes in the warehouse; Kane and his first wife Emily sitting farther and farther apart at the breakfast table as the years pass; and Kane plodding to the end of the huge den with the gigantic hearth in Xanadu, as his second wife, Susan, plies her jigsaw puzzle.

Often commentators have assumed this represents Welles's attempt to create pure auditory realism. It would be more accurate to say that—consistent with his approach to all the performing arts—what he strove to create was *the illusion of realism*. Evan William Cameron seems inclined in this direction when he notes that the aural moments in *Kane*, following from Welles's work in radio, are "constructed not reproduced."[9] A more recent study of the subject by film/sound historian Rick Altman extends this notion via a technically detailed assessment of what he calls the "deep focus sound" employed in the film.[10]

Altman notes, using some of the examples already discussed, how Welles's use of sound in *Kane*, as was the case with his work in radio, serves not the tenets of realism but the "narrative/discourse interplay" and emotional tone of a scene. As he points out, scenes in the film may open with spatial realism in sound, but they can soon deviate (in volume and reverberation, for example) to serve the interplay between and fate of the characters involved. Also the distance between the actors in some scenes is represented by sound differences that are not as wide as they would be in reality. Welles of course had already explored such auditory conjuring in radio, albeit in a more limited way, given the technical constraints of the medium at that time. With *Kane* he brought into being what Altman refers to as the "first modern movie," representing "the first effective meeting place of the century's two most powerful media, broadcasting and film."[11]

Sometimes an auditory shift in the film is connected not to the actors, as discussed above, but directly to the movement of the camera. The first instance occurs early in the film. It is a memorable tracking shot during a thunderstorm through the skylight of the El Rancho (using a dissolve through the semiopaque glass), the nightclub in which an aging Susan Alexander Kane sits forlornly after completing a singing performance. As the camera stalks her, we hear the sounds of the storm gradually fade and those inside the nightclub increase. Although this is a purely cinematic use of sound, it has antecedents in radio—for example, when we enter the Casbah in the 8 October 1939 *Campbell Playhouse* production of *Algiers*. Now, in filmmaking, the camera allows Welles to explore this kind of effect in a way that transcends the logical parameters of radio drama.

Finally, when a scene involves a conversation with more than two people, such as the sequence involving the gaggle of reporters, extensive use is made of overlapping dialogue. The film also uses dialogue whereby one person finishes another's sentence with his or her own thoughts, such as during the speculations surrounding what Rosebud might be or mean. Both techniques, although they might have been used in radio prior to Welles's *Mercury* and *Campbell* productions, were never more fully exploited than in those broadcasts. Screwball comedies such as *His Girl Friday* (1940) possibly introduced them into the movies, but it was in *Kane* where they were first integrated into a dramatic motion picture.

Commiserating over the score of Citizen Kane *with composer Bernard Herrmann. Courtesy of MPTV.net.*

Of Bernard Herrmann's music, not enough can be said. He regarded the Kane score as his best and most challenging work.[12] It is certainly one of the best in motion picture history. He credited his abilities as a film composer to having worked extensively in radio drama. Since much of this experience was with Welles, their artistic sympatico while making *Kane* was exceptional. Although most composers worked after the fact of a shoot, adding a palette of tonal colors following the editing, Herrmann composed before the shoot, with script in hand, and during production. As a result, the music so intimately permeated the film's conception that major visual and dialogue edits were done so as to be consonant with phrases and rhythms in the score. In the editing room Welles oversaw a young Robert Wise, who would later describe the experience to Frank Brady: "We both learned from each other, but he overwhelmed me with his radio background and his masterful use of sound, stretching the boundaries of how I thought sound could be used."[13]

Herrmann's score covers an enormous range of musical genres, sometimes in rapid succession. Nowhere is this more apparent than in the "News on the March" segment, where quick cuts give us a panoramic glimpse of Kane's life. Here, and throughout the film, Herrmann used the full orchestra sparingly. He preferred, as he often did in scoring radio drama, to employ unorthodox instrument combinations to get the desired effect or to voice a particular motif. For the dark and brooding opening sequence, for example, he states that he used "eight flutes (four being alto), four bass flutes, very deep contrabass clarinets, clarinets, tubas, trombones, deep lower percussion, and a vibraphone."[14] Original motifs were used to highlight the music of folk songs, a marching band, jazz combo, and grand opera. And as in radio, the score was used to indicate transitions that lead to a scene change. This is particularly effective in the historical flashbacks, where the music evokes the period, coloring the way we are supposed to interpret the images, be it the time of Kane's childhood in the post–Civil War era, or his entry into the lively milieu of 1890s New York as a newspaper publisher.

A major musical moment in the film occurs when the score itself becomes the subject, during the grand opera Salammbô. Welles suggested the stage setting. He wanted something lavish and exotic, set in ancient Rome and Carthage. Ernest Reyer's opera of the same name, based on the novel by Gustave Flaubert, inspired the visual scenario. For the music, Herrmann had something in mind along the lines of Jules Massenet's excursion into high Romanticism, *Thaïs*.

The script called for Kane's wife Susan to be coerced by her husband into pursuing an operatic career, with her efforts eventually embarrassing them both. Herrmann knew that for the idea to be convincing, subtlety was required. In other words, Susan should be modestly talented rather than blatantly incompetent, but thrust into a performance situation beyond her abilities. He had her voice dubbed by a young soprano, Jean Forward, who was forced to sing at the limits of her range and against a heavy-handed orchestration. The visual setting complements this. It had to, because the singing does not sound *that bad* to nonmusically trained ears; operaphobes might also puzzle over it by assuming she is just as good as any singer they have heard doing a similar aria. Visually, Susan sits alone on the operatic stage, garishly costumed, in a vast sea of a set in which she appears to be drowning, metaphorically. The music itself is highly evocative and was later performed in concert and recorded.

Welles's intent in making Charles Kane a stage husband was to parody William Randolph Hearst's attempts to promote his paramour Marion Davies's film career. A difference is that she did have talent, especially as a comedienne. Hearst, however, wanted her to do more dramatic and uplifting roles, for which, as it turned out, she was ill suited. As a result her career floundered. It also seems that in the character of Susan Alexander, Welles and Herrmann had in mind the career of Ganna Walska, the second wife of Harold McCormick, the farm machinery tycoon.[15] He was a patron of the Chicago Opera and shamelessly promoted the aspirations of his modestly talented wife, although stardom would elude her.

During the filming (from July 1940 to February 1941) Welles's extracurricular activities were limited, but he did manage to make several radio appearances. On 30 August he appeared on *This Is Radio*, an hour-long paean to the medium. The program originated from the site of the New York World's Fair, the location, ironically, where the previous year television was given its first widespread unveiling to the American public.

In October Welles went on a brief lecture tour. On the 28th he encountered H. G. Wells on station KTSA San Antonio, Texas, for a cordial reminiscence of the Panic Broadcast. On 10 January he made the first of what would be several appearances on Rudy Vallee's radio show, *The Sealtest Program* on NBC. The other invited star was Welles's former radio guest, John Barrymore. The two chided each other relentlessly. When Vallee refers to Orson as "Boy Wonder," Barrymore responds, "I know, I look at him and boy, do I wonder." A series of spoofs follow, of commercials, soap operas, quiz shows, and several other radio genres. A brief return to sobriety punctuates the hilarity when the two thespians do a short scene from Shakespeare's *Julius Caesar*. The idea of doing comedy and drama routines within a single program would later become the staple of one of Welles's wartime programs, *Orson Welles's Almanac*.

Waiting for *Kane* to premiere, and trying to thwart the attempts of Hearst and his supporters to block from release or destroy the film, was a difficult period for Welles. However, there were other ventures to keep him busy: several guest appearances on radio and a chance to direct theater once again. Apparently the break with Houseman was not as final as Houseman had thought, since much to his surprise he did "what I vowed I would never do again," which was work with Boy Wonder.[16] The project was an adaptation by Richard Wright and Paul Green of Wright's incendiary novel, *Native Son*. Wright, an African American, had written an uncompromising story about the results of racial prejudice. Transposed into a Mercury production by Welles, it was both successful and controversial . . . another moment in his career of great use to his enemies, such as Hearst and J. Edgar Hoover, who wished to portray him as a subversive with communist leanings. On 6 April, two weeks after *Native Son* opened, radio would provide them with even more ammunition.

The program was a rare example of an original radio play written by Welles. Called *His Honor the Mayor*, it ran as an episode in *The Free Company*. The series was a government encouraged venture coordinated by novelist James Boyd and geared toward presenting stories that illustrate the fundamental freedoms in America guaranteed by the Bill of Rights. It was broadcast on CBS as a minimally budgeted sustaining program. In writing for the series, Welles joined a list of luminaries, among them his former colleague, Archibald MacLeish; also the likes of William Saroyan, Sherwood Anderson, Maxwell Anderson, and Stephen Vincent Benét. Actors who had appeared in previous episodes include Paul Muni, Canada Lee (Banquo in Welles's Voodoo *Macbeth*), John Garfield, Franchot Tone, and Edmund Gwenn.

The Free Company was hosted by Burgess Meredith and proved to be both popular (for a sustaining show) and controversial. The political ideals expressed in Welles's program, particularly as they sought to counter racial prejudice, had in fact been championed in earlier broadcasts. *His Honor the Mayor* broached the issues with directness but without dogma. Using a *Kane* cast that included Ray Collins as the mayor, Agnes Moorehead, Everett Sloane, Erskine Sanford, and Paul Stewart, the thirty-minute drama chronicles a dilemma facing the nonpartisan mayor of a small town near the Mexican border. He must deal with a group known as the White Crusaders who wish to hold a rally to disseminate their views. Various people are interviewed who hold conflicting positions on the issue, while Welles, as the announcer, urges listeners to draw their own conclusions. In the end, despite fervent opposition, the mayor upholds the First Amendment and the racists are allowed to stage their meeting.

The next day the political fireworks in the radio play extended to the press as the Hearst papers came down on *The Free Company* in general, and Welles in particular. Accusations that the whole enterprise was communistic and an attack on American values were timed so as to jeopardize Welles's career and thwart the release of *Kane*. The non-Hearst media, however, were quick to point this out, as did Welles in a lengthy press release and several radio interviews. He also emphatically denied being a communist. Welles's defense was similar to what Kane says in the film when similar accusations are made (he is called a fascist as well as a communist): "I am now what I have always been, an American."

Kane eventually opened on 1 May 1941. There is no evidence that the May Day premier was intended to further provoke Hearst. Ultimately, the theaters willing to show it were few and the public, despite the controversy, was not lured to see it, even out of curiosity. *Kane* did win high critical acclaim and several Oscar nominations, which resulted in boos for Welles every time his name was called; fortunately, he was not present. The film did garner a best original screenplay award for him and Mankiewicz, who was also absent. Legend has it that this was a slap at Welles rather than a kudo, given the controversy surrounding the sharing of credit with Mank.

Hearst, it appeared, had won the battle. But he would lose the war, decisively. Not only would *Kane* achieve greatness in later decades, it would become the vehicle through which posterity would largely recall the life and legacy of the megalomaniacal press baron.

Having proved he could make a great picture, Welles now had to show he could make one that was merely good, but also successful. *The Magnificent Ambersons* would turn out to be very good—downgraded by critical posterity from great because of the studio's postproduction cuts and additions—but it was even less viable at the box office than *Kane*. Shooting would begin on 28 October. In the months previous, Welles had toyed with several film project ideas, toured as a stage magician with paramour of the moment Delores Del Rio, and launched a national tour for *Native Son*. Radio, however, was never far away. It came easily and he was good at it. CBS again approached him, this time for something light. The result was *The Orson Welles Show*, sometimes known as *The Orson Welles's Almanac*. The initial sponsor was Lady Esther cosmetics—a mostly female audience being assured. The show had two incarnations; the first ran from 15 September 1941 to 2 February 1942. The format of this version was variable. There was comedy, music, readings from literature, and drama, in shifting proportions. Occasionally a complete radio play would be featured. In several of the more comedic broadcasts, Orson would banter with Jiminy Cricket

(Cliff Edwards)—inspiration for these routines may have come from Edgar Bergen and his dummy, Charlie McCarthy.

The second installment of the show ran from 26 January to 19 July 1944 and was sponsored by Mobil Oil. It featured a live studio audience, which brought out more spontaneity in Welles, and followed a more predictable variety show format, and for the most part dispensed with full-length radio plays. The primary ingredients were skits with guest stars, banter, and music. The program was as hilarious and hip as anything on radio at the time.

Notable moments in the first incarnation of *Almanac* include Welles reading from the *Song of Solomon* on 29 September, and Poe's *Annabel Lee* on 6 October. On 30 October Lucille Ball was the guest. She did a hilarious sketch with Orson, "Noah Webster's Library," and then read four poems by Dorothy Parker. The 17 November broadcast was given over to an original radio play rather than an adaptation from a literary source (a rarity in a Welles program, especially when he did not write it himself), *The Hitch Hiker*, by Louise Fletcher, wife of Bernard Herrmann.

The story, which would appear two decades later on television's *Twilight Zone*, concerns a young man, Ronald Adams, driving from Brooklyn to Los Angeles. Almost immediately he spots a hitchhiker as he crosses the Brooklyn Bridge. As Adams traverses the country he sees the mysterious man again, and again, and again. At one point he actually tries to run down the phantom figure. Eventually, he picks up a female hitchhiker for company. She is unable to see the stalking specter obsessing him and bolts from the car, thinking he is crazy. In New Mexico, he fills up his tank for $1.49 (!) and then spends a pricey, even by today's standards, $3.85 for a three-minute phone call to Brooklyn. At his wit's end, Adams calls his mother, whom he discovers is in the hospital with a nervous breakdown. Apparently, her son was killed in a traffic accident on the Brooklyn Bridge a week earlier.

Welles played the lead and narrates in diary fashion the plight of Adams. He adds a progressive tremolo to his voice as the succession of phantom sightings gradually unhinges the perplexed driver. The sound effects are simple but effective: the car; the distant and haunting voice of the hitchhiker hailing Adams; and the deadpan voice of the telephone operator. The final phone call is particularly chilling, as we hear the amplified clanging of coins being dropped into the slot. As they trigger bells of different pitch we sense that somehow this tolls a death knell for our protagonist. The success of the radio play led Welles to repeat it—as an episode of *Suspense* on 2 September 1942, and as part of *The Mercury Summer Theatre* on 21 June 1946. On that occasion Welles briefly profiled Louise Fletcher, mentioning that in his opinion her *Sorry, Wrong Number* (which featured Agnes Moorehead and was first broadcast on 25 May 1943 as an episode of *Suspense*) is the "greatest single radio script ever written."

On 29 December, the accent of *Almanac* was on comedy; not short sketches this time, but a full-length radio play, *There Are Frenchmen and Frenchmen*. The story, by Richard Connell, was adapted for radio and seems narrated (no credits are given) by Joseph Cotten. Welles plays a teacher from France involved in a faculty exchange at an Oklahoma college. The coeds swoon over him, but the acting dean, Ona Birdsong (Rita Hayworth), is not impressed. He, however, is impressed with her and not with his entourage of admirers. Eventually, of course, the two see eye to eye. The story is silly and Orson's accent overblown and unconvincing. The surprise is Miss Hayworth . . . playing a college dean! She is excellent. Without the "distraction" of her stunning features and seductive tresses, it soon becomes obvious that she possessed a rich and nuanced voice that makes listening to her on radio a pleasure. Orson, at this point—reputedly their first meeting—must have been impressed as well, with the whole package. He would eventually court and marry her.

While these broadcasts were going on, *Ambersons* was in production. Once again Welles was able to utilize a nucleus of Mercury actors, Joseph Cotten (Eugene Morgan), Agnes Moorehead (Fanny Minafer), Ray Collins (Uncle Jack Amberson), and Erskine Sanford (Roger Bronson). The other principals included Tim Holt (George Minafer), better known for his westerns, and newcomer Ann Baxter (Lucy Morgan), along with veterans from the silent era, Dolores Costello (Isabel Amberson) and Richard Bennett (Major Amberson). Back from their work on *Kane* were editor Robert Wise, sound man James G. Stewart, and special effects maestro Vernon L. Walker. Gregg Toland was unavailable to handle cinematography. Stanley Cortez and sundry assistants had to suffice. Welles found him slow[17]—after working with the fastest lens in the West on *Kane*, how could he not? Nevertheless, the film has a very Tolandesque look about it that seems consistent with what Welles wanted. Bernard Herrmann again provided the music, although he asked that his name be deleted from the credits after the studio's post-production cuts and additions.

Of all Welles's films, it is *Ambersons* that perhaps comes closest to being a radio picture. He recorded many scenes during rehearsal, making changes as he listened to the playback. But when he tried to use these recordings to coordinate the way the actors performed before the camera, by getting them to lip-synch to the disks, it just did not work. His vision of the film was strongly influenced by the successful version of *Ambersons* he had broadcast on *Campbell Playhouse* two years earlier. He used a recording of that performance as a basis for the movie, and to convince George Schaefer to approve the project, although according to Welles, Schaefer nodded off after five minutes.[18] Nevertheless, there are differences in the story line between the film and radio versions. The most notable one is the addition of the character of Aunt Fanny (Agnes Moorehead), who is crucial to the novel but omitted in the radio play, perhaps so as not to overly complicate the story, given the forty-five-minute length allowed for it in a commercial broadcast. Also, a radio drama tends to work better with fewer characters than a film, given a similar story framework.

Little did Schaefer know that everything about the film would also be darker than the radio play: the characters, Herrmann's music, and the Amberson mansion, which we can now see as opposed to imagine. The house is Gothic to the core, a scaled-down version of *Kane*'s Xanadu, or perhaps the kind of home Count Dracula would have chosen had he been forced to live in late nineteenth-century middle America. There is of course a good deal of pleasant decor, but it always seems to cast shadows. This suggests an era and way of life on the wane, a central theme of the film.

The first thirty minutes of *Ambersons* is a seamless evocation of time and place and serves to introduce the principal characters. After the title card, the screen goes black for fifteen seconds and we hear Welles, as he did on radio, begin narrating Tarkington's sociological description of the setting for the story. Then the images come: a stately house (not the Amberson mansion but the one across the street), a horse-drawn streetcar hailed from the window, and a humorous montage of male fashions of the time. Welles elected to comment on these clothes because he felt that what the men of the time wore was far more odd than the women's apparel.

With a context established, we are then told about the individuals whose destiny will unfold. How years earlier, a somewhat inebriated and love-struck Eugene Morgan (Joseph Cotten) made a fool of himself by falling into a bass fiddle while serenading the lovely Isabel Amberson (Dolores Costello). The Morgan character in the film was much inspired by Orson's father, whom he often claimed knew Booth Tarkington. Isabel, however, opts to marry someone more stable, Wilbur Minafer (Don Dillaway). Not only do we have Welles's narration informing us of these events, several townsfolk function as a kind of chorus and add their impressions. We learn from these voices that since Isabel could never truly love Wilbur, she would vent all her affection on her offspring . . . just one, as it turned out, George Amberson Minafer (Bobby Cooper as the child, Tim Holt, the adult).

We are further told the boy is a spoiled holy terror and then witness him in action, looking all the world like a young Louis XIV with his long curls and skirt. To those in the know, the demeanor of George Amberson in both film and novel bears a striking resemblance to that of young George Orson. The townsfolk chorus half-prophesy, half-hope that someday the arrogant hellion will get his comeuppance, a fate that many in Hollywood hoped would befall Orson. They would not have to wait long following the completion of *Ambersons*.

The story then jumps forward in time to when George returns from college. This chronological leap is almost identical to the one in *Kane*, from when young Charlie is being taken away from home by his new guardian, Thatcher, to the resumption of the story when we hear that he has been expelled from several colleges and has decided to try his hand at running a newspaper. George's return happens to coincide with that of Eugene Morgan, now a successful inventor and widower with an eighteen-year-old daughter, Lucy. A soirée is held at the Amberson mansion in George's honor. The scene is an extraordinary marriage of image and sound. It foreshadows several stunning sequences in Welles's later films, such as the hall of mirrors dénouement in *The Lady from Shanghai* (1946), the opening tracking shot in *Touch of Evil* (1958), and the Battle of Shrewsbury in *Chimes at Midnight* (1966).

We enter the Amberson ball through the front door with Eugene and Lucy, via a tracking camera. Once inside, it sweeps the dance floor in marvelous synch to Herrmann's music. Like a paint brush, the lens seems to highlight the characters it touches, while snippets of conversation provide details of their relationship to each other. Once again, as in Welles's radio work, dialogue fades in, overlaps, and fades out. Sound provides most of the information. But what visuals accompany it! Remarkably, most of the dialogue in this scene was later dubbed, since during the actual filming the camera cranes were too heavy for the floor and elicited loud creaks.

During the ball George meets Lucy, with whom he becomes smitten; Eugene admits to still adoring Isabel; and Aunt Fanny (Agnes Moorehead) who has always carried a torch for Eugene, is left in the lurch once again. The festivities carry over to the next day and yield another remarkable scene. George takes Lucy on a sleigh ride while Eugene chauffeurs Isabel, Fanny, and Uncle Jack Amberson (Ray Collins) in his horseless carriage. It is an exhilarating moment (all the more remarkable since it was shot in a raw and uncomfortable icehouse, steeped in the stench of fish, which led Ray Collins to contract pneumonia). Once again the images seem to flow from the sounds and words we hear, since in conception the sequence is very close to the way it was constructed in the radio version: the jingling sleigh bells and horses' hooves in counterpoint to the sputtering gasoline engine, with Herrmann's music and laughter-laced conversation completing the scene.

The sleigh eventually tips over and George protects Lucy during the tumble. He then steals a kiss, an act absent from both the novel and radio version, but it works well in the movie. Both are forced to return in Eugene's vehicle, which George disdains but is forced to push-start. As they return, they sing "The Man Who Broke the Bank at Monte Carlo." In the novel it is "The Star Spangled Banner." Welles's substitution, both here and in the radio version, seems more apropos and was inspired by his own father's escapades in Monte Carlo. This sequence also presented sound man James G. Stewart with one of his biggest challenges. It was shot in an ice house, which made recording the dialogue virtually impossible. Stewart responded to the challenge by recording the dialogue of each character separately, then mixing and rerecording it with the sound of the old car engine. Welles was not satisfied. He told Stewart that the voices evidenced no movement in response to the bouncing car. Stewart then went back to square one and rerecorded the dialogue by having the actors speak their lines while sitting on a plank suspended between two sawhorses, which he repeatedly bounced, thus achieving the illusion of motion Welles sought.[19]

The outing in the snow ends with an auditory fade-out as we see Eugene's contraption recede in the distance. But it is the visual resolution of the scene that is memorable. It ends with an iris-out. This technique, often used in silent cinema, is a fade to black through a gradually constricting circle. In this case all we see before the screen goes dark is a tiny oval embracing the vehicle on the horizon; an iris-in does the reverse. Symbolically, the shot, in light of the story of the Ambersons, signifies the end of an era—the genteel preindustrial way of life in which the family thrived. Unfortunately, it also marks the end of the most compelling section of the film, for what follows is more dialogue dependent and less effective.

Wilbur Minafer dies and Eugene begins to court Isabel, much to the frustration of Fanny. She subtly provokes George to anger over the situation, especially since his courtship of Lucy is being stalled by her reticence. George's simmering animosity toward Eugene surfaces in a family dinner where the inventor is present while his daughter is away visiting a friend. George berates the automobile, knowing full well that Eugene has become successful manufacturing them. Eugene, always the diplomat, says that George may well be right, and that this step forward in technology may be a step backward in civilization. The exchange is, as it was in the radio version, faithful to the novel. Part of Welles's fascination with the book has to do with Tarkington's sociological commentary on the way industrialism, particularly the coming of the automobile, ended a way of life that, although not idyllic, was more emotionally fulfilling than what succeeded it.

Eventually, George takes Isabel to Europe to keep her away from her suitor. In the novel she dies there, but the movie puts her death throes in the Amberson mansion where, as was the case in an earlier scene, Eugene is not allowed to see her. Isabel's death starts a chain of events that finally brings George his comeuppance, in spades. The family patriarch, Major Amberson (Richard Bennett), dies. There is no inheritance, and because of debts, not even the family home can be retained. Scenes more fully explaining this demise were removed when the studio lopped forty minutes from Welles's original cut after uninspiring previews—reducing it to its current length of eighty-eight minutes.

As the Amberson empire unravels, Fanny becomes hysterical, Uncle Jack heads east, and George is forced to work for the first time in his life, dangerous work with explosives. In a wrenching scene he revisits the boarded-up family home and prays for forgiveness at his mother's bed. But there is more comeuppance to come, and of the ironic variety. George is hit by a car and has both his legs broken. In the novel, the radio play, and the film, a reconciliation with Eugene and Lucy seems possible. Welles's original ending for the movie, however, was less optimistic and more in tune with the rest of the picture. The new, studio-imposed finale, explicitly suggesting the couple will reconcile, is totally different in look from what precedes it, and Herrmann's music has been replaced by composer Roy Webb's "violins." Fortunately, those responsible left intact the way Welles presented the final credits, orally, with cameos of the actors when their names are cited. Finally, we hear him take a bow for the writing and directing credits, as he signs off with "My name is Orson Welles."

The missing footage, which was destroyed by RKO while Welles was in Brazil working on the abortive *It's All True* project, has become the stuff of legend. Nevertheless, we do have a good sense of what it contained from segments of the script and stills. Peter Bogdanovich and Jonathan Rosenbaum in *This Is Orson Welles*, and Robert Carringer's *The Magnificent Ambersons: A Reconstruction*, have collated and assessed the pieces of this cinematic puzzle.

Would an original print of *Ambersons*, if found, truly be, as Welles has intimated, his greatest film? Although the first thirty minutes of what now exists are close to the best thirty minutes of celluloid ever turned, the rest of the film, even if we imagine the missing footage, would be hard-pressed to match it. In any case, the acting remains exceptional throughout. Joseph Cotten has rarely been better, and Ray Collins affirms his position as one of the best supporting actors to ever appear in Welles's films. He is also in *Kane* and *A Touch of Evil* (1958). It also sounds like his voice on the exquisitely produced *Ambersons* trailer; and no one else in the Mercury Company had appeared as frequently and successfully on Welles's radio broadcasts.

For her portrayal of Aunt Fanny, Agnes Moorehead won the New York Critics award for best actress, an Oscar nomination, and the accolades of later film commentators. It is an intense performance, but on several occasions it goes a bit too far. Preview audiences at the time laughed at her emoting; younger viewers today, even film students, also laugh. As great an actress as she was, and her bit in *Kane* is the first of many remarkable performances, the histrionics Welles induced out of her for *Ambersons* do not, in my estimation, hold up well, although the scenes would probably be effective in a theatrical or radio production. She in fact had considerable radio experience, and her intense performances in the several broadcasts of *Sorry, Wrong Number* stand with the greatest in the history of the medium.

There are also occasions in the film when the script, which was Welles's responsibility, seems stilted. In part this resulted from his extraordinary fidelity to the novel. He later told Peter Bogdanovich, "If the movie of *Ambersons* has any quality, a great part of it is due to Tarkington. What doesn't come from the book is a careful imitation of his style."[20] But literary fidelity does not a great movie make. Welles's reverence for the Indiana novelist at times caused him to lose sight of the 1942 filmgoing public, who would probably have been more comfortable reading than hearing some of the lines. Tim Holt as the lead also posed problems for the audiences at the time.[21] But more recently his convincing portrayal of George is finally getting the recognition it deserves from film aficionados.

Sometimes, but not often, Welles's injection into film of what worked well in novels, theater, and radio strained rather than enhanced the medium. Nevertheless, no matter what form his original cut of *Ambersons* might have taken, audiences in 1942 would not have been appreciative. The United States had just entered the war. To moviegoers at the time (and attendance was up), *Ambersons* countered what was acceptable. The dark, brooding glimpse it presents of a forgettable period in history was neither uplifting, relevant, nor escapist. Once again, and the tendency would both plague and bless him, Welles tried to make a movie that would be of interest to the audience of his time but succeeded only in creating another one for posterity. The idea of a remake, which eventually yielded Alfonso Arau's highly publicized A & E television movie (2002), seemed to hold much promise. Inspired by Welles's original screenplay, it nevertheless took both idiosyncratic liberties with the story and made casting decisions that were not well received by critics or audiences—much to A & E's credit, some of this negative reaction was documented on their website.

As *Ambersons* was being completed, Welles began work on a third film he was obliged to do as part of his RKO contract. *Journey into Fear* (1943) began shooting on 6 January 1942, and although it was produced by and starred Welles, Norman Foster directed. It is an uninspired second-rate thriller, somewhat in the manner of early Hitchcock. By this time Orson's contract had been renegotiated and he lost final cut privileges on this film as well as *Ambersons*. If it were not enough to be working on two films at once, he still managed to perform his *Almanac* radio program for Lady Esther cosmetics and CBS. Through the entirety of his controversial career, he maintained an enormous capacity for work, as his collaborators attest, which contrasted markedly with his public image. Beneath the ballooning weight and reputation for debauchery lurked an uncompromising dedication.

Soon after shooting began on *Journey into Fear*, Welles's radio program yielded two of its most renowned broadcasts. The first, which aired on 12 January, was John Galsworthy's *The Apple Tree*, adapted by Roger Quayle Denny. It featured Geraldine Fitzgerald, who had performed in the Mercury stage production of *Heartbreak House* four years earlier. The second broadcast came one week later, *My Little Boy*, written and adapted by Carl Euwald and featuring Ruth Warrick from *Citizen Kane*.

The Apple Tree is haunting reminiscence. Welles plays Frank Aschers, who with his wife Stella visits England's West Country twenty-five years after they first met there. A particular apple tree triggers a flashback and the memory of someone else encountered there at the same time. Frank had made the original trip with a college friend, but an injured knee from football acted up and he is forced to recuperate at a farm while the friend returns to London. Frank soon becomes enthralled with the farmer's niece, Megan, a simple but lovely country girl. The feeling is more than mutual. She agrees to meet him under an apple tree one evening. They kiss in the moonlight and he promises to take her to London. She loves him, but expresses doubt that the relationship would work, since she is such an unsophisticated country lass. She also fearfully tells him of the ominous presence of mysterious spirits known as the Gypsy Bogles, who seek to thwart human happiness.

The next day Frank goes into town to shop and meets an old friend who is accompanied by his sister, Stella. They spend the day together, and the next, since the bank is closed and Frank cannot return to the farm. Stella is of his world and a perfect match; Megan, he surmises, might be a fantasy of the spring—how could she fit into his life in London? Reason wins out. After observing Megan longingly from a distance, Frank goes back to London and a year later marries Stella. When they return twenty-five years later, he seeks news of Megan, only to find out she drowned herself in a pond under the apple tree after he failed to return. In her hair was an apple blossom he had placed there.

The mood of fantasy and longing throughout the performance is beautifully buoyed both by Herrmann's music and by the faint sounds of birds in the distance. Much of Welles's narration and dialogue is barely above a whisper—neither theatrical nor cinematic, it is a style in tune with the possibilities of radio.

Welles introduces *My Little Boy*, which he previously performed on 8 August 1938, by claiming it had been the most popular and requested of the *Mercury* radio plays. This is a somewhat surprising claim, since that broadcast took place in only the second month of the show, at a time when it had barely found an audience.

The story is largely a first person narrative of a man observing the development of, and teaching life's lessons to, his young son. Among the issues broached are death—a discussion inspired by the demise of a local dog; honesty—the boy uses money earmarked for rolls to buy candy, but after a sympathetic lecture the father "allows" him to find some change and make the original purchase; and anti-Semitism—the boy joins others in beating up a Jewish playmate for no reason other than the victim's ethnicity, whereby the father lectures him on the contributions Jews have made to world history. All in all it is a pleasant enough if somewhat saccharine drama, which did little to stretch Welles's abilities as a radio actor.

After two more broadcasts of the show, Welles entered one of the most bizarre and frequently interpreted periods of his life. He had in mind several documentarylike films, one of them set in Mexico, and another dealing with the history of jazz, in which Duke Ellington was put on retainer. As these projects were being planned, Nelson Rockefeller, a large RKO shareholder and admirer of Orson's talent, arranged through the Good Neighbor Policy, the Office of Inter-American Affairs' propaganda voice, to have Welles sent to Brazil. Some of his docudrama ideas could be realized there, especially through the filming of events such as Carnival. It would also be a chance for him to do his part in the war effort, especially since he had assiduously avoided military service (his flat feet finally a blessing), by being a kind of goodwill ambassador and convincing Latin Americans to stay on the non-Axis side of the conflict.

The project, called *It's All True*, was funded by the American government for $300,000 against any loss RKO would incur. Welles, however, ran the bill close to the million mark. While in Brazil, he also tried unsuccessfully to supervise at a distance the editing of *Ambersons*. No feature film emerged from the Brazilian assignment. In the early 1990s, longtime Mercury assistant

Richard Wilson was instrumental in making much of the *It's All True* footage available as a documentary film that is now on video. Did Welles do the best he could under the terms of the project, or did he treat it in cavalier fashion while behaving like a prima donna party boy at the government and RKO's expense, as some have claimed? The weight of recent Welles scholarship, as well as thousands of feet of remarkable film, strongly suggest the former, as Jonathan Rosenbaum persuasively argues.[22]

Meanwhile, back at the RKO, Schaefer paid the price for his support of Welles. He was fired as production head by Charles Koerner.[23] After screening *Ambersons* and being told about the escalating tab in Brazil, Koerner became acutely Orsonphobic. He released *Ambersons* with virtually no publicity on what must remain as one of the oddest double-bills in movie history, alongside *Mexican Spitfire Sees a Ghost* starring Lupe Velez. On 1 July, with Welles still in Rio, Mercury Productions was ordered off the RKO lot and all contractual agreements with them were terminated. This action did leave Orson with an option to sue, which he refrained from doing. But Kaiser Koerner was not yet through with his nemesis. He came up with a motto for RKO to inform the world that hereafter the studio would be producing only Welles-free pictures: "Showmanship in place of genius."

Welles returned from South America at the end of August. His sojourn there, which started in Brazil, had developed into a goodwill tour of several other countries on behalf of the State Department. He was now without resources or facilities with which to continue his film career. But, as in the past, there was radio, now more than ever, given the war.

Almost immediately he was in demand as a guest performer. He did dramas, panel shows, variety shows, and literary readings. Of particular note are his appearances on NBC's *Information Please,* where he answered more questions than any other panelist and in friendly jest regularly one-upped the host, Clifton Fadiman (this talent would later come into play when, near the end of his life, he frequented the television talk-show circuit). In almost every instance he managed to get in a pitch on behalf of some aspect of the war effort. NBC's *Cavalcade of America* called on him several times. Two of his more notable appearances were *Juarez: Thunder from the Hills* on 28 September, and *Admiral of the Open Ocean* on Columbus Day, 12 October.

The *Juarez* production was adapted as a verse play by Arthur Miller from N. B. Baker's biography, *Juarez: Liberator of Mexico.* Using this resource and NBC's technical facilities, Welles was given carte blanche to weave his audio magic. The gist of the broadcast, which is heavily dependent on narration, compares Mexico's struggle for liberation with that of the United States. Juarez is portrayed in a very Lincolnesque manner. This kind of simplistic cultural-historical comparison would certainly raise the eyebrows of postcolonial theorists today, but there was a war on and ideologies could be easily reconfigured to serve it, as George Orwell would point out a few years later.

The drama makes the point that in the mid-nineteenth century the United States surreptitiously aided Mexico in resisting French designs on her. It is, of course, not mentioned that this occurred only a few years after the states drubbed Mexico in a quasi-imperialistic war prompted by western expansion. What is mentioned is that our southern neighbor has much to fear from the Axis powers and might again need our help—after Welles's several visits to Mexico one wonders whether he sensed that a number of its inhabitants felt it might be the other way around.

The subsequent Columbus Day broadcast aired throughout the Western Hemisphere. It was based on the book by Samuel Eliot Morison and adapted by Welles, Robert Meltzer, and Norris Houghton. The format alternates between Welles's first person narration and dramatization. From the outset, the narration has to contend with a fact-obsessed professor who says Columbus "was not the first." Orson admits knowing this but says Columbus is also the embodiment of all who went before. His cause is helped by a little girl's probing questions, along with a crewman reflecting on the meaning of the voyage. Before the program ends, however, the politics of the times must be served. Welles likens the talk of mutiny among Columbus's sailors to the views of those who believe that Hitler cannot be defeated, and urges that on this day we should all rediscover America and the democratic principles we are fighting for.

Welles's semiregular appearances on *Cavalcade of America* for NBC were augmented by a widely rebroadcast guest spot on that network's *Texaco Star Theatre* hosted by Fred Allen. This must have given CBS concern. After all, they did have some proprietary claim on his radio stardom. In November, they again offered him his own series, two in fact, both of which were geared to provide entertainment that would inspire the war effort: *Ceiling Unlimited*, which debuted on 9 November, and *Hello Americans*, launched six days later.

Ceiling was sponsored by the Lockheed-Vega Corporation, whose planes were integral to the war effort. Welles would be producer, writer, director, narrator, and occasional actor in a series of fifteen-minute inspirational stories about the men and women in the aviation industry, past and present. According to Frank Brady, Welles suggested the show be called *Ceiling Unlimited*, while Lockheed-Vega wanted its name in the title.[24] Orson held out until the eleventh hour and was victorious, which was fortunate, since it is hard to imagine a more evocative or appropriate title for the program.

An important collaborator and frequent writer for the show was playwright Arthur Miller, who Brady contends was invited by Welles to suggest a format for the show. Miller, for his part, after a few flattering remarks about Welles's abilities as a narrator—"Your voice is a format," he told him—let Orson conceptualize the kind of story presentation the show would follow.[25] To prepare for the broadcasts Welles visited various Lockheed-Vega plants, familiarized himself with their flagship plane, the B-17 Flying Fortress, and read widely on aviation, especially literary sources such as Antoine de Saint-Exupéry. It must also be remembered that back in the days of *Campbell Playhouse* he had acquired considerable flying experience as a passenger. He traversed the country weekly in all kinds of weather, gaining as intimate a knowledge of the DC-3 as any nonaviation industry person could have had.

The program ran until 1 February 1943. It featured a variety of topics as well as familiar guest stars from the Mercury Company. The debut broadcast was called *Flying Fortress* and, as one might expect, it is a paean to that assemblage of military hardware; Welles seems much impressed with its ability to take many hits and still make it home. On 30 November he narrated Saint-Exupéry's *Wind, Sand, and Stars*, with the then Lieutenant Burgess Meredith playing the lead. On the Pearl Harbor anniversary broadcast, an imagined scenario is created whereby Philip II of Spain, Napoleon, and Kaiser Wilhelm discuss Hitler's attempt to follow in their footsteps. Welles then urges us to always be vigilant regarding the designs of such men. A week later the featured story had to do with a hypothetical Axis secret agent at the Vega plant—shades of an episode of *The Shadow* called *Sabotage* (discussed in chapter 2) which aired on 16 January 1938.

The first broadcast of the New Year, 4 January, opened with Edward G. Robinson pinch-hitting for an indisposed Welles, and deals with the submarine patrol. The next two programs were scripted by John Steinbeck. In the first, we learn of a boy whose love of flying leads him to join the Lafayette Escadrille during World War I, followed by a career in barnstorming in the 1920s, and then his own airline business in the next decade. Much to his dismay he is later deemed too old to serve in World War II. In Steinbeck's second offering, a klutzy, shy boy becomes a competent flyer. He is shot down over the Pacific but fortunately is rescued. The story is narrated by former Mercury stalwart Betty Garde, as the mother.

Welles's final hosting of the series, on 1 February—he would be succeeded by Ronald Colman—takes place in an imagined future at La Guardia Airport. It portrays a harmonious world where passports are unnecessary. "This is a broadcast, but not a hoax," intones Orson, who certainly knew how to perpetrate the latter. Playing himself, he glimpses the new America that will be possible if we make a concerted effort to resolve the global conflict.

The *Hello Americans* series allowed him greater artistic and entertainment latitude. It was funded by Inter-American Affairs, who obviously forgave whatever indiscretions he committed in Brazil; after all, when he ran the tab over their ante, it went on RKO's bill. A variety show with a message would be one way of describing the program. That message was hemispheric unity. Latin America, especially the southern continent, was not immune to fascist contagion and Welles wanted to rally Americans to be as supportive a neighbor as possible for the democratic option. Once again, as he had done in the *Juarez* program on *Cavalcade of America*, he stressed, and often overstressed, a case for commonalities in the social and political history of the United States and her southern neighbors.

The first show was called *Brazil*, presented as if it were originating from Rio. Having been there for the abortive *It's All True* project, Welles's pronouncements about the country, her flora, fauna, architecture, and racial mixing were informed by experience. But most of all, this debut episode celebrated the samba, its infectious rhythms filling the airwaves. Even the explanation of the music is entertaining. Welles's and the listeners' (there was also a small studio audience) teacher was Brazilian bombshell Carmen Miranda. She gives a thoroughgoing description of the music's format and the instruments used to play it, replete with examples of how they each sound. Orson even sings along with her, in Portuguese, putting so much effort into articulating the words that he does not quite find the musical groove.

The following week's broadcast dealt with the Andes. Edmond O'Brien was the guest, and Welles welcomed Bernard Herrmann back to the musical fold. Herrmann did a credible job with the Latin numbers; after all, he *was* Ramon Raquello in *War of the Worlds*. Using sound effects in the inimitable Mercury tradition, the program dramatizes the Andes crossings of Pizarro and Bolívar. On 29 November, Haiti was the topic. The program highlights the rise and fall of the slave liberator turned tyrannical emperor, Jean Christophe. This was a subject with which Orson had some familiarity, having broached it in his Voodoo *Macbeth* in 1936.

The next three offerings in the series use the letters of the alphabet to cover various Latin American themes. On 6 December, the Andes, Bolívar, and Christophe are reprised and augmented with additional material. The letters D to R follow the week after. The experiment concluded on 20 December with S prompting a feature dramatization of the Caribbean slave revolt led by Abednego.

The 27 December program changed the tone somewhat. Called *The Bad Will Ambassador*, it deals with the phenomenon that would later become known as "the ugly American." In this case, he is an arrogant and ignorant tourist in Argentina at Christmas anxious to get home, but who must first learn that the world does not revolve around him. Illness subsequently prevented Welles from doing most of the January broadcasts. Nevertheless, he returned on the 31st to close out the series. The finale is a plea for pan-American unity in the face of Axis barbarism, using flashbacks from earlier episodes and all the radio pyrotechnics in the Mercury arsenal.

With the two CBS series now over, Welles was hoping to reenter motion pictures. In February, *Journey into Fear* was finally released. It impressed neither the critics nor the moviegoing public and quickly vanished from theaters. Other film opportunities would come, but most would be of the acting variety, with Orson's creative input limited to suggestions regarding his lines. Well, maybe not completely. Later that year he starred in the 20th Century-Fox production of *Jane Eyre*, in which he was also de facto producer. He claimed he could have received on-screen credit in this capacity but was uncomfortable with the notion of a lead actor being the producer *and* not the director as well.[26] Robert Stevenson directed, and although Welles has given him full credit, the film has a very Wellesian look to it reminiscent of the Gothic moments in *Kane* and *Ambersons*.

Before embarking on *Jane Eyre*, miscellaneous radio work was available, as per usual. In mid-March Welles began a five-week stint pinch-hitting for an indisposed Jack Benny. He had appeared on Benny's show before and not only had the chemistry between them been good, Welles seemed very comfortable with the show's format. It involved a live audience and outlandish skits, in which comedy could spill over into drama, the actors might comment directly to the audience about a scene (a tradition that goes back at least as far as Shakespeare), and it was the duty of the star to be parodied and insulted. With Benny it had been his skinflint persona and attempts at violin playing that had been mocked. Welles, in contrast, was set up to be a prima donna artiste, snobbish and full of himself. The audience loved it, but he began to be dismayed over how widespread this conception of him was becoming on the part of the public at large.

When Benny returned in April, Welles was the guest for another three weeks. Listening to the banter between them is a delight. The experience also fueled the idea that he could perhaps mount a similar show of his own. In the New Year he would reprise an invigorated version of *Almanac*, using a live audience.

A much lower-key form of radio had been tried and died on 3 September. Called *Reading Out Loud*, this CBS offering had Welles reading passages from literature, most notably John Donne's "Meditation XVII," "No Man Is an Island." Unfortunately, fifteen minutes of Welles's voice, minus a dramatic context involving sound effects and other actors, was more than audiences at the time were willing to appreciate. In any case, if it was razzle dazzle they wanted, he could and did accommodate them with a theatrical package called *The Mercury Wonder Show*, which ran that August and September.

It was an adult circus, with magic, skits, and audience interaction. Agnes Moorehead, Joseph Cotten, Rita Hayworth, and Marlene Dietrich were part of the act. Held in a large tent on Cahuenga Boulevard in Los Angeles, the two-and-a-half-hour show was geared to servicemen, who were allowed in free. The paying civilians in the audience—Welles called them "suckers"—included many Hollywood notables. Orson loved it. "It's one of our great works" he later told Peter Bogdanovich.[27] The energy he brought to the show is evident in a radio interview done during intermission of the 7 September performance. Perhaps some of his enthusiasm resulted from the fact that earlier that day he had married Rita Hayworth. A scaled-down *Wonder Show* would later tour various military installations. The famous act whereby he saws Marlene Dietrich in half can be seen in the film *Follow the Boys* (1944).

After several appearances on *Suspense* and *Inner Sanctum* that fall, he finally got another show of his own when the *Orson Welles Almanac* came back on the air for CBS in January 1944 with Mobil Oil as the sponsor. *Almanac* built on its previous incarnation, incorporated a few things learned from doing Jack Benny's show, and added a new wrinkle or two. It would air weekly until 19 July. Each program would open with a slice of homespun humor from the *Almanac*, and then feature a prominent guest star in a comedy skit. This would usually be followed by a musical interlude performed by Lud Gluskin and his orchestra, or an invited performer; finally, a dramatic reading usually closed out the half hour. There were also several

The Carnivalesque exterior of The Mercury Wonder Show. Courtesy of Lilly Library, Indiana University.

The magician with Marlene. Courtesy of Lilly Library, Indiana University.

regular characters: a secretary capable of wielding deft insults; an Orson Welles Swoon Club, consisting of three giggly girls who called him "Wellesy" or "Orsey"; the folksy Prudence Pratt, who dispensed household tips; and a Doctor Snake Oil who handled all matters medicinal.

The first installment aired on 26 January. Mercury regular Ray Collins did the announcing and Groucho Marx was the guest. When Orson tells him "This is my new show," Groucho responds with "You look used to me," then off they go insulting one another and lampooning Hollywood. Gluskin performs a Latin number and Orson closes the show by reading excerpts from Thomas Paine.

At times either the material or the guest did not click. The former was the case when Lionel Barrymore appeared on 2 February, and the latter occurred when an overly low-key Robert Benchley visited the show on 10 February. But, more often than not, *Almanac* was a successful mélange of outrageous comedy mixed with social satire. Several of the more notable programs are worth mentioning.

On 23 February Hollywood gossip columnist Hedda Hopper bantered with Welles about Tinseltown and stardom. It seems from their exchange

Part of the Orson Welles Show entourage—the *"Swoon Club?"* Courtesy of Lilly Library, Indiana University.

that Welles had a rival for the status of reigning male heartthrob, Frank Sinatra. Both here and in subsequent programs, he would make jokes about the skinniness of the renowned crooner; but he more than made up for these insults with reference to his own burgeoning corpulence. The musical guest on this program was the King Cole trio (they would appear again the following week and be more renowned in a few years as the Nat King Cole trio). Welles had a fondness for jazz and supported African American performers whenever he had the chance. During the sign-off he refers to Hedda as "Louella," her arch rival. She responds by noting how much she enjoys the way he says "obediently yours" at the end of his broadcasts, "because then I know it's over."

Lucille Ball was the guest on 8 March. Although she was not that well known at the time, Welles was quick to recognize her comedic talents. They joke about the Oscars as the Swoon Club comes by, calling him "master," while the secretary, trying to get his attention, refers to him as "Fatso." Orson and Lucy then do a radio drama spoof with a commercial that parodies Rice Krispies. During the skit a burglar endeavors to shoot Orson. Miss Ball intercedes by saying, "You can't shoot him. Don't you know the government is trying to save waste fat?" A sonorous reading of John Donne's "No Man Is an Island" ends the half hour.

The 15 March program featured Charles Laughton and is a gem. They trade insults, with Welles of course taking the brunt. "It has been said that Welles has a figure to brag about, " quips Laughton. "Yes," replies the secretary, "and what he brags about he drags about." Laughton later peruses Orson's tax form, to which the host replies, "I've worn myself down to a shadow." Both men then go to a reducing salon, and the manager, upon looking at them, waxes Shakespearean, "Too too solid flesh would melt." The musical guest is the great jazz trombonist Kid Ory. "This is," Welles rightly intones, "real jazz." The program ends with a scintillating rendition of the quarrel between Brutus (Welles) and Cassius (Laughton) in Shakespeare's *Julius Caesar*. Rarely has a radio variety show so perfectly married popular entertainment and high culture.

On the 5th, 12th, and 19th of July, *Almanac* featured part of the traveling *Mercury Wonder Show* and was broadcast from military installations in Los Angeles, Sacramento, and Long Beach. Lana Turner, Susan Hayward, and Ruth Terry were the guests, with the skits built around their charismatic glamour. Servicemen or no in the audience, Welles ended the second of these programs with a reading from Shakespeare's *Richard III*. The third program was the last in the series. Orson bid the audience adieu, said he hoped to return with a similar show next season, and, as

Auld Lang Syne played in the background, urged listeners to write in with their opinions.

During his stint on *Almanac*, Welles appeared as a guest on several other radio shows. On 2 April he did *The Chase and Sanborn Hour* with Edgar Bergen and Charlie McCarthy. This was the program that had been his prime competition during the heady days of *Mercury Theatre on the Air*. That May saw him do yeoman service in two productions on *Suspense*. His debut on the series had been on 2 September 1942 in *The Hitch Hiker*, which reprised his successful *Almanac* staging of the radio play (17 November 1941). In all he would make seven guest appearances on the show, which had a long and successful run from 1942 to 1962. His 4 May 1944 vehicle was a black comedy, *The Dark Tower*. On the 18th and 25th of the month it was a two-part production of *Donovan's Brain*, now considered a radio classic and one of Welles's most famous performances in a program other than his own.

The Dark Tower is a send-up of Welles himself written by Alexander Woollcott and George S. Kaufman. Welles plays a stage actor, Damon Wellington (note the name similarity), with an overinflated ego who has a penchant for being a ham. "You dare call me a ham?" he intones while casually tossing off lines from Shakespeare in casual conversation. He refers to Hollywood as a "cesspool of the arts" and, when his sister Jessica urges him to drink less and eat more, the response is, "Would you have me subsist entirely on food and reach the gargantuan proportions of Orson Welles? That ought to needle the 'Boy Wonder.'" At one point he even notes, "I have a pressing engagement with a pinup girl," an obvious reference to wife Rita Hayworth. Of Jessica, also an actor, he remarks, "She has talent but no genius"—the reverse of a phrase that had been occasionally applied to Welles himself.

As the story unfolds we find out that Jessica has been institutionalized after a bad marriage to a Svengali-like psychoanalyst, Stanley Vance (Hans Conried), who has supposedly been killed. Her release and recovery is thwarted by his unexpected return. Resuming power over her, he withholds her services from a new theatrical production, *The Dark Tower*, in the hopes of a payoff. Stanley is then visited by an investor, Max Hartsfeld. Greed soon turns to panic as Hartsfeld reveals himself to be Damon, in character, and proceeds to strangle Stanley in order to free Jessica from his control. He succeeds and the play eventually goes into production. What makes this scenario so remarkable is the character of Stanley, whose pan-European accent bears an uncanny resemblance, or is deliberately inflected, to sound like John Houseman. For insiders, the radio play must have seemed like Welles symbolically killing Houseman out of resentment for Houseman's role in managing the Mercury Theatre.

The now legendary *Donovan's Brain* broadcasts were produced and directed by William Spier and based on the novel by Curt Siodmak. Although no credit is given for the adaptation, it is possible that Welles provided significant input; he certainly had latitude in developing his characters. The story involves Doctor Patrick Corey (Welles) who tries to keep alive the brain of a wealthy industrialist, Donovan (Welles), mangled in a plane crash. The brain sporadically influences Corey's actions and speech, causing him to kill his son in the hope of using the body for Donovan. Eventually, Corey asserts enough of his own individuality and conscience to destroy the brain, killing himself in the process.

In playing dual roles, Welles's Doctor Corey speaks with British inflections, such as "Wait heah," reminiscent of Lamont Cranston as the Shadow; the portrayal also contains elements of the Professor Richard Pierson persona he donned during *War of the Worlds*. For the Donovan character, he employs a gruff assertive Eastern urban tone. Both voices, especially the doctor's, are used in the first person narration. The story is of course farfetched, but the production, especially the sound effects and music, makes it exciting radio fare.

On 5 June, he reprised *Jane Eyre* on *Lux Radio Theatre*, hosted by Cecil B. De Mille. Welles, having performed the story on radio under his own direction, and on film with some input regarding the performance, was here at the mercy of the format he did not like—a live audience and theatrical pretensions. Nevertheless, he played his Rochester, opposite Loretta Young's Jane, with great gusto. De Mille would call him into service for another *Lux* production on 11 September: an adaptation of the film *Break of Hearts* (1935), a melodrama scripted by Sarah Y. Mason and Victor Herman from the Lester Cohen story. Welles plays an arrogant symphony conductor, with Rita Hayworth as a talented but unknown composer (in the film the roles are played by Charles Boyer and Katherine Hepburn). This is maudlin fare, even for *Lux*. In the chitchat following the performance, Rita is asked how she copes with Orson, and replies, "He goes his own way and I go with him." Not for very much longer, however.

The remainder of the year, and the first few months of the next, found him busy on the political front making speeches on behalf of the war effort and Roosevelt's upcoming campaign. A number of these occasions were broadcast. Radio guest appearances were also frequent, and included *Inner Sanctum*, *The Kate Smith Show*, and *The Philco Radio Hall of Fame*, on which he adapted and performed with Bing Crosby on Christmas Eve a memorable version of Oscar Wilde's *The Happy Prince*.

Orson at RKO 185

At the CBS microphone during one of his wartime broadcasts. Courtesy of Lilly Library, Indiana University.

In March, CBS let him try yet another program format, a half-hour series called *This Is My Best*, sponsored by Cresta Blanca wine. Ostensibly, the show allowed him to reprise previous Mercury successes, or at least give the Mercury touch to similar untried material. However, since this was only a thirty-minute program with a studio audience, anything truly new and exciting would be impossible; it also featured one of the corniest commercial sign-ons in radio, whereby Cresta Blanca was spelled out to the accompaniment of chimes.

The debut broadcast on the 13th was a somewhat ambitious *Heart of Darkness*. It is actually a better production than the earlier *Mercury Theatre* rendering on 6 November 1938, and follows in part the screenplay Welles wrote for RKO before opting to do *Kane*. Welles plays both Marlow and Kurtz, affecting a sinister German accent for the latter. Kurtz's speeches echo overarching Nazi ambitions, which, as Orson's interpretation of the story implies, will be brought to heel by destiny. The acting and production values, especially during the journey upriver, are superb, but the merciless time limitation of the program makes the story seem sketchy and incomplete.

The following week, true to a formula often used when doing the *Campbell Playhouse*, comedy followed drama with *Miss Dilly Says No*. It featured Ann Sothern as Miss Dilly, Rita Hayworth as her friend, and Francis X. Bushman as her boss. Adapted by Robert Tallman from the Theodore Pratt novel, the story is about a producer's secretary, Miss Dilly, who has aspirations to sell her screenplays. After numerous rejections she finally sells one as a novel, and film studios begin clamoring for the rights—one is even called "Mercury" (!) and another "Tantamount." As it turns out she derives great pleasure turning down their offers and only wants to stay at her original job, with a raise. She gets one, along with a marriage proposal from her boss, which she duly accepts. This radio play is all-around great fun, with Rita hilarious as she affects a Brooklyn accent.

On 26 March *Lux Theatre* called upon Welles to once again do his "far, far better thing" in *A Tale of Two Cities*. The next day he was back at the helm of *This Is My Best* with a version of *Snow White and the Seven Dwarfs*, replete with musical numbers and dedicated to his daughter Christopher on her seventh birthday. Welles narrates, Jane Powell plays the lead, Jeanette Nolan, who would become Orson's Lady Macbeth in his 1948 film, is the evil queen, and John McIntire voices the mirror. It is an exhilarating and flawless presentation, and greatly benefits from not being interrupted by a Cresta Blanca commercial—a concession to young listeners?

The following week featured an effective thriller, *A Diamond as Big as the Ritz* by F. Scott Fitzgerald. The 10 April broadcast yielded an intense production of Robert Lewis Stevenson's *The Master of Ballantrae*, featuring Mercury notables Agnes Moorehead and Ray Collins. Set in Scotland, and opening with a curse, the story has remarkable similarities with *Macbeth*. Bret Wood makes a convincing case for connections back from *Ballantrae* to Welles's previous stagings of the Shakespeare play, both the Voodoo *Macbeth* in 1936 and the more traditional version recorded on disc by the Mercury Company in 1940.[28] He also shows how the production of *Ballantrae* foreshadows the film version of *Macbeth* Welles would direct and star in three years later.

On 17 April, an unannounced version of Milton Geiger's *I'll Not Go Back* was performed as a tribute to President Roosevelt following his death. Welles notes how the president wrote to him personally only six weeks earlier. He truly admired FDR and had become one of the strongest voices speaking on his behalf. The story, which chronicles the human journey, is mostly performed through Orson's narration. It seems heavy-handed as well as sentimental, and it is perhaps best appreciated in light of the moment for which it was intended.

The final *This Is My Best* program aired a week later, with the lighthearted *Anything Can Happen*, adapted by Robert Tallman from the novel by George and Helen Papashvily. At the conclusion Welles announces that the next week's production would be Richard Powell's *Don't Catch Me*, featuring Rita Hayworth. He had purchased the rights to it the previous November and, in collaboration with two of his *Almanac* writers, Bud Pearson and Les White, rendered it into a screenplay he was planning to flog. The sponsor apparently did not like the idea of such a self-serving radio broadcast and dropped the show. Arguments had already arisen regarding Orson's frequent last-minute script changes and belligerent attitude. It is also possible that low ratings influenced the termination.

Most of Welles's radio appearances from this point to the Japanese surrender in August were war related. On 7 May he spoke on a special V-E Day broadcast; on 17 July, he narrated *French Press: The Liberation of Paris*, an NBC special about underground radio in France during the occupation; and on 9 August he was a guest speaker on *Town Meeting of the Air* on NBC, the theme discussed being "What Does the British Election Mean to Us."

On 10 July he began the first of several appearances on *Columbia Presents Corwin*. If anyone had inherited the mantle of creative radio drama that began with Irving Reis and was imparted to Welles, it was Corwin. With the war ending in atomic fashion, Corwin scripted a tribute to the victors and the cooperative spirit that had wrought the ultimate weapon. Called *God and Uranium*, it aired in an abbreviated fifteen-minute format on 14 August, and in the full-length thirty-minute version on the 19th. It is a nonlinear pastiche of observations rather than a coherent story, with Orson's boosterism sounding a bit forced.

188 ～ Chapter Eight

Welles (front right) in the studio with Norman Corwin (glasses and mustache) for a wartime broadcast, probably supervised by Corwin. Courtesy of Lilly Library, Indiana University.

With the war now over, Welles wanted to reenter moviedom as a director. That summer he had started work on his most conventional film, *The Stranger*, for Sam Spiegel and Bill Goetz at International Pictures. He had worked with Goetz before, on *Jane Eyre*, and in the melodrama *Tomorrow Is Forever*, which would be released the following February. Welles brought *The Stranger* in on time and under budget—to show he could do it, he would later claim. Still, he felt he was whoring, which he was willing to do as an actor to fund his projects, but no longer as a director. Opportunities to work on his own terms, however, would be hard to come by and fraught with conflict when they did. The comeuppance he had endured at RKO would yield several sequels.

Going over some radio scripts at CBS, September 1945. Courtesy of MPTV.net.

CHAPTER NINE

The Last Radio Shows

> I'm only safe here as long as they can use me.
>
> —Harry Lime (Welles) in *The Third Man*

Welles was a gifted humorist. Biographers have rarely given the comedic side of his artistic persona much consideration. This is probably because all his films are dramas, although a few, such as *Chimes at Midnight* (where he plays Falstaff), contain comic moments. His forays into the funny in theater, especially with plays such as *Horse Eats Hat* and *The Shoemaker's Holiday*, were somewhat more extensive. However, it was on radio where Welles's humor was most prominent. The *Mercury* and *Campbell* programs featured some notable comedies, and his *Almanac* show ranks with the best of classic radio's laugh fests.

Following the war, this talent was evident in the guest appearances he did on various comedy and variety shows. Of note is his visit to the *Fred Allen Show* on 3 March 1946. Allen, like Jack Benny—with whom he had a long-running "staged" feud to drum up ratings—had a dry, self-deprecating wit. It seems that Welles was as comfortable working with him as he had been with Benny, probably because the humor was poignant, the host's ego capable of withstanding a lively performance by the guest, and the insults distributed with equanimity.[1] The program featured a hilarious spoof of *Les Misérables*, a sketch they had performed together several years earlier (18 October 1942) when the show was known by its sponsor's eponym, as the *Texaco Star Theatre*.

In the 1946 version, Allen introduces Welles by making reference to the recently completed film, *Tomorrow Is Forever*, in which Orson played one of his inimitable character parts. We are then led to believe that following its release, Welles had a crisis of confidence to the point where he could not even speak his name aloud! Allen tries to draw him out by suggesting they do segments from *Les Misérables*. This experiment in boosting a fallen ego turns out to be more than successful. Welles blares out his name incessantly as he exalts his role as producer, director, writer, and star. He then monopolizes the sketch to the point of thwarting at every turn the participation of an increasingly frustrated Allen.

If radio was a major forum for Welles's humor, it also did the same for his social and political views. On 16 September 1945, he began a weekly fifteen-minute spot on ABC called *Orson Welles Commentaries*, sponsored initially by Lear Radios. Editorializing over the air was not something new to him. He had done it on a semiregular basis during the war, but the topics broached were usually related to that struggle. His opinions had also been voiced in print. Several invited columns eventually led to a regular stint with the *New York Post*, starting in January 1945. Syndicated to several other major papers, the column at first bore the same title (this time with an apostrophe added) as his defunct radio show, *Orson Welles Almanac*. It was a mélange of politics, gossip, and trivia. After the death of FDR that April, he changed the title to *Orson Welles Today*, upped the intensity of the political quotient and, much to the editor's chagrin, minimized his lively discussions of Hollywood and Broadway. This shift, coupled with his legendary tardiness in meeting deadlines, led to the column's termination in June.

The early broadcasts of *Orson Welles Commentaries* were a grab bag in which his liberal advocacy of several causes was tempered by reminiscences and literary readings. However, during the postwar recovery, a diminution in global injustice made the domestic variety more obvious. Never was this more apparent than in a run of five programs, starting on 28 July 1946, in which he took up the cause of Isaac Woodard Jr., a decorated black war veteran who was beaten and blinded by police in South Carolina. Welles pursued his cause relentlessly, demanding justice. One hears in his voice a strident and dramatic tone—ham in the service of justice—that must have alienated some listeners, despite the merits of his argument.

Welles's publicizing of the incident, in which he eventually named the officer and demanded justice, managed to arouse many. It prompted national news coverage, a fund-raising campaign on behalf of the victim, and some unsettling hate mail still available for perusal in the Welles Collection at Indiana University's Lilly Library. The officer involved would eventually be given a one-year sentence, with Welles receiving a commendation from the NAACP for helping to bring it about.[2] Just prior to the Woodard editorials, Lear had dropped its sponsorship of *Commentaries* on the grounds of poor ratings. ABC kept it going, with Welles's salary dropping from $1,700 to $50 a week. Not surprisingly, on 6 October they finally pulled the plug, since the size of the audience did not match that of Welles's causes. ABC insisted the reasons were not political; Orson believed otherwise. Then, as now, controversy in network broadcasting can only be tolerated when it does not threaten ratings. There were also critics who felt Welles should confine his media appearances to entertainment only, as well as some who wished he would not appear at all.

At this point, what he wanted most was another film contract allowing him to direct. This would come in just over a year when Harry Cohn of Columbia (Rita Hayworth's boss) let him make *The Lady from Shanghai* (1948). In the meantime he secured a radio commitment more in tune with past efforts, the *Mercury Summer Theatre*, and undertook another "shirt-losing" theatrical venture, *Around the World*, based on Jules Verne's novel, *Around the World in 80 Days*. *Summer Theatre* was an attempt to reprise the spirit of his earlier *Mercury* broadcasts. The format was, unfortunately, more limited: thirty minutes, plus time for the sponsor, Pabst Blue Ribbon beer, versus the sixty minutes he had enjoyed in the earlier sustaining format. Nevertheless, he was back with CBS and enjoying the occasional presence of Bernard Herrmann, now well ensconced in Hollywood, thanks to Welles.

Not coincidentally, the program launched its season with *Around the World in 80 Days* on 7 June 1946. A week earlier, the stage version had opened at the Adelphi Theatre in New York, after chaotic previews in Boston, New Haven, and Philadelphia. The stage play was an ambitious mélange of drama, comedy, carnivalesque themes, musical numbers by Cole Porter, and film segments à la the ill-fated *Too Much Johnson* (1938). With most of the bugs ironed out for the New York run, critical reaction was largely positive and the house near capacity for the first several weeks. But interest eventually waned and Welles's debts mounted.

The radio version was conceived in part as a promotion for the play, which Welles laughingly plugs in his introduction. He adds that some Mercury aficionados might remember the company's earlier (23 October 1938) broadcast of the story. Drawing on nostalgia for those halcyon days, he goes on to point out that "Summer Theatre will reprise former Mercury favorites." But, by his own admission, this rendering of Verne's classic will be "minus many scenes" (an understatement). It is a less than stellar example of his radio art. The narration is too rapid and assumes a knowledge of the story on the part of listeners. Much of it is told through Cole Porter's musical numbers. Given Porter's astoundingly inventive work, however, this effort seems lame in comparison. One yearns for Mercury's nonmusical 1938 version, with its exhilarating sense of geography and fully developed characters.

Summer Theatre ran until 13 September. From the former *Mercury* repertoire Welles reprised *The Count of Monte Cristo* on 14 June, *Jane Eyre* on 28 June, *A Passenger to Bali* on 5 July, and *Hell on Ice* on 9 August. He also sourced two of his other series: from the Lady Esther incarnation of *Almanac* he resurrected *The Hitch Hiker* on 21 June and *The Apple Tree* on 6 September; and *Hello Americans* yielded *Abednego the Slave* on 16 August. The all-new productions were *The Search for Henri Le Fevre* on 12 July, *Life with Adam* on 19 July, *The Moat Farmer Murder* on 26 July, *Golden Honeymoon* on 2 August, *I'm a Fool/The Tell-Tale Heart* on 23 August, *Moby Dick* on 30 August, and *King Lear* on 13 September. Most of these broadcasts suffer from being reduced to a half-hour format in which Pabst Blue Ribbon had to have its due. Nevertheless, several merit more than a passing mention.

Life with Adam is one of the most unusual broadcasts of Welles's career, since he did not produce, direct, write, or star in it. The previous week, Canadian actor and writer Fletcher Markle had played him a recording of a Stage 46 production that had aired over CBC, Toronto. Andrew Allan was the producer of this radio play by Hugh Kemp, which mercilessly parodied Welles. Orson loved it and arranged for a rebroadcast in which Markle would play him as well as direct. Perhaps Welles wanted to show that if Hearst could not be a good sport about *Kane*, he would be in this radio send-up of his own life. In the introduction he refers to it as a "light hearted little libel . . . something less than a compliment, and something more than a comment." The plot centers on "boy wonder" Adam Barneycastle, who has attained success on Broadway and radio, but not in romance. After Barneycastle's performance in a broadcast of *A Tale of Two Cities*, he meets bored socialite Eve Holiday (Grace Mathews). There then ensues a series of encounters that recall the battle of the sexes often depicted on screen in screwball comedies: he makes a move and she resists with a barrage of insults. . . . She makes a move and he does likewise.

Few of the references are veiled. Barneycastle is portrayed as a multitalented prima donna, an arrogant, sexist, workaholic who even uses (as Welles once did) an ambulance to get to his various theater and radio commitments! An important stabilizing force in his life is his devoted female manager, Jenkins (Mercury's Betty Garde). Her organizational abilities recall the role that John Houseman once played in keeping the Mercury Company afloat. In a poignant exchange, Jenkins admits that she loves Barneycastle and will never stop being supportive, but she has no romantic illusions. He continues his pursuit of Eve, along with his hesitation to commit to her. Eventually, after a torrent of insults, Adam and Eve agree to attempt a relationship.

"WHEW!" says Welles at the close of the performance. Rightly so. Markle, who would eventually go on to a distinguished career on Canadian radio and television, gives an extraordinary performance. Everything rings true. At times it is hard to believe we are not hearing the voice of Welles.[3] Although the romance in the radio play was fictitious, a real one did emerge from it. Markle would go on to marry Mercedes McCambridge, whom he met as a result of a bit part she had in the production; he would also work for Welles again, as a writer on several projects, including *The Lady from Shanghai*.[4]

The following week, *The Moat Farm Murder* took radio entertainment one hundred and eighty degrees. The story is based on confessional transcripts of a forty-one-year-old English murder case. Norman Corwin, whom Welles had worked with before (*We Hold These Truths* on 15 December 1941, *God and Uranium* on 14 and 21 August 1945, and the version of *Jane Eyre* that aired during the first month of *Summer Theatre*), did the adaptation, adding fictional moments of dialogue to impart continuity. Welles opens the production by suggesting that it might be deemed a "radio documentary"—today we might prefer the term *docudrama*. In this sense it can be seen as having a kinship with the *Mercury* production of *Hell on Ice* (9 October 1938), which was based on actual transcripts. Like that production, it features an eerie and effective score by Bernard Herrmann. In it we hear sonorities that he would later use in his films with Alfred Hitchcock, such as *Vertigo* (1958) and *Psycho* (1960).

The story is simple but unsettling. Welles plays Dougal, who shares a farm owned by a spinster, Cecile Holland (Mercedes McCambridge), whom he falsely believes has hidden a substantial amount of money in the house. They quarrel often, then reconcile, until Dougal decides that it would be best for him to do away with her. He shoots her one night and buries the body in a ditch. Haunted by guilt, he begins to have sleepwalking episodes that take him to the site of the crime. Eventually, he confesses and is hanged. If the story is sparse, the range of emotions and details of the incident that Welles recounts in the confessional are not. Most disturbing is the killer's uncertainty that his victim is dead, which is followed by a moment of necrophilia when he affectionately strokes the corpse. The radio play is largely done as a monologue and stands as one of Welles's greatest on-air performances.

His *Moby Dick* broadcast a month later, although a minimal production, is notable because Welles reading Melville is nothing less than mesmerizing—a near-perfect blend of voice and text. A decade later (1955) he would create an ingenious stage version called *Moby Dick: Rehearsed*. His voice also seems a perfect match for one of Shakespeare's richest characters, King Lear. With the *Summer Theatre* program ending, Welles decided to close it with this bit of classic drama, although his *Lear* is ostensibly a highlights package— "scenes from *Lear*," he calls it in his introduction. As per all the *Mercury* broadcasts, the program opens with the moving strains of Tchaikovsky's Piano Concerto in B Flat Minor, a tradition that began on 11 July 1938 and would end here. Fittingly, three of the company's players are present who were there during its first radio run: Agnes Moorehead, Edgar Barrier, and the redoubtable William Alland. One does wonder if Welles's choice of *Lear*, with its agonizing end of the king, his daughters, and his world, possibly held symbolic resonance in terms of the end of a kingdom on the air he had ruled for almost a decade.

How ironic also that one of Shakespeare's most complex plays and a sterling example of "high art" in a popular medium should be sandwiched between speeches of a far different order that also incorporate alliteration, to champion "blended, splendid, Pabst Blue Ribbon Beer." The *Lear* production is made easier (but not easy) to follow through a voice-over (Barrier's?) to set scenes and indicate transitions. Sound effects are minimal—thunder and rain—with the orchestra's role limited to fanfares at the outset of several scenes. Welles, however, seems in rare form as he pounds out his lines with clarity and emotion. He would get a chance to reprise the role in a 1953 television production for a sustaining program, *Omnibus*, on CBS. Unlike the radio version, however, this *Lear* was not staged by Welles, but by Peter Brook. Given the constraints of live television, it was an impressive production, as a kinescope of the broadcast reveals. The sets (especially the tower) and effects are compelling. But despite adroit camera work, the miking is uneven in several scenes.

Following the end of the radio play, the sign-off is done quickly and with a taint of sadness. Welles thanks the sponsor for a "grand summer" and urges listeners to "look for us again." He bids us adieu by remaining, "as always, obediently yours."

Welles would not command another series until 1951, when without the Mercury Company, he was given the opportunity to do the *Adventures of Harry Lime*, following the success of *The Third Man* and his residency in Europe. However, the immediate postwar years did grant him several filmmaking opportunities, although not always on his own terms. In 1946 *The Stranger* was released. It is a well-made thriller in which Welles plays Franz Kindler/Charles Rankin, an ex-Nazi now ensconced as a teacher in a small New England town and married to a dutiful wife (Loretta Young). Edward G.

Robinson plays the Nazi hunter seeking to find and expose him. The film includes the first clips of Holocaust footage used in a motion picture and has garnered increasing respect in recent years. Nevertheless, Welles would eventually go on to disdain, if not disown the work—claiming he did it to show that he could bring in a production on time and under budget. Such would not be the case with *The Lady from Shanghai*.

Shooting for the picture began a month after the end of *Summer Theatre*. Welles would use his earnings as director, writer, and star to pay off debts incurred in mounting his *Around the World* theatrical venture. The studio was Columbia, headed by Harry Cohn. He was an outspoken, self-consciously vulgar mogul whose honesty Welles appreciated, to a point. Cohn wound up having second thoughts about ceding so much control of the film to Welles. But the studio ultimately held the trump card: final cut. The slash and reshoot campaign Cohn ordered during postproduction was not as severe as the strafing of *Ambersons* that Charles Koerner had ordered at RKO. It did, nevertheless, diminish the quality of the film—by twenty percent, according to Welles's estimate.[5] The original rough cut was 155 minutes; the released version 86 minutes. Close-ups were added, especially of Rita Hayworth. Schmaltz music was inserted over the source music in several places and also put into scenes where no music was intended.

The film is an overly ambitious noir thriller featuring Rita as the femme fatale. The complex plot led Harry Cohn to offer $1,000 to anyone who could explain it to him. There were no takers. No less an authority on Welles than Joseph McBride confesses that it took him eight screenings to figure out the story.[6] Needless to say, a synopsis is not attempted here, save to mention that it involves a con game, seduction, and betrayal. Rita, in the classic noir tradition, plays the archetypal "double-crossing dame." By cutting her long red hair and dyeing it blonde for the part, Welles shocked and annoyed many, including Cohn and gossip columnist Louella Parsons. However, this new role for her necessitated a new look, and the makeover helps give her character the necessary edge. She performs superbly, a fact overlooked by many at the time. Still married to Welles, the couple were separated and on their way to divorce when the project came up. A few romantic sparks were rekindled during the shooting, but they soon fizzled.

Not surprisingly, the film lost money, lots of it. The release was delayed for over a year. Originally budgeted as an A picture, it wound up being treated by the studio as a B and consigned to the tail end of double bills. The film has been viewed as a laboratory for Welles's unconventional stylistics and is loaded with more unusual shots and symbolism than most of his films. He later insisted that he was merely trying to tell the story (based on Sherwood

King's novel, *If I Die Before I Wake*) as he saw it. What others viewed as celluloid pyrotechnics, he felt were appropriate devices to further the narrative.[7] The most celebrated scene in the film, and a landmark one in the history of cinema, is the final shootout in the Hall of Mirrors. Images distort, regress, and then deconstruct in a kaleidoscope of broken glass. When the shards clear, Rita lies fatally wounded.

This visual tour de force would seem to be far removed from the world of radio drama that Welles once inhabited. But only because of studio meddling. He originally intended the scene to play without music: gunshots and glass only, as he most likely would have staged it on radio. Crashing chords were subsequently added. He also complained about several other scenes where, when music was inserted, it overrode the evocative sonority of the locations. Such intrusions were never part of his work with Bernard Herrmann in radio and film. In those collaborations, music always complemented, never interfered or competed with location sounds.

Auditory concerns also characterize several scenes that remain as intended. Welles cast Everett Sloane, who plays a shady lawyer, as a cripple. This, he later told Peter Bogdanovich, was to capitalize on Sloane's radio background. By keeping the actor's physical movements within a narrow range, Sloane might, Welles believed, more effectively voice his role.[8] There were several other points in the film when Welles wanted his actors to deliver their lines convincingly, without having to worry about how they were supposed to appear. He achieved the desired result by using a new technology: the magnetic tape recorder. The actor's speeches were prerecorded and later dubbed in during postproduction. Rita's death scene finale is an example. Her diction is strong, clear, and emotionally powerful, despite the fact that she has been shot. The scene does seem a bit unnatural, almost operatic, but is nonetheless effective—and quite antithetical to the way it would be played according to the canons of method acting.

While *The Lady from Shanghai* was awaiting release, Welles went to work on a film version of *Macbeth* (1948) for Republic Pictures. Part of the preparation entailed staging the play in Salt Lake City, Utah, under the auspices of the Utah Centennial Commission and University Theatre, along with the American National Theatre and Academy. The head of Republic, Herbert Yates, did not know Macbeth from Mack Brown, although he did know the latter fairly well. Along with Roy Rogers and Gene Autry, Johnny Mack Brown was part of Republic's stable of actors featured in the studio's specialty: low-budget westerns. Somehow, Yates was persuaded that *Macbeth*'s modest budget of just under $900,000 (although not so modest by Republic standards) was reasonable enough for such a project. He approved the film, surmising that even if it did little more than break even, it would nonetheless add cachet to the studio.

Welles turned the twenty-one days of shooting into another film for posterity rather than for its time. Shakespeare had always been a hard sell for American moviegoers. To make matters worse, Orson's reshuffling and editing of the text alienated the highbrows and educators who might have otherwise championed the project. Their darling would remain Laurence Olivier, whose *Henry V* (1944) and *Hamlet* (1948) were regarded as the standard bearers of bardic cinema.[9] Welles's film is something else entirely—Bard noir. Not surprisingly, the film, which James Naremore has suggested might be the "purest example of expressionism in the American cinema,"[10] is now earning the respect denied it during Welles's lifetime. He had of course done noteworthy *Macbeth* productions before: the all-black voodoo version in 1936, and the radio adaptation for the CBS *Columbia Workshop* a year later. The film version recalls the mysticism of the Harlem production, but with Celtic paganism rather than voodoo ritual facing off against Christianity.

Welles's radio experience is also evident in the film. Several of the actors had previously worked with him over the airwaves: Jeanette Nolan (Lady Macbeth) was a *March of Time* alumnus; and from the old Mercury Company he cast Edgar Barrier (Banquo), Erskine Sanford (Duncan), and William Alland (second murderer). Welles also wanted Bernard Herrmann to do the music, which is somewhat ironic in that in the radio *Macbeth* he kept Benny's orchestration at bay in favor of a bagpiper, much to the annoyance of the composer. Had Herrmann been available, he no doubt would have provided an inspired score. Welles used instead Jacques Ibert, whom he had recruited in Europe. Ibert's music is more than adequate, and at times even seems laced with Herrmannesque touches.

Another possible radio (and theater) influence, although Welles claimed the reason for the technique was budgetary, is the use of long takes (with few, if any retakes) similar to those we find in *Kane* and *Ambersons*. Finally, as might be expected, the audio portion of the film is a tour de force. Welles creates a soundscape that complements the dark and exotic sets—sets that recall those of 1930s horror films. This *Macbeth* would also work splendidly as a radio play. The emotional context of the story is greatly enhanced by the sound of wind, ravens, pigs, an unforgettable owl, thunder, and the relentless beating of a drum.

To speed up production and help stay under budget, Welles recorded the dialogue on disk and had the actors mouth their lines during the shoot. He made this a bit easier by having lines, such as soliloquies that are normally spoken out loud when an actor is alone, be uttered as thoughts we overhear as we see the contemplative face of the actor in question. The whole experiment was partly frustrated when the studio insisted that the Scottish accents Welles employed were inappropriate for American audiences. Much to Welles's chagrin, they insisted that a more familiar English dialogue be substituted, and that 21 minutes be cut from the running time of 107 minutes. Fortunately, a restored version of the original cut—the dialogue is clear and effective—became available on video in 1992.

After the *Macbeth* filming, Welles went to Europe, partly as a break, partly to commiserate with British producer Alexander Korda. They discussed the possibility of collaborating on several projects, particularly a version of *Cyrano de Bergerac* with Welles in the lead. When funding fell through, the project was soon picked up by Hollywood, with José Ferrer starring in the 1950 film. Eventually Welles did get a chance to act in a European production when he was offered the part of Cagliostro, and the chance to direct several scenes, in Gregory Ratoff's *Black Magic* (1949). Given Welles's background as a stage magician and interpreter of exotic characters, Cagliostro—a Svengali-like eighteenth-century conjurer and charlatan—seems a role to which he was ideally suited. Yet, despite fine production values, the film falters because of its lead. Welles seems to have added an extra slice of ham to an already overdrawn character. The near-comic result seems unintended. He would fare better as Cesare Borgia in Henry King's version of *The Prince of Foxes* (1950), which was shot in Italy.

Through his work on these films, and the earlier meetings with Korda, Welles had established a European beachhead. The creative possibilities there appealed to him, but funding was still a scramble. Still, this was preferable to Hollywood, where he was shut out on both fronts. He soon began planning another Shakespeare film, *Othello* (1952; 1955 in the United States), which would wind up as a much interrupted, multiyear project, with unintended location and wardrobe changes. What the film lacks in continuity, it more than makes up for in originality and cinematographic brilliance. To secure funding he continued acting in other people's films. Eventually, he was offered what would become his most famous role—until the reappreciation of *Kane* over the past several decades.

When Korda asked Welles to play Harry Lime in *The Third Man* (1949), it came in the form of a contract proposal Welles both accepted and declined. He acquiesced to a $100,000 acting fee, but claimed he turned down an alternate arrangement that would have ceded to him 20 percent of the profits.[11] Big mistake as it turned out. Never one to know, or even surmise, how the public would react to a film (he made more of an effort when it came to theater), he could not have foreseen what would transpire: that *The Third*

Man would go on to become the biggest grossing European film up to that time. It could have made him a millionaire. Instead it raised his acting profile another notch. Over the next several decades he would never be wanting for work in front of the camera, work that bequeathed to him the funds needed to be behind it as well.

The idea to make the film was Korda's. The story and script came from Graham Greene, with direction by Sir Carol Reed. Yet it is often regarded as a Welles picture. He did script most of his character and suggest how several scenes should be shot. The film also reunited him with Joseph Cotten, who had played Jed Leland in *Kane*. Their interplay as Harry Lime and Holly Martins recalls the friendship that ended in estrangement between their characters in the earlier film. The overall look of *The Third Man*, with its frequent oblique camera angles, although not Welles's doing, seems, nevertheless, to have been influenced by *Kane* and *Ambersons*.

The Third Man also features a memorable chase through the sewers of Vienna. It recalls the Paris sequence in *Les Misérables* that Welles staged in the 1937 radio play. In the film version of the chase there are moments where we, along with the characters, have to get our bearings through what we can hear rather than see. The rest of the movie is full of evocative sounds but devoid of an orchestral score. Reed, along with Welles, agreed that Anton Karas's zither should provide the only music. It was a daring decision, with extraordinary results.

The success of *The Third Man*, along with the rich auditory world it created, made reprising the character of Harry Lime, along with the atmosphere of the film, a good bet for radio. But the series was two years away, and in the meantime there was a film to complete. *Othello* reunited him with Hilton Edwards, Micheál MacLiammóir, and Joseph Cotten. It became a cinematic odyssey that took Welles from Italy, where he was building a home base, to Morocco and back again . . . and again. Because of the recurring shortfall of funds, and difficulty getting everyone together at one time and in one place, the project suffered regularly from *cinema interruptus*. This was frustrating, but it did allow Welles to pursue other projects. In June 1950, he launched a quirky theatrical venture called *The Blessed and the Damned*, which consisted of two plays running back to back that he wrote himself: *The Unthinking Lobster*, "a Hollywood fable," and *Time Runs*.

The lobster in *Lobster* is the Hollywood studio system. The play satirizes the production of a religious epic—all the rage at the time—not unlike *The Song of Bernadette* (1943). The director within the play brings in cripples who are in turn cured by a secretary turned actress. Tinseltown becomes a new Lourdes, with pieces of MGM celluloid sold as sacred relics. All this diminishes the business of filmmaking and the accompanying revenues, until an archangel comes to Earth to commiserate with the moguls. He promises to suspend the miracles if they refrain from making religious pictures. Although written by Welles, the play bears a spiritual kinship to the 15 January 1939 *Campbell Playhouse* production of *I Lost My Girlish Laughter*. Both works lampoon the studio system as artless and market driven. *Lobster* provides a more cutting critique, since *Girlish Laughter* was, for Welles at the time, the perception of a Hollywood he had yet to experience. After he had run Tinseltown's gauntlet, *Lobster* was a revenge gesture.

The second play in the double bill, *Time Runs*, explicitly declared its source of inspiration. Based on Marlowe's *The Tragical History of Dr. Faustus*, which Welles had staged in 1937, *Time Runs* updates the story to a modern context and featured Hilton Edwards as Mephistopheles. It also contained a touch of exotica. Eartha Kitt played Helen, and her inimitable breathy voice purred several songs to the accompaniment of Duke Ellington's orchestration. The two-play production opened in Paris to mostly positive reviews. Although program notes in French helped non-English speaking members of the audience, the run there lasted only one month. Welles subsequently took parts of the work, along with his magic act, to Germany in a package called *An Evening with Orson Welles*. Needless to say, this endeavor did not provide him with the kind of funding he needed to sustain *Othello*. But as had happened so often in the past, radio income would come to the rescue—for one last time—in the form of two series over the next year. The first required declawing the character of Harry Lime.

The astonishing box office success of *The Third Man*, were it to happen today, might lead to a sequel or two or three—perhaps even a television series. Interestingly enough, it did come to the small screen in a 1959–1962 program with Michael Rennie in the role Welles made famous. This was an unusual British-American co-production. The television version of *The Third Man*, although inspired by events in the film, based its format on the radio series, with Rennie's Lime, although still tainted with a shady past, a touch more concerned with justice than we find in Welles's radio portrayal of the character.

Always on the lookout for financially rewarding projects that would not compromise his status as auteur-director, Welles's attitude toward reprising Harry Lime for radio would hover between blasé and mildly interested. When he listened to the producer pitch the series, it was perhaps with visions of what must be done next with *Othello* dancing in his head. That producer was Harry Alan Towers, who worked for the BBC during the war. Just after it, at the age of twenty-five, he became an independent producer. Much of what we know about *The Adventures of Harry Lime* comes from a remarkable Ph.D. dissertation by Frank Tavares—a rare treatise on the radio side of Welles's many artistic accomplishments—for which he was able to interview Towers in 1975.[12]

When Towers approached Graham Greene about doing an adaptation of his story for radio, he asked whether it was Greene or the film's producer, Alexander Korda, who owned the character of Harry Lime. As it turned out Korda only held rights to the screenplay. Lime belonged to Greene and he was willing to sell the character. Towers was delighted. Welles was almost as easy to secure. Towers found him in Rome trying to raise money for *Othello*. Welles somewhat flippantly wondered how a radio series could be made about someone who had already died in his film incarnation. Tower's solution—today we might call it a prequel—is explained in the program's opening sequence. Following a series of crashing orchestral chords, an announcer intones, "Presenting Orson Welles as the Third Man." We then hear the familiar zither music from the film, followed by a gunshot, which Welles's familiar voice tells us

> was the shot that killed Harry Lime. He died in a sewer beneath Vienna, as those of you know who saw the movie *The Third Man*. Yes, that was the end of Harry Lime. But it was not the beginning. Harry Lime had many lives, and I can recount all of them. How do I know? It's very simple. Because my name is Harry Lime.

With Welles inked for the series all that remained was to secure the services of Anton Karas, whose zither gave the film an unforgettable musical coloring. When he came on board, his theme, and innumerable variations on it, were prerecorded for subsequent use. With the *Lime* now ready for production, Towers discovered that Korda was livid over what he believed was a pilfering of his cinematic legacy. He was placated with a percentage.[13] Graham Greene retained script approval.

The show's format was a first for Welles. It was not done as a series of live network broadcasts but recorded on the relatively new medium of magnetic tape and syndicated globally. This made production similar to filming a movie, in that retakes were possible, as was recording parts of an episode out of sequence and doing postproduction edits. It also resembled a Welles film shoot because not all the programs were done at Tower's primary venue, the International Broadcast Company in London. With Welles often on the move, Rome and Paris occasionally served as production venues. Fifty-two half-hour episodes resulted. Sixteen were purchased for regular broadcast in two installments by the BBC on their *Light Programme*. The first aired from 3 August to 21 September 1951; the second from 3 July to 21 August 1952. Once again, as with *Les Misérables* in 1937, and *First Person Singular* (the original name for *Mercury Theatre on the Air*) in 1938, a Welles series was used as a summer replacement. Popular in British Commonwealth countries, it suffered from uneven distribution and a lukewarm reception in the United States, where it was called *The Third Man: The Lives of Harry Lime*.

Several episodes were usually recorded in one session. More often than not Welles would pass up a morning rehearsal only to arrive energized in the afternoon and able to continue until well past midnight with a by-then exhausted crew.[14] This scenario recalls his halcyon days with *Mercury*. And, as with *Mercury*, he enjoyed the support of a solid stable of actors throughout the series, which included Robert Arden, Agnes Bernelle, Sebastian Cabot, Dino Galvani, Ferdy Mayne, Betty McDowell, Irene Prador, Robert Rietti, and Dana Wynter. Sometimes the show's writers were credited, occasionally not. Welles himself was responsible for at least ten scripts and fine-tuned all the others. A regular (and usually uncredited) collaborator was Ernest Borneman, who had worked with him on a never-completed screenplay for *Ulysses* (Homer's version). Because of the way the show was syndicated globally, slightly different versions (the most common alteration being length—often a reduction to accommodate commercials) and even different titles for the same program abound. It is hoped that in the near future the complex history of the series will be more fully sorted out.

The show's association with the film doubtlessly contributed to its success. However, there was a fundamental problem to be surmounted even when taking the character back in time prior to the events depicted in the film. Lime was a despicable villain in the movie. He needed a makeover for radio, one that would appeal to postwar audiences. Rather than erasing completely his dark side, the radio version turns him into a bon vivant adventurer; not quite a scoundrel, but someone who is concerned with justice only when it appears there is something in it for him. Part of Lime's roguish trickster persona—he loves confronting and at times humiliating his criminal adversaries—seems to bear a touch of Welles's former incarnation as the Shadow.

The stories are often formulaic and the situations implausible. What drives and makes engaging the episodes is Welles's narration, which sets the context for each story and explains transitions. His dialogue is always fast-paced and laced with humor and wisecracks. One of my favorite lines occurs at the end of program #21, *It's a Knockout*. After Lime has been stiffed by his girlfriend Jenny, who absconds with the take from a rigged boxing match that Lime arranged to swindle a wealthy businessman, he decides not to pay his collaborators. They should have known, he says unapologetically in an aside, "that Lime doesn't pay."

The series also gave Welles the chance to once again showcase his talents as a writer of original radio plays. The results are uneven: sometimes better than what the regular coterie of writers yielded, occasionally, not as good. Several are worth assessing. Program #1, *Too Many Crooks*, has Lime going to Budapest at the behest of a bank manager who wants to hire him to catch thieves planning to rob the bank before they actually do the job. The robbery plan involves a bank employee, a flower shop girl, and an underground tunnel from her shop to the bank. Lime soon finds out that the manager is actually planning to rob his own bank and pin the rap on his employee. He is being helped, and duped, by the girl, whom he hopes will run away with him afterward. Double- and triple-cross result. The manager finds that the money he hid in the filing cabinet is nothing but strips of newspaper, while the actual take is in the hands of the girl, whose accomplices are locked in the tunnel. Everyone involved is eventually caught. Lime is found guilty of no crime and still manages to collect the money originally promised him by the manager.

Program #4, A *Ticket to Tangier*, is somewhat less baroque. Lime, now in Paris—exotic global locales were de rigeur for the series—is summoned through a classified ad. He has to identify himself by whistling the *Third Man* theme. A beautiful and mysterious woman then picks him up and they go to a castle in Tangier. She turns out to be a baroness and the wife of a Corsican gangster whom she killed, and now she wants Lime to use his contacts to help her sell her ex's stash of heroin on the black market. When her husband's former partner shows up, she shoots him. With the police on the way, the baroness and Lime make a run for it. The woman is caught but Lime escapes with the heroin. He dumps it into the sea, substitutes sugar in the packages, and sells it as the real thing to the Corsican's contacts in France. (In the movie, a Lime drug switcheroo involves penicillin earmarked for children, with dire consequences.)

Perhaps the most notable program in the series is #37, *Man of Mystery*, in that it provided the outline for a later Welles film: *Mr. Arkadin* (1955), sometimes referred to as *Confidential Report*. In the radio version, Arkadian (note the different spelling), claiming to have amnesia, hires Lime to find out about his past. Not surprisingly, he has a beautiful daughter who enthralls Lime and later tells him that her father is not an amnesiac after all. Lime eventually discovers that Arkadian has a criminal past that the man wants to cover up by eliminating those who know too much about it as soon as he finds out who and where they are, information Lime will unwittingly provide. Soon realizing that knowledge in this instance is not only power, it might be his own death sentence, Lime goes on the lam. He eventually contacts the daughter and tells her about her father's past, something she was unaware of. Arkadian subsequently commits suicide by jumping out of a plane. The show was recorded in Paris with Frédérick O'Brady in the role of Arkadian. Welles would play Arkadin in the movie, with Robert Arden (a *Lime* radio alumnus) in the role of the adventurer/investigator Guy Van Stratten.

Welles also scripted the series' last program, #52, *Greek Meets Greek*. One of the weakest entries, it involves Lime being quarantined in his hotel with measles. A beautiful woman seeks to hide in his room. She convinces him her fears are well founded by showing him a murdered corpse in her own room. The act, she claims, was perpetrated by a jealous suitor. When shots are fired through his window, Lime suspects the scenario might be a bit more complex. Indeed it is. The woman turns out to be a countess, and an arms smuggler of an unusual ilk. She abhors violence so is selling guns with packages of ammunition that will not work in them. The ruse recalls the sugar for heroin switch in program #4.

Certain elements recur throughout the series. Lime clearly has a criminal past. Smuggling is mentioned often. His favorite prey are criminals and shady businessmen. Since their original take is usually the result of nefarious activities, in trying to get his hands on it, Lime is therefore somewhat below the law. Occasionally, he is the one duped, usually by a beautiful woman—a Lime weakness. They are, however, usually caught. These deceitful lovelies often bear an aristocratic lineage: a countess here, a baroness there.

Despite the convenience of taping, some of the programs are poorly structured, with the sound effects less ambitious than they were in the *Mercury* productions. The acting, however, is uniformly good. If the writing seems uninspired at times, it must be remembered that the *Lime* scripts are original radio plays, not adaptations of carefully hewn literary works, as was the case with *Mercury*. Nevertheless, I feel that one of the best *Lime* broadcasts, program #10, *Operation Music Box*, is as fine an original story idea and script as Welles ever created for the airwaves. It goes as follows.

In London, Lime meets an American, Myrna Chafic, in an antique shop. She is trying to find a music box the store acquired the previous year. The shopkeeper had purchased four and sold three. She buys the remaining one and smashes it with a hammer—it is an amusing scene, especially due to the sound of a dying music box. Bribing the shopkeeper, she then secures the addresses of the three other music box purchasers. Lime is incredulous at these goings-on and follows the woman. He manages to find out that a year earlier she was given a music box that was eventually sold. Only recently did she learn that it contained a cache of jewels bequeathed to her by a supposed uncle. After subtly stealing her address list, Lime heads to one of the names on it, buys the box, and smashes it. No jewels.

The woman and Lime arrive simultaneously at the home of the next person on the list. A bidding war ensues over the music box. The owner could not care less for music boxes per se but will not sell. It seems he bears a distant relationship to the Russian monarch whose image is depicted on the box. That evening Lime decides to play cat burglar. He snatches this box, which promptly starts to play its tune, waking the man and bringing the police. Lime tries to play innocent with an officer who stops him outside the house, but the box begins to play again and the chase is on. It is a hilarious scenario. Somehow, he gets away, eluding the police but not Myrna. Together they smash the box. Empty again.

They finally track down the last person on the list, only to find out that he so hated the tune the box played that he donated it to a foundling home. Harry and Myrna rush there, only to find a new building being dedicated. They learn this was made possible through the sale of jewels discovered when a boy accidentally dropped the box, which was later repaired. They look at it, open the lid, and hear the awful tune that led the previous owner to get rid of it: Anton Karas's *Third Man* theme!

After *Harry Lime* wrapped production, Welles remained committed to living in Europe and frequently stayed in London—his stage version of *Othello* would open in October 1951. Towers made good use of this situation by signing him to another radio series. Fifty-two half-hour episodes of *The Black Museum* were produced and syndicated following their broadcast on the BBC beginning in January 1952. The series drew its stories from the files of Scotland Yard. Welles hosted but did not star in the programs, although he did act in a number of them. Given that none of the actors received on-air credit, and Orson would have played heavily accented character parts in any case, it is difficult to be sure in which of the stories he performed. Taut, superbly acted, and often gruesome in its details, *The Black Museum* is superb radio. Welles not only introduces the stories, he narrates throughout. Two basic openings are used, with minor variations. Both are preceded by the same unnerving musical signature, which slowly oscillates between a plucked double bass fiddle in the low register, and violins, flutes (a piccolo?), and a celeste exuding dissonant high tones. It sounds, as does the music throughout the series, very much in the style of Welles's former concert meister—soon to be Hitchcock's—Bernard Herrmann.

The first and more frequently heard opening yields "This is Orson Welles speaking from London," followed by the sound of Big Ben, and then, "The

Black Museum. A repository of death. Here in the grim stone structure on the Thames, which houses Scotland Yard, is a warehouse of homicide where everyday objects. . . . " Welles then mentions several of them, eventually arriving at the one that will launch that evening's episode. The second opening has the voice of an announcer intoning, "From the annals of the criminal investigation department of the London Police, we bring you the dramatic stories of the crimes recorded by objects in Scotland Yard's gallery of death—the Black Museum." Welles's voice then beckons us in the manner of a tour guide: "Well here we are, in the Black Museum, Scotland Yard's museum of murder. . . . " We hear his footsteps as he continues by describing the layout of the space in a voice that reverberates through the ominous archive. Then, as in the other introduction, he describes several of the objects before alighting on the one to be featured.

Each episode showcases Scotland Yard investigating a murder by gathering clues and interviewing witnesses, acquaintances of the victim, and eventually suspects. It is a formula that partly resembles television's *Dragnet*, which also went on the air in January 1952. Sometimes the featured murder occurs at the outset of the program. Such is the case in *The Raincoat*, in which a woman's bludgeoned body is discovered wrapped in her husband's raincoat. He is convicted of the crime on the basis of feeble circumstantial evidence, but in a later appeal is acquitted. In *The Centre Fire Bullet*, death also occurs early in the program, in a robbery gone awry. The police slowly close in on the perpetrators by puzzling together meager evidence and using subterfuge in the interrogation of suspects.

By contrast, in episodes such as *The Gladstone Bag*, where a married man murders one of his two girlfriends, the crime does not occur until well into the story. In this instance, the killer leaves a baggage claim ticket in his coat. It is discovered by his wife who takes it to a private detective, since she suspects adultery—he was allegedly out of town on the date the ticket was issued. The implements found in his checked bag, a bloodstained knife and saw, suggest a more heinous transgression.

Welles's narration helps us grasp the context of the stories more fully and serves to bridge transitions in time and place. Occasionally he makes comments about the characters, such as "That was an astute observation by the detective" or "Murderers sometimes make these mistakes." The sign-off is vintage *Mercury*. After he says, "Till we meet again and I'll tell you another story about the Black Museum," we hear a familiar line, "I remain, obediently yours," for what would be the last time in a radio series.[15] But that inimitable voice can still haunt us. As of this writing, a television remake of *The Black Museum* is being proposed. It would use a digitally transposed version of

Welles's original narration, fronted by an actor in silhouette. Again, over fifty years after the original, it is slated to be produced by Harry Alan Towers and offered for worldwide syndication.

Welles would of course go on to make, and try to make, films for the next twenty-five years. That output, largely unheralded during its time, grows in stature with each passing year. But our radio story is not quite over. There is one more broadcast to acknowledge. In 1952, Towers was still producing in London and Welles was occasionally in the neighborhood. Towers offered him the lead in a Sherlock Holmes series. Alas, the *Othello* odyssey precluded acceptance. Welles did, however, agree to do the concluding episode, *The Final Problem*. In it he played the evil Professor Moriarty, who faces off against Holmes (John Gielgud) and Dr. Watson (Ralph Richardson).

Welles's radio career ended as it had begun. Not with Mercury, nor with educational fare on CBS, but, as pointed out in chapter 1, with an adaptation of *Sherlock Holmes;* the first version having been done during his adolescence for a small radio station set up by the Todd School in Woodstock, Illinois. Now, in his final radio play, he is again in the Conan Doyle oeuvre: this time as Moriarty struggling with Holmes in a fight to the death on a ledge in the Alps. They both go over. The bodies are never found. Lost, too, would be Orson Welles's voice from a medium he had enriched with artistry and wonder for nearly twenty years.

Epilogue

> He was a great artist in the theatre and in film but I think that if there was one natural medium for Orson, it was radio.
>
> —John Houseman

A major segment of his career still lay ahead, but none of it would be in radio. The medium was changing. Like silent film after the coming of sound in the late 1920s, or black and white cinematography in the last quarter of the twentieth century, radio drama in the 1950s was rapidly becoming the art form of a bygone era. Welles called it "a victim of technological restlessness" and lamented the situation: "For me, radio's a personal loss, I miss it very much."[1] Today the history of the medium he so enriched is becoming increasingly forgotten. One reason is television, which has strongly skewed our cultural-historical memory toward the visual.

On 8 June 1998, *Time* magazine published the second installment in its "100" series profiling the most influential people of the twentieth century. It was devoted to artists and entertainers. Welles's name does not appear in any category. Under the heading "Auteurs Who Made Some of the Movies' Milestones," we find listed instead the likes of Preston Sturges and François Truffaut—one wonders what Truffaut, who greatly admired Welles, would make of his own inclusion and the latter's exclusion.[2]

Even more lamentable is how the *Time* commemorative seems ill-informed on the first half of the century. There is no category for radio, the dominant mass medium from the 1920s to the 1950s. Welles would most certainly merit mention here, or perhaps in the theater section; after all, he did make the cover of *Time* for accomplishments in these areas sixty years previous. But apart from the Welles radio legacy, what about one of the most successful shows in the history of broadcasting, *Amos 'n' Andy*? When two white entertainers, Freeman Godsen and Charles Correll, brought their controversial but wildly entertaining brand of blackface humor to radio in 1928, they created a show that enjoyed unprecedented popularity during the medium's first decade and then endured as a legend for another twenty years. Instead of acknowledging this phenomenon, the *Time* poll saw fit to cite such second-tier television fare as *My Little Margie* and *Mod Squad*.

Welles's radio legacy has not gone unacknowledged by biographers. David Thomson credits it with powerfully influencing Orson's cinematic vision, and Barbara Leaming has noted that listening to the *Mercury* broadcasts was the most exciting part of her research. But they, along with other worthy chroniclers, were nevertheless, as Thomson puts it, "anxious to get to Hollywood." This is understandable. Welles's rich and diverse film legacy is far from being fully assessed, especially the work he did after *Citizen Kane*, both in and out of Hollywood.

Kane itself remains the ultimate motion picture. It began to top the best film lists of critics in the late 1960s and early 1970s. Early in the new millennium it was appearing as the number one movie of all time in less highbrow polls—one in *Newsweek* provides an ironic counter to the omission of Welles in the aforementioned issue of *Time*. The power and influence of *Kane* has prompted ongoing references to it in unlikely places, such as television sitcoms. *The Simpsons* even presented an homage. One hopes that this led some younger viewers to rent the video or DVD, although the film's scope, as is the case with other great films that fully utilize cinematic resources—for example, Griffith's *Intolerance* or Kubrick's *2001: A Space Odyssey*—is somewhat diminished on the small screen. If we accept that motion pictures have been the preeminent art form of the twentieth century, both as high culture and mass-mediated popular entertainment, can we not see *Kane* as the era's equivalent of the Sistine Chapel? Similarly, American cultural historian Michael Denning suggests, although admittedly somewhat tongue in cheek, that Welles's legacy might be regarded in more inclusive terms: "If our Elizabethan age is called Rooseveltian, and classic Hollywood, for better or worse, is our theater, then Welles is our Shakespeare, the Mercury our Globe."[3]

Unfortunately, as an awareness of Welles's masterwork *Citizen Kane* increases, a sense of who he was and what he did apart from celluloid seems to be diminishing. The situation was quite different on 15 October 1956 when he appeared on an episode of the *I Love Lucy* show. Most viewers probably knew him from his radio days, his larger than life reputation as an enfant terrible of Broadway and Hollywood, and his appearances in other people's films. Only a minority would have seen *Kane* or been aware of the other films he directed. The skits in the program do nothing to alter this perception. They involve his magic act and status as a Shakespeare thespian. When Lucy tries to ingratiate Orson into allowing her to perform one of the Bard's scenes with him, she trumpets that his stage acting is superior to that of John Gielgud, Maurice Evans (whom he despised), and Ralph Richardson. He adds, playing on his prima donna persona, that she left out Laurence Olivier. Actually, the rivalry with Olivier was more in terms of Shakespeare on screen.

As Michael Anderegg's recent work reveals, Olivier's three efforts, *Henry V* (1944), *Hamlet* (1948), and *Richard III* (1955), have often been used as benchmarks from which to unfairly downgrade Welles's trio of *Macbeth* (1948), *Othello* (1952), and *Chimes at Midnight* (1966).[4] Anderegg also argues convincingly that no twentieth-century artist has done as much as Welles to bridge the divide between high and popular culture, a view strongly echoed in the work of Michael Denning just cited.

What makes *Kane* a great film is what makes Welles's work in a variety of other art forms noteworthy: his understanding of the limits and potential of his chosen medium, especially the way it could be used to further storytelling. Conjuring was his gift; that inimitable voice his first magic wand. When he later encountered the resources of radio and film, he developed their potential for multidimensionality in ways that had only been hinted at previously. Nowhere is this more evident than in the infamous *War of the Worlds* broadcast. Even before the horrific events of September 11, 2001, many believed America was under attack. Marx notes in the opening to his *Eighteenth Brumaire of Louis Bonaparte* (1852) that "All facts and personages in world history occur, as it were twice. The first time as tragedy, the second as farce."[5] Welles has shown us how, in the age of electronic entertainment media, that equation can sometimes be reversed.

The late and notorious Canadian communications scholar, Marshall McLuhan, in his most famous work, *Understanding Media*, drew parallels between what Welles did in the Panic Broadcast and what Hitler would later do in Europe. Parallels could also be drawn between McLuhan himself and Welles. Both had an extraordinary grasp of the nature of modern mass media—McLuhan as a commentator and pundit, Welles in order to use this ability to further his artistic ends.

In film as in radio, Welles did not create the techniques often identified with him, such as overlapping dialogue, deep focus cinematography, and first person narration, any more than D. W. Griffith invented the close-up, intercutting, tracking shot, or the various other innovations often attributed to him. Yet, like Griffith, he configured these elements into a unique and influential cinematic language. This was his genius and the basis of the auteurship posterity has bestowed on him. He found it a mixed blessing. Late in life he worried about being renowned more for his style than his art. He may have also felt insecure over what we now perceive as a less than stellar ability to create original stories. When he wrote the scripts for and starred in *An American Cavalcade: The Things We Have*, on radio, and *Mr. Arkadin*, the movie, they were among his least noteworthy projects in their respective media. It is also clear that the controversy surrounding the authorship of the script of *Kane* haunted him to the end. However, as an auteur by means of adaptation, he was nonpareil. The audio alchemy of *The Mercury Theatre on the Air* remains unsurpassed in bringing literature to radio. And who in the annals of moviedom has been as successful at making films from both high literature—his three Shakespeare efforts—and pulp fiction—*Touch of Evil*?

The work Welles did in radio, although widely acknowledged, is often underappreciated as art, especially since the medium itself has been eclipsed. Things were otherwise in the 1930s. On one hand radio threatened film in the realm of popular entertainment; on the other, it laid claim to being a purveyor of high art—CBS had its *Columbia Workshop* and NBC its Toscanini-led symphony orchestra. Not until the 1950s did motion pictures come to be widely regarded as a serious art form. Ironically, this occurred following the rise of television—which threatened the industry in ways that were similar to the challenge radio once posed—and in response to the influx of non-Hollywood films into North America.

Radio presented Welles with an intriguing set of auditory smoke and mirrors with which to conjure his stories. It also allowed him more latitude as an actor than any other medium, since he did not have to look the part he voiced. Not surprisingly, he would later tell Peter Bogdanovich that in his radio work he was "the happiest I have ever been as an actor."[6] From the outset Welles realized that conventions drawn from the stage had only minimal relevance for radio drama. Narration took precedence over theatricality. He usually did it with a character or characters in the story. When this was not feasible, he had the narrator speak from the time and place of the events being chronicled—as opposed to using the kind of disembodied "Once upon a time" or "Meanwhile back at the ranch" voice other radio productions employed.

Additional props in what long-time assistant Richard Wilson has called Orson's "Theatre of the Imagination" include the use of overlapping dialogue, as opposed to the "I talk, you talk" format employed in theater and conventional radio plays; the indication of space through auditory depth of field, coupled with the notion that sonority in the dialogue should reflect the location where it was supposed to be taking place—into the washroom he went for the sewer sequence in *Les Misérables*; and occasionally making the medium self-referential, which he demonstrated with the use of radio news techniques in *War of the Worlds*, right down to those unnerving moments of dead air.

Toward the end of his film *Radio Days*, Woody Allen has one of his characters wonder out loud "if future generations will ever hear about us." Narrator Allen continues the lament by noting that with each passing year those radio voices "seem to grow dimmer and dimmer." For a time it seemed as if this would be the fate of Welles's radio legacy. Fortunately, his increasing stature as a cineast should compel posterity to at least consider what he did before; and the Internet is now making available many of his better and lesser known broadcasts.

When Welles first strolled onto the RKO soundstage in 1939 to begin a career that would revolutionize the cinema, he wondered why movies could not be as creative as radio had been under his reign. He soon made it so, in part by applying some of the innovations he had already used to mesmerize a generation of listeners.

Selected Radiography

The following radiography charts most, but not all of the broadcasts Welles did during his radio years, 1934–1952. The previous chapters provide a commentary and credit listings for many of those listed. For a complete tabular compilation of each of Welles's radio appearances, see Bret Wood's *Orson Welles: A Bio-Bibliography*, and Jonathan Rosenbaum's chronology of Welles's career in Welles and Bogdanovich, *This Is Orson Welles*.

1934

Welles begins his radio career as an anonymous voice for the educational series *School of the Air of the Americas* (CBS), also known as the *American School of the Air*. He meets Joseph Cotten while working on the program.

1935

Further anonymous work in educational radio follows with appearances on *America's Hour* (CBS) and *Cavalcade of the Americas* (NBC).

In March he begins a series of semiregular appearances on *The March of Time*, which will continue until March of 1938.

1936

Welles performs in his own two-part adaptation of *Hamlet* that fall for Irving Reis's *Columbia Workshop*. He works with Bernard Herrmann for the first time during the production.

Toward the end of the year he begins a six-week run as both narrator and The Great McCoy on *The Wonder Show* (Mutual Broadcasting System).

1937

In March, Welles becomes the unbilled star of *The Shadow* (Mutual), a commitment that would last until March of the following year.

On 11 April he plays the announcer in Irving Reis's acclaimed *Columbia Workshop* production of Archibald MacLeish's verse play *The Fall of the City*.

From 23 July to 3 September he directs, writes, and stars in a seven-part adaptation of Victor Hugo's *Les Misérables* (Mutual).

1938

On 11 July Welles's *Mercury Theatre* goes on the air each week under the title *First Person Singular* (CBS). The debut broadcast is Bram Stoker's *Dracula*. The series, which began as a summer replacement for *The Lux Radio Theatre*, is regularized as a sustaining (network funded) program on 11 September and assumes a new name, *The Mercury Theatre on the Air*. Shakespeare's *Julius Caesar* launches the new season.

On 30 October *Mercury* broadcasts the infamous *War of the Worlds* Panic Broadcast.

On 9 December, having attracted a sponsor, *Mercury* would hereafter be known as *The Campbell Playhouse*. Daphne du Maurier's *Rebecca* is the first broadcast under this new format.

1939

There are thirty-nine *Campbell Playhouse* productions. One of the most notable is the 24 December broadcast of Charles Dickens's *A Christmas Carol*, in which Lionel Barrymore played Scrooge.

1940

Welles appears as a guest on Jack Benny's *The Jell-O Program* (NBC) on 17 March, moments before his *Campbell Playhouse* broadcast of Mark Twain's *Huckleberry Finn*. The following week Benny reciprocates and appears in the *Campbell* production of Ring Lardner and George S. Kaufman's *June Moon*.

On 31 March, Charlotte Bronte's *Jane Eyre* becomes the final *Campbell* broadcast.

On 28 October, Orson Welles meets H. G. Wells in a radio interview broadcast from station KTSA in San Antonio, Texas.

1941

Welles appears as a semiregular guest on *The Sealtest Program* (NBC) hosted by Rudy Vallee.

On 6 April *The Free Company* performs *His Honor—the Mayor*, which is written, directed, and narrated by Welles.

The Orson Welles Show: Almanac, also known as *Orson Welles's Almanac* (CBS), sponsored by Lady Esther Cosmetics, debuts on 15 September. On 15 November the format shifts from variety to drama and the program is referred to as *The Orson Welles Show*. The following week Welles broadcasts the first version of what would become a radio classic: *The Hitch Hiker*, written by Lucille Fletcher, wife of Bernard Herrmann.

On 15 December Welles appears in the *Cavalcade of America* (CBS) production of *The Great Man Votes*, based on the Peter Lyon script of the Gordon Malherne Hillman story. Later that evening he performs in Norman Corwin's production of *The President's Bill of Rights* for *We Hold These Truths* (CBS).

1942

On 2 February, the last broadcast of *The Orson Welles Show* is Norman Corwin's *Between Americans*.

Guest appearances on *The Kate Smith Show* and *Information Please*.

On 28 September, Welles directs and stars in Arthur Miller's verse play, *Juarez: Thunder from the Hills*, for *Cavalcade of America* (NBC).

Welles is Fred Allen's guest on *Texaco Star Theatre* (NBC) on 18 October.

First installment of Welles's new dramatic series, *Ceiling Unlimited* (CBS): *The Flying Fortress*, on 9 November.

First installment of Welles's new variety show, *Hello Americans* (CBS): *Brazil*, on 15 November.

1943

Hello Americans concludes its run with *Bolivar's Idea* on 31 January. *Ceiling Unlimited* follows suit the next day with *The Future*.

During March–April Welles hosts the Jack Benny program five times due to Benny's illness.

Four appearances on *Suspense* (CBS) during September-October. Welles would make almost a dozen appearances on the show over the next several years.

1944

Welles's *Almanac* (CBS) series is reprised on 26 January with an exclusively comedy/variety format. Groucho Marx is the first guest.

Welles continues his guest appearances on *Suspense*, with the two-part broadcast of *Donovan's Brain* on 18 and 24 May being one of his most memorable.

Almanac concludes its run on 19 July. The last three broadcasts feature *The Mercury Wonder Show* and are performed before a live audience of servicemen.

Throughout the fall, Welles does numerous political broadcasts on behalf of the war effort.

1945

On 13 March Welles launches his new series, *This Is My Best* (CBS), sponsored by Cresta Blanca Wines. The debut broadcast is Joseph Conrad's *Heart of Darkness*.

This Is My Best concludes on 24 April with *Anything Can Happen*, adapted by Robert Tallman from the book by George and Helen Papashvily.

On 19 August *Columbia Presents Corwin* features Welles in *God and Uranium*.

Orson Welles Commentaries (ABC) begins on 16 September.

1946

The Mercury Summer Theatre (CBS), sponsored by Pabst Blue Ribbon Beer, begins on 7 June. Jules Verne's *Around the World in 80 Days* is the first broadcast.

Summer Theatre ends its run on 13 September with a Shakespeare adaptation: *Scenes from Lear*.

Final broadcast of *Orson Welles Commentaries* on 6 October.

1947

On 24 May Welles is the featured guest on the *Command Performance Anniversary Program* for the Armed Forces Radio Service.

1951

In Europe that March Welles begins recording the first of fifty-two episodes of Harry Alan Towers's syndicated radio series *The Lives of Harry Lime*, also known as *The Adventures of Harry Lime*. The program begins airing in August on the BBC. Worldwide distribution follows.

1952

In January, Towers recruits Welles as host and occasional actor for fifty-two episodes of another syndicated series, *The Black Museum*.

Later in the year Towers produces yet another syndicated series, *Sherlock Holmes*. Welles's commitments preclude him from a regular involvement, but he is able to co-star in the finale, *The Final Problem*, where he played Professor Moriarity opposite John Gielgud (Holmes) and Ralph Richardson (Watson).

Notes

Chapter One: A Voice Is Born

1. Lynn Kear, *Agnes Moorehead: A Bio-Bibliography* (Westport, CT: Greenwood Press, 1992), 37.
2. This bizarre incident is recounted in David Thomson, *Rosebud: The Story of Orson Welles* (New York: Knopf, 1996), 25–26.
3. Richard Jr. was emotionally unstable and periodically institutionalized.
4. He confessed this to Barbara Leaming, *Orson Welles: A Biography* (New York: Viking, 1985), 32–33.
5. Todd School File, "Orson Welles Mss. Collection," Lilly Library, Indiana University.
6. MacLiammóir, *All for Hecuba* (Boston: Branden Press, 1967), 127.
7. MacLiammóir, *All for Hecuba*, 127.
8. Quoted in Leaming, *Orson Welles*, 46.
9. MacLiammóir, *All for Hecuba*, 131.
10. Leaming, *Orson Welles*, 54–55.
11. *As It Happens*, 28 September 1997.
12. Leaming, *Orson Welles*, 60–61.
13. Houseman, *Run-Through: A Memoir* (New York: Simon and Schuster, 1972), 144.
14. Houseman, *Run-Through*, 144.
15. The audition is described in Houseman, *Unfinished Business* (New York: Applause Theatre Books, 1989), 76.

Chapter Two: Theatrical Notoriety, Radio Anonymity

1. Houseman, *Run-Through: A Memoir* (New York: Simon and Schuster, 1972), gives an extended account of the production and the responses to it.
2. MacLeish, *Six Plays* (Boston: Houghton Mifflin, 1980), reflects on the impact of the play.
3. Orson Welles and Peter Bogdanovich, with Jonathan Rosenbaum, ed., *This Is Orson Welles* (New York: HarperCollins, 1992), 10.
4. Welles and Bogdanovich, *This Is Orson Welles*, 10.
5. Rosenbaum, in Welles and Bogdanovich, *This Is Orson Welles*, 331.
6. In his autobiography, Joseph Cotten, *Vanity Will Get You Somewhere* (San Francisco: Mercury House Inc., 1987), puts the date of this encounter as 1931, but it would have been 1934, or more likely, 1935.
7. Cotten, *Vanity Will Get You Somewhere*. Cotten claims to have never had an argument with Welles.
8. Lawrence W. Lichty and Thomas W. Bohn, "Radio's March of Time: Dramatized News," *Journalism Quarterly*, vol. 51, no. 3 (autumn 1974), gives a complete account of the history of the program.
9. Lichty and Bohn, "Radio's March of Time."
10. Lichty and Bohn, "Radio's March of Time."
11. Barbara Leaming, *Orson Welles: A Biography* (New York: Viking, 1985), 93. As his "official" biographer, she was told this by Welles himself.
12. Raymond Fielding, *The March of Time: 1935–1951* (New York: Oxford University Press, 1978), provides a history of the newsreel version.
13. Erik Barnouw, *A History of Broadcasting in the United States* (New York: Oxford University Press, 1966–1970), vol. 1, 277–78.
14. Welles and Bogdanovich, *This Is Orson Welles*, 74.
15. Leaming, *Orson Welles*, 78–79.
16. Houseman, interview in "The Mercury Company Remembers," in *Theatre of the Imagination* (boxed set of audiocassette tapes, Santa Monica, CA: Voyager, 1988).
17. Houseman, *Run-Through*, has attributed the idea to Virginia, something Welles has neither affirmed nor denied.
18. This incident has justly impressed biographers Simon Callow, *Orson Welles: The Road to Xanadu* (London: Jonathan Cape, 1995), and David Thomson, *Rosebud: The Story of Orson Welles* (New York: Knopf, 1996).
19. Welles and Bogdanovich, *This Is Orson Welles*, 74.
20. Contract dated 17 August 1936 in the "Orson Welles Mss. Collection," Lilly Library, Indiana University.
21. Rosenbaum, in Welles and Bogdanovich, *This Is Orson Welles*, 13.
22. Welles and Bogdanovich, *This Is Orson Welles*, 13.
23. Welles, along with several of his colleagues and biographers, all remark on this unusual way of coping with New York traffic.
24. Welles and Bogdanovich, *This Is Orson Welles*, 11.

25. Welles and Bogdanovich, *This Is Orson Welles*, 11–12.

26. Archibald MacLeish, *The Fall of the City: A Verse Play for Radio* (New York: Farrar and Rinehart, Inc., 1937), ii.

27. Frank Brady, *Citizen Welles* (New York: Scribner's, 1989), 109.

28. Thomson, *Rosebud*, 76.

29. Houseman, *Unfinished Business* (New York: Applause Theatre Books, 1989), 136.

30. In Altman, "Deep Focus Sound: *Citizen Kane* and the Radio Aesthetic," *Quarterly Review of Film and Video* 15, no. 3 (December 1994), 12. Altman also suggests that Welles may have invented this type of narration. At the very least he brought to the airwaves a distinctive way of doing it.

31. John Dunning, *Tune in Yesterday: The Ultimate Encyclopedia of Old Time Radio, 1925–1976* (New York: Oxford University Press, 1998), 209.

32. Richard Jewell, "Hollywood and Radio: Competition and Partnership in the 1930's," *Historical Journal of Film Radio and Television*, vol. 4, no. 2 (1984), and Michele Hilmes, *Hollywood and Broadcasting: From Radio to Cable* (Urbana, IL: University of Illinois Press, 1990), discuss the origins of the *Lux Radio Theatre*.

33. Quoted in Hilmes, *Hollywood and Broadcasting*, 218.

34. Quoted in Dunning, *Tune in Yesterday*, 144.

35. Leaming, *Orson Welles*, 121.

36. "Orson Welles Mss. Collection."

37. Houseman, *Unfinished Business*, 140.

38. Michael Denning, *The Cultural Front: The Laboring of American Culture in the Twentieth Century* (New York: Verso, 1998), 362.

39. Interview in *The Battle over Citizen Kane*, PBS documentary, 1996.

Chapter Three: *Mercury Theatre on the Air*

1. William S. Paley, in *As It Happened: A Memoir* (Garden City, NY: Doubleday, 1979), gives a personal account of his role in the history of CBS.

2. Houseman, *Unfinished Business* (New York: Applause Theatre Books, 1989), 176.

3. Welles makes this declaration quite overtly in his introductory remarks to the 9 December 1938 broadcast of *Rebecca*.

4. This incident is described in Orson Welles and Peter Bogdanovich, with Jonathan Rosenbaum, ed., *This Is Orson Welles* (New York: HarperCollins, 1992), 332.

5. John Houseman, in *Run-Through: A Memoir* (New York: Simon and Schuster, 1972), reflects on how the Welles/Herrmann partnership began.

6. Ted Gilling, "The Colour of Music: An Interview with Bernard Herrmann," *Sight and Sound* 41, no. 1 (Winter 1971–1972), 36.

7. Herrmann's biographer, Steven C. Smith, recounts this and other bizarre incidents in the composer's life in *A Heart at Fire's Center: The Life and Music of Bernard Herrmann* (Berkeley: University of California Press, 1991).

8. Smith, *Heart at Fire's Center*, 48.

9. Simon Callow, *Orson Welles: The Road to Xanadu* (London: Jonathan Cape, 1995), 527.

10. Quoted in Houseman, *Unfinished Business*, 179.

11. Herrmann interview in "The Mercury Company Remembers," in *Theatre of the Imagination* (boxed set of audiocassette tapes, Santa Monica, CA: Voyager, 1988).

12. "Orson Welles Mss. Collection," Lilly Library, Indiana University.

13. The session is vividly described in Houseman, *Unfinished Business*, 177–79.

14. Welles and Bogdanovich, in *This Is Orson Welles*, 13–14.

15. Robert L. Mott, *Radio Sound Effects* (Jefferson, NC: McFarland and Company, Inc., 1973), 103–5.

16. Mott, *Radio Sound Effects*, 103–5.

17. The incident is recounted in Callow, *Orson Welles: The Road to Xanadu*, 387–88.

18. Frank Brady, *Citizen Welles* (New York: Scribner's, 1989).

19. Houseman, *Unfinished Business*, 180.

20. The incident is described by Houseman in *Theatre of the Imagination*.

21. Bret Wood, *Orson Welles: A Bio-Bibliography* (Westport, CT: Greenwood Press, 1990), 91.

22. Houseman, *Unfinished Business*, 190.

23. Howard Koch reflects on his early years in *As Time Goes By: Memoirs of a Writer* (New York: Harcourt Brace Jovanovich, 1979).

24. Koch, *As Time Goes By*, 3.

25. Houseman, *Unfinished Business*, 192.

Chapter Four: Genesis

1. Arthur Lovejoy in *The Great Chain of Being* (New York: Harper Torchbooks, 1960) discusses the "plurality of worlds" and the principle of plenitude.

2. William Sheehan in *The Planet Mars* (Tucson, AZ: University of Arizona Press, 1996) discusses the nomenclature of Schiaparelli and Secchi.

3. Susan J. Douglas, *Inventing American Broadcasting* (Baltimore: Johns Hopkins University Press, 1987), 304–5.

4. Howard Koch, *The Panic Broadcast: Portrait of an Event* (Boston: Little, Brown, 1970), 30.

5. Houseman, *Unfinished Business*, (New York: Applause Theatre Books, 1989), 192.

6. Howard Koch, *As Time Goes By: Memoirs of a Writer* (New York: Harcourt Brace Jovanovich, 1979), 12.

7. Koch, *The Panic Broadcast*, 14.

8. Houseman, *Unfinished Business*.

9. Houseman, *Unfinished Business*, 193.

10. Summarized in Simon Callow, *Orson Welles: The Road to Xanadu* (London: Jonathan Cape, 1995), 400.

Chapter Five: Exodus

1. Hadley Cantril, *The Invasion from Mars: A Study in the Psychology of Panic* (Princeton, NJ: Princeton University Press, 1940), contains data regarding radio listenership at the time of the Panic Broadcast.
2. Cantril, *Invasion from Mars*.
3. Geduld, "Welles or Wells? —A Matter of Adaptation." In Morris Beja, *Perspectives on Orson Welles* (New York: G. K. Hall and Co., 1995), 268.
4. Houseman interview in "The Mercury Company Remembers" in *Theatre of the Imagination* (boxed set of audiocassette tapes, Santa Monica, CA: Voyager, 1988).
5. Herrmann's musicological evolution is discussed in Bruce Graham, *Bernard Herrmann: Film Music and Narrative* (Ann Arbor: UMI Research Press, 1985), and in Steven C. Smith, *A Heart at Fire's Center: The Life and Music of Bernard Herrmann* (Berkeley: University of California Press, 1991).
6. Koch, *As Time Goes By: Memoirs of a Writer* (New York: Harcourt Brace Jovanovich, 1979), 8.
7. Houseman in *Run-Through: A Memoir* (New York: Simon and Schuster, 1972) is one of the few commentators on the Panic Broadcast to assess the contribution of Dietz to the *Mercury* programs.
8. Houseman interview in *Theatre of the Imagination*.
9. Alland interview in *The Battle over Citizen Kane* (PBS Television Documentary, 1995).
10. Alland interview in *The Battle over Citizen Kane*.
11. It is still uncertain whether Delmar did this of his own creative volition or at Welles's urging. I suspect the former.
12. *War of the Worlds Radio Report* (audiocassette tape produced by Radio Yesteryear, Vancouver, BC Canada, nd.).
13. Geduld, "Welles or Wells?" 262–65.
14. MacLeish, *Six Plays* (Boston: Houghton Mifflin, 1980), v.
15. MacLeish, *The Fall of the City: A Verse Play for Radio* (New York: Farrar and Rinehart, Inc., 1937), iii.
16. Brady, *Citizen Welles* (New York: Scribner's, 1989), 166.
17. Houseman interview in *Theatre of the Imagination*.

Chapter Six: Revelation

1. Houseman interview in "The Mercury Company Remembers" in *Theatre of the Imagination* (boxed set of audiocassette tapes, Santa Monica, CA: Voyager, 1988).
2. Houseman interview in *Theatre of the Imagination*.
3. In Simon Callow, *Orson Welles: The Road to Xanadu* (London: Jonathan Cape, 1995), 404.
4. Cited in Frank Brady, *Citizen Welles* (New York: Scribner's, 1989), 173–74.

5. My data on *War of the Worlds* listenership are drawn from Hadley Cantril, *The Invasion from Mars: A Study in the Psychology of Panic* (Princeton, NJ: Princeton University Press, 1940).
6. Howard Koch, "Orson Welles—Some Reminiscences," in *Orson Welles on the Air* (New York: Museum of Broadcasting, 1988), 30.
7. Koch, "Orson Welles—Some Reminiscences," 30.
8. Orson Welles and Peter Bogdanovich, with Jonathan Rosenbaum, editor, *This Is Orson Welles* (New York: HarperCollins, 1992), 18.
9. "Orson Welles Mss. Collection," Lilly Library, Indiana University.
10. Brady, *Citizen Welles*, 175.
11. Brady, *Citizen Welles*, 176.
12. David Hughes in "'The War of the Worlds' in the Yellow Press," *Journalism Quarterly* vol. 43, no. 4 (winter 1966), assesses these American adaptations of the novel.
13. The original Welles family name did not have the "e." It was added by Orson's grandfather, Richard.
14. Cantril, in *The Invasion from Mars*, assesses these polls.
15. Cantril, *The Invasion from Mars*.
16. *War of the Worlds Radio Report* (audiocassette tape produced by Radio Yesteryear, Vancouver, BC Canada, nd.).
17. *War of the Worlds Radio Report.*
18. *War of the Worlds Radio Report.*
19. *War of the Worlds Radio Report.*
20. An interesting response to the broadcast on the part of rural African Americans is chronicled in Virginia Hamilton's novel, *Willie Bea and the Time the Martians Landed* (New York: Greenwillow Books, 1983).
21. *War of the Worlds Radio Report.*
22. *War of the Worlds Radio Report.*
23. *War of the Worlds Radio Report.*
24. Brady, *Citizen Welles*, 176.
25. Although she does not discuss the Panic Broadcast, Gwenyth Jackaway in *Media Wars: Radio's Challenge to the Newspapers, 1924–1939* (Westport, CT: Praeger, 1995), gives a concise history of that rivalry.
26. Both Houseman and Koch felt that it was Thompson's editorial that most stemmed the tide of negative opinion.
27. Telegram in the "Orson Welles Mss. Collection."
28. Callow, *The Road to Xanadu*, 490.
29. Telegram in "The Orson Welles Mss. Collection."
30. Telegram in "The Orson Welles Mss. Collection."
31. Geduld, "Welles or Wells?—A Matter of Adaptation." In Morris Beja, *Perspectives on Orson Welles* (New York: G. K. Hall and Co., 1995).
32. Howard Koch, "Orson Welles—Some Reminiscences," in *Orson Welles on the Air* (New York: Museum of Broadcasting, 1988), 30.

33. Koch's travails are documented in Aljean Harmetz's *Round Up the Usual Suspects: The Making of Casablanca, Bogart, Bergman, and World War II* (New York: Hyperion, 1992).
34. Harmetz, *Round Up the Usual Suspects*.
35. Cantril discusses this broadcast in *Invasion from Mars*.
36. *Newsweek*, 27 November 1944.
37. *Time*, 21 February 1949.
38. Another notable example of television fakery was the pseudo-documentary, *Ghostwatch*, which the BBC aired in the UK on 31 October 1992. Presented as the live investigative report of an alleged haunted house, the clever special effects terrified thousands and the program drew considerable criticism. It was not rebroadcast until the Scream Channel in North America aired it in 2004. The pseudo-documentary format, this time in the context of a feature film, would eventually attain worldwide notoriety with the release in 1999 of *The Blair Witch Project*.
39. Nowhere does he make this point with more humor and poignancy than in his brilliant 1974 "mockumentary," *F for Fake*.

Chapter Seven: *Campbell Playhouse*

1. John Houseman, *Unfinished Business* (New York: Applause Theatre Books, 1989), 186.
2. Harold Clurman, *The Fervent Years* (New York: Hill and Wang, 1964), 202.
3. Robert L. Mott, *Radio Sound Effects* (Jefferson, NC: McFarland and Company, Inc., 1973), 105, discusses how this sequence was achieved.
4. Houseman, *Unfinished Business*, 203, describes the visit.
5. Richard Jewell, "Hollywood and Radio: Competition and Partnership in the 1930's," *Historical Journal of Film Radio and Television*, vol. 4, no. 2 (1984), gives a history of the program.
6. Simon Callow, *Orson Welles: The Road to Xanadu* (London: Jonathan Cape, 1995), 422.
7. Donald Spoto assesses the Selznick/Hitchcock relationship in *The Dark Side of Genius* (New York: Ballantine, 1993).
8. Houseman, *Unfinished Business*, 174.
9. Houseman, *Unfinished Business*, 206.
10. Barbara Leaming, *Orson Welles: A Biography* (New York: Viking, 1985), 167–68.
11. "Orson Welles Mss. Collection," Lilly Library, Indiana University.
12. "Orson Welles Mss. Collection."
13. "Orson Welles Mss. Collection."
14. "Orson Welles Mss. Collection."
15. This information was sent to Orson Welles and John Houseman in a letter from Diana Bourbon dated 25 August 1939. "Orson Welles Mss. Collection."
16. Letter dated 9 October 1939. "Orson Welles Mss. Collection."

17. "Orson Welles Mss. Collection."
18. Keith J. Fennimore, *Booth Tarkington* (New York: Twayne Publishers, Inc., 1974), and James Woodress, *Booth Tarkington: Gentleman from Indiana* (New York: Greenwood Press, 1969), assess the writer's legacy.
19. Houseman, *Unfinished Business*, 217.
20. Orson Welles and Peter Bogdanovich, with Jonathan Rosenbaum, editor, *This Is Orson Welles* (New York: HarperCollins, 1992), 137.

Chapter Eight: Orson at RKO

1. Orson Welles and Peter Bogdanovich, with Jonathan Rosenbaum, editor, *This Is Orson Welles* (New York: HarperCollins, 1992), 92.
2. Richard B. Jewell and Vernon Harbin, *The RKO Story* (London: Octopus Books, 1982), and Betty Lasky, *RKO: The Biggest Little Major of Them All* (Englewood Cliffs, NJ: Prentice-Hall Inc., 1984), provide detailed histories of the studio.
3. Pauline Kael, with Herman J. Mankiewicz and Orson Welles, *The Citizen Kane Book* (Boston: Little, Brown, 1971).
4. Many of the arguments against Kael are raised by Peter Bogdanovich in Welles and Bogdanovich, *This Is Orson Welles*, 494–503. Bernard Herrmann also takes issue with Kael's charges, most vociferously, in "Bernard Herrmann, Composer," in Cameron, ed., *Sound and the Cinema: The Coming of Sound to American Film* (Pleasantville, NY: Redgrave Publishing Company, 1980), 128–29.
5. Steven C. Smith, *A Heart at Fire's Center: The Life and Music of Bernard Herrmann* (Berkeley: University of California Press, 1991), 77.
6. James G. Stewart, "The Evolution of Cinematic Sound: A Personal Report," in Cameron, *Sound and the Cinema: The Coming of Sound to American Film* (Pleasantville, NY: Redgrave Publishing Company, 1980), 53.
7. Quoted in Joseph McBride, *Orson Welles* (New York: Da Capo Press, 1996), 41.
8. Welles and Bogdanovich, *This Is Orson Welles*, 41.
9. Evan Cameron, ed., *Sound and the Cinema: The Coming of Sound to American Film* (Pleasantville, NY: Redgrave Publishing Company, 1980), 126.
10. Rick Altman, "Deep Focus Sound: Citizen Kane and the Radio Aesthetic," *Quarterly Review of Film and Video* 15, no. 3 (December 1994).
11. Altman, "Deep Focus Sound: Citizen Kane and the Radio Aesthetic," 25.
12. Ted Gilling, "The Colour of Music: An Interview with Bernard Herrmann," *Sight and Sound* 41, no. 1 (winter 1971/1972).
13. Frank Brady, *Citizen Welles* (New York: Scribner's, 1989), 271.
14. Herrmann, "Bernard Herrmann, Composer," 54–55.
15. Leaming, *Orson Welles*, 211.
16. Houseman, *Unfinished Business*, 231–33.
17. Welles and Bogdanovich, in *This Is Orson Welles*, 104.
18. Leaming, *Orson Welles*, 223.

19. This incident is discussed more fully by Stewart in "The Evolution of Cinematic Sound."

20. Welles and Bogdanovich, *This Is Orson Welles*, 96.

21. Robert Carringer, *The Magnificent Ambersons: A Reconstruction* (Berkeley, CA: University of California Press, 1993), assesses early reactions to the film.

22. Rosenbaum, in Welles and Bogdanovich, *This Is Orson Welles*.

23. It was Koerner who ordered the destruction of the footage edited from Welles's original cut of *Ambersons*.

24. Brady, *Citizen Welles*, 351.

25. Brady, *Citizen Welles*, 351.

26. Welles and Bogdanovich, *This Is Orson Welles*, 175.

27. Welles and Bogdanovich, *This Is Orson Welles*, 177.

28. Bret Wood, *Orson Welles: A Bio-Bibliography* (Westport, CT: Greenwood Press, 1990), 139.

Chapter Nine: The Last Radio Shows

1. Excellent portraits of Jack Benny and Fred Allen can be found in Gerald Nachman, *Raised on Radio* (Berkeley, CA: University of California Press, 2000).

2. Barbara Leaming, *Orson Welles: A Biography* (New York: Viking, 1985), 331.

3. Several people for whom I have played the tape find it hard to believe that it is not the voice of Welles they are hearing.

4. Rosenbaum, in Orson Welles and Peter Bogdanovich, *This Is Orson Welles* (New York: HarperCollins, 1992), 397.

5. Leaming, *Orson Welles*, 340.

6. Joseph McBride, *Orson Welles* (New York: Da Capo Press, 1996), 103.

7. Welles and Bogdanovich, in *This Is Orson Welles*, 200.

8. Welles and Bogdanovich, in *This Is Orson Welles*, 198.

9. Michael Anderegg, *Orson Welles, Shakespeare, and Popular Culture*, assesses the reaction Welles's Shakespeare films have received.

10. James Naremore, *The Magic World of Orson Welles* (New York: Oxford University Press, 1978), 142.

11. Leaming, *Orson Welles*, 362.

12. Frank Tavares, A Critical Analysis of Selected Dramatic Elements in the Radio Series "The Adventures of Harry Lime," with Orson Welles (Ph.D. dissertation, University of Texas, 1976).

13. Tavares, Critical Analysis, 48.

14. Tavares, Critical Analysis, 50.

15. In a remarkable 1952 short film directed by Hilton Edwards, *Return to Glennascaul* (also known as *Orson Welles's Ghost Story*), Welles introduces himself as "your obedient servant."

Epilogue

1. Orson Welles and Peter Bogdanovich, with Jonathan Rosenbaum, editor, *This Is Orson Welles* (New York: HarperCollins, 1992), 10.

2. In Pauline Kael, with Herman J. Mankiewicz and Orson Welles, *The Citizen Kane Book* (Boston: Little, Brown, 1971), 3, Truffaut is cited for his belief that *Citizen Kane* has probably inspired the careers of more filmmakers than any other movie.

3. Denning, *The Cultural Front: The Laboring of American Culture in the Twentieth Century* (New York: Verso, 1998), 363.

4. Michael Anderegg, *Orson Welles, Shakespeare, and Popular Culture* (New York: Columbia University Press, 1999).

5. Karl Marx, *The Eighteenth Brumaire of Louis Bonaparte* (1852; reprint New York: International Publishers, 1969), 1.

6. Welles and Bogdanovich, in *This Is Orson Welles*, 18.

Bibliography

Altman, Rick. "Deep Focus Sound: *Citizen Kane* and the Radio Aesthetic." *Quarterly Review of Film and Video* 15, no. 3 (December 1994).
———, ed. *Sound Theory, Sound Practice*. New York: Routledge, 1992.
Anderegg, Michael. *Orson Welles, Shakespeare, and Popular Culture*. New York: Columbia University Press, 1999.
As It Happens. Canadian Broadcasting Corporation radio program, 28 September 1997.
Barfield, Ray. *Listening to Radio*. Westport, CT: Praeger, 1996.
Barnouw, Erik. *A History of Broadcasting in the United States*. New York: Oxford University Press, 3 vols., 1966–1970.
———, ed. *Radio Drama in Action*. New York: Rinehart and Company Inc., 1945.
The Battle over Citizen Kane. PBS Television Documentary, 1995.
Bazin, André. *Orson Welles: A Critical View*. New York: Harper and Row, 1972.
Beja, Morris, ed. *Perspectives on Orson Welles*. New York: G. K. Hall and Co., 1995.
Bessy, Maurice. *Orson Welles*. New York: Crown, 1971.
Blue, Howard. *Words at War: World War II Era Radio Drama and the Postwar Broadcasting Industry Blacklist*. Lanham, MD: Scarecrow Press, 2002.
Bogdanovich, Peter. See Welles and Bogdanovich.
Brady, Frank. *Citizen Welles*. New York: Scribner's, 1989.
Brown, Robert J. *Manipulating the Ether: The Power of Broadcast Radio in Thirties America*. Jefferson, NC: McFarland and Company, 1998.
Brown, Royal S. "Herrmann, Hitchcock, and the Art of the Music of the Irrational." *Cinema Journal* 22, no. 2 (spring 1982).
Callow, Simon. *Orson Welles: The Road to Xanadu*. London: Jonathan Cape, 1995.
Cameron, Evan William. "Citizen Kane: The Influence of Radio Drama on Cinematic Design." In Cameron, ed., *Sound and the Cinema: The Coming of Sound to American Film*. Pleasantville, NY: Redgrave Publishing Company, 1980.

———, ed. *Sound and the Cinema: The Coming of Sound to American Film.* Pleasantville, NY: Redgrave Publishing Company, 1980.
Cantril, Hadley. *The Invasion from Mars: A Study in the Psychology of Panic.* Princeton, NJ: Princeton University Press, 1940.
Cantril, Hadley, and Gordon W. Allport. *The Psychology of Radio.* New York: Arno Press, 1935.
Carringer, Robert L. *The Making of Citizen Kane.* Berkeley, CA: University of California Press, 1985.
———. *The Magnificent Ambersons: A Reconstruction.* Berkeley, CA: University of California Press, 1993.
Clurman, Harold. *The Fervent Years.* New York: Hill and Wang, 1964.
Cotten, Joseph. *Vanity Will Get You Somewhere.* San Francisco: Mercury House Inc., 1987.
Cowie, Peter. *The Cinema of Orson Welles.* London: A. Zwimmer Limited, 1965.
Denning, Michael. *The Cultural Front: The Laboring of American Culture in the Twentieth Century.* New York: Verso, 1998.
Douglas, Susan J. *Inventing American Broadcasting.* Baltimore: Johns Hopkins University Press, 1987.
———. *Listening In: Radio and the American Imagination.* New York: Random House, 1999.
Dunning, John. *Tune in Yesterday: The Ultimate Encyclopedia of Old-Time Radio, 1925–1976.* New York: Oxford University Press, 1998.
Fennimore, Keith J. *Booth Tarkington.* New York: Twayne Publishers, Inc., 1974.
Fielding, Raymond. *The March of Time: 1935–1951.* New York: Oxford University Press, 1978.
Flanagan, Hallie. *Arena.* New York: Duel, Sloan, and Pierce, 1940.
Foot, Michael. *The History of Mr. Wells.* Washington, DC: Counterpoint, 1995.
Fowler, Roy Alexander. *Orson Welles: A First Biography.* London: Pendulum Publications, 1946.
France, Richard. *The Theatre of Orson Welles.* Cranbury, NJ: Bucknell University Press, 1977.
———, ed. *Orson Welles on Shakespeare: The W. P. A. and Mercury Theatre Playscripts.* Westport, CT: Greenwood Press, 1990.
Gabler, Neal Winchell. *Gossip, Power, and the Culture of Celebrity.* New York: Vintage Books, 1995.
Geduld, Harry M. "Welles or Wells?—A Matter of Adaptation." In Morris Beja, *Perspectives on Orson Welles.* New York: G. K. Hall and Co., 1995.
Gilling, Ted. "The Colour of Music: An Interview with Bernard Herrmann." *Sight and Sound* 41, no. 1 (winter 1971/1972).
Gottesman, Roland, ed. *Focus on Citizen Kane.* Englewood Cliffs, NJ: Prentice-Hall Inc., 1971.
Graham, Bruce. *Bernard Herrmann: Film Music and Narrative.* Ann Arbor: UMI Research Press, 1985.

Greenfield, Thomas Allen. *Radio: A Reference Guide.* Westport, CT: Greenwood Press, 1989.

Hamilton, Virginia. *Willie Bea and the Time the Martians Landed.* New York: Greenwillow Books, 1983.

Harmetz, Aljean. *Round Up the Usual Suspects: The Making of Casablanca, Bogart, Bergman, and World War II.* New York: Hyperion, 1992.

Harmon, Jim. *The Great Radio Heroes.* New York: Doubleday, 1967.

Herrmann, Bernard. "Score for a Film." *New York Times,* 25 May 1941.

———. "Bernard Herrmann, Composer." In Cameron, ed., *Sound and the Cinema: The Coming of Sound to American Film.* Pleasantville, NY: Redgrave Publishing Company, 1980.

Heyer, Paul. "America under Attack I: A Reassessment of Orson Welles' 1938 *War of the Worlds* Broadcast." *Canadian Journal of Communication,* vol. 28, no. 2 (2003).

Higham, Charles. *Orson Welles: The Rise and Fall of an American Genius.* New York: St. Martin's Press, 1985.

Hilmes, Michelle. *Hollywood and Broadcasting: From Radio to Cable.* Urbana IL: University of Illinois Press, 1990.

———. *Radio Voices: American Broadcasting, 1922–1952.* Minneapolis, MN: University of Minnesota Press, 1997.

Hilmes, Michelle, and Jason Loviglio, eds. *Radio Reader: Essays in the Cultural History of Radio.* New York: Routledge, 2002.

Houseman, John. *Run-Through: A Memoir.* New York: Simon and Schuster, 1972.

———. *Front and Center.* New York: Simon and Schuster, 1979.

———. *Final Dress.* New York: Simon and Schuster, 1983.

———. *Entertainers and the Entertained.* New York: Simon and Schuster, 1986.

———. *Unfinished Business.* New York: Applause Theatre Books, 1989.

Hughes, David Y. "'The War of the Worlds' in the Yellow Press." *Journalism Quarterly* vol. 43, no. 4 (winter 1966).

Hughes, David Y., and Harry M. Geduld. Introduction and Notes. *"The War of the Worlds": H. G. Wells' Scientific Romance.* Bloomington, IN: University of Indiana Press, 1993.

Jackaway, Gwenyth. *Media at War: Radio's Challenge to the Newspapers, 1924–1939.* Westport, CT: Praeger, 1995.

Jewell, Richard B. "Hollywood and Radio: Competition and Partnership in the 1930s." *Historical Journal of Film Radio and Television,* vol. 4, no. 2 (1984).

Jewell, Richard B., and Vernon Harbin. *The RKO Story.* London: Octopus Books, 1982.

Kael, Pauline, with Herman J. Mankiewicz and Orson Welles. *The Citizen Kane Book.* Boston: Little, Brown, 1971.

Kear, Lynn. *Agnes Moorehead: A Bio-Bibliography.* Westport, CT: Greenwood Press, 1992.

Klass, Phillip. "Wells, Welles, and the Martians." *The New York Times,* 30 October 1988.

Knight, Arthur. "Citizen Kane Revisited." *Action Magazine*, no. 4 (1989).
Koch, Howard. *The Panic Broadcast: Portrait of an Event*. Boston: Little, Brown, 1970.
———. *Casablanca: Script and Legend*. Woodstock, NY: The Overlook Press, 1973.
———. *As Time Goes By: Memoirs of a Writer*. New York: Harcourt Brace Jovanovich, 1979.
———. "Orson Welles—Some Reminiscences." In Museum of Broadcasting, *Orson Welles on the Air*. New York: Museum of Broadcasting, 1988.
Lasky, Betty. *RKO: The Biggest Little Major of Them All*. Englewood Cliffs, NJ: Prentice-Hall Inc., 1984.
Leaming, Barbara. *Orson Welles: A Biography*. New York: Viking, 1985.
Lichty, Lawrence W., and Thomas W. Bohn. "Radio's March of Time: Dramatized News." *Journalism Quarterly*, vol. 51, no. 3 (autumn 1974).
Loggia, Marjorie, and Glenn Young, eds. *The Collected Works of Harold Clurman*. New York: Applause Books, 1994.
Lovejoy, Arthur O. *The Great Chain of Being*. New York: Harper Torchbooks, 1960.
MacLeish, Archibald. *Panic: A Play in Verse*. Boston: Houghton Mifflin, 1935.
———. *The Fall of the City: A Verse Play for Radio*. New York: Farrar and Rinehart, Inc., 1937.
———. *Six Plays*. Boston: Houghton Mifflin, 1980.
MacLiammóir, Micheál. *All for Hecuba*. Boston: Branden Press, 1967.
Maloney, Russell. "Orson Welles: 'This Ageless Soul.'" *The New Yorker*, 8 October 1938.
Marx, Karl. *The Eighteenth Brumaire of Louis Bonaparte*. 1852; reprint New York: International Publishers, 1969.
McBride, Joseph. *Orson Welles*. New York: Da Capo Press, 1996.
McLuhan, Marshall. *Understanding Media: The Extensions of Man*. New York: Signet, 1964.
Merryman, Richard. *Mank: The Wit World and Life of Herman Mankiewicz*. New York: William Morrow, 1978.
Metz, Robert. *CBS: Reflections in a Bloodshot Eye*. Chicago: Playboy Press, 1975.
Mott, Robert L. *Radio Sound Effects*. Jefferson, NC: McFarland and Company, Inc., 1973.
Museum of Broadcasting. *Orson Welles: On the Air*. New York: Museum of Broadcasting, 1988.
Nachman, Gerald. *Raised on Radio*. Berkeley, CA: University of California Press, 2000.
Naremore, James. *The Magic World of Orson Welles*. New York: Oxford University Press, 1978.
Noble, Peter. *The Fabulous Orson Welles*. London: Hutchinson, 1956.
"Orson Welles Mss. Collection." Lilly Library, Indiana University.
Paley, William S. *As It Happened: A Memoir*. Garden City, NY: Doubleday, 1979.
Rosenbaum, Jonathan. *Movie Wars: How Hollywood and the Media Conspire to Limit What Films We Can See*. Chicago: Capella, 2000.

Rosenbaum, Jonathan, ed. See Welles and Bogdanovich.
Sheehan, William. *The Planet Mars*. Tucson, AZ: University of Arizona Press, 1996.
Smith, Stephen C. *A Heart at Fire's Center: The Life and Music of Bernard Herrmann.* Berkeley: University of California Press, 1991.
Spoto, Donald. *The Dark Side of Genius: The Life of Alfred Hitchcock*. New York: Ballantine, 1993.
Stewart, James G. "The Evolution of Cinematic Sound: A Personal Report." In Cameron, *Sound and the Cinema: The Coming of Sound to American Film*. Pleasantville, NY: Redgrave Publishing Company, 1980.
Tarkington, Booth. *The Magnificent Ambersons*. New York: Sagamore Press Inc., 1957.
Tavares, Frank. A Critical Analysis of Selected Dramatic Elements in the Radio Series, "The Lives of Harry Lime." Ph.D. dissertation, University of Texas, 1976.
Theatre of the Imagination: Radio Stories by Orson Welles and the Mercury Theatre (boxed set of audio cassette tapes). Santa Monica, CA: Voyager, 1988.
Thomas, François. "La Radio d' Orson Welles." *Positif*, October 1988.
Thomson, David. *Rosebud: The Story of Orson Welles*. New York: Knopf, 1996.
Thomson, Virgil. *Virgil Thomson*. New York: Knopf, 1966.
Time Magazine. "George Orson Welles: Shadow to Shakespeare, Shoemaker to Shaw." 9 May 1938.
———. "Boo!" 7 November 1938.
Vogue (French edition). "Interview with Orson Welles." December–January, 1982–1983.
War of the Worlds Radio Report. Cassette tape produced by Radio Yesteryear. Vancouver BC, Canada, n.d.
Welles, Orson, and Peter Bogdanovich, with Jonathan Rosenbaum, ed. *This Is Orson Welles*. New York: HarperCollins, 1992.
Wells, H. G. *The War of the Worlds*. Thorndike, ME: G. K. Hall and Co., 1995 (orig. 1988).
Wolfe, Joseph G. "'War of the Worlds' and the Editors." *Journalism Quarterly*, vol. 57, no. 1 (spring 1980).
Wood, Bret. *Orson Welles: A Bio-Bibliography*. Westport, CT: Greenwood Press, 1990.
Woodress, James. *Booth Tarkington: Gentleman from Indiana*. New York: Greenwood Press, 1969.

Index

Aaroyan, William, 162
Abbey Theater, 8
ABC, 19, 38, 192, 193
Abednego the Slave, 194
Abe Lincoln in Illinois, 64
Abraham Lincoln, 11, 54, 63, 64, 131
Actor's Equity, 34
Adams, Alice, 139
Adelphi Theatre, 193
Adler, Stella, 117
Admiral of the Open Ocean, 173
The Adventures of Harry Lime, xiv, 196, 203
The Adventures of Huckleberry Finn, 147–48, 149, 153
Adventures of Robin Hood, 40
The Affairs of Anatole, 64
AFRA (American Federation of Radio Artists), 38
Aherne, Brian, 13
Ah! Wilderness! 136
Air Raid, 32, 90–92
Algiers, 136, 137, 138, 158
Algonquin Round Table, 12
Allan, Andrew, 194

Alland, William, 19, 59, 87, 98, 148, 154, 156, 196, 199
Allen, Fred, 174, 192
Allen, Gracie, 152
Allen, Jane, 124, 125
Allen, Woody, 81, 95, 124
Allison, Joan, 110
Altman, Rick, 158
Altman, Robert, 124
American, 143
American Broadcasting, 78
An American Cavalcade: The Things We Have, 214
American Institute of Public Opinion (AIPO), 100, 101
American Mercury, 41
America's Hour, 18
Amos 'n' Andy, 129, 212
Anderson, Arthur, 58, 59
Anderson, Maxwell, 162
Anderson, Sherwood, 63, 140, 162
Andrews, Robert Hardy, 25
anti-Semitism, xv, 172
Anything Can Happen, 187
The Apple Tree, 171–72, 194

Apropos of Dolores, 99
Arau, Alfonso, 170
Archer, William, 63, 126
Arlen, Harold, 18
Around the World, 193, 197
Around the World in 80 Days, 69, 70, 80, 81, 130, 147, 193
The Arrival, 75
Arrowsmith, 125, 126, 134, 144
Associated Press, 102
Astaire, Fred, 152
As Time Goes By, 110
Astor, Mary, 134
Autry, Gene, 198

Badge of Evil, 11
The Bad Man, 130
The Bad Will Ambassador, 177
Baker, N. B., 173
Ball, Lucille, 146, 164, 182
Bankhead, Tallulah, 40
Barnes, Marion, 140
Barneycastle, Adam, 194
Barnouw, Erik, 20, 32
Barr, Richard, 80, 96
Barrie, J. M., 136
Barrie, Wendy, 138
Barrier, Edgar, 70, 130, 150, 196, 199
Barrymore, John, 146, 161
Barrymore, Lionel, 123, 143, 146, 180
The Battle over Citizen Kane, 98
Baxter, Ann, 165
Bay, Richard, 154
Bay, Victor, 40
BBC Radio, 67, 111
Beatrice, Lillie, 134
Beery, Noah, 127
Benchley, Robert, 180
Benefield, Barry, 124
Benet, Stephen Vincent, 162
Bennett, Richard, 165, 169
Benny, Jack, 32, 148–50, 152, 177–78, 191

Bergen, Edgar, 65, 81, 82, 84, 85, 92, 98, 102, 164, 183
Bernstein, Dr. Maurice, 4, 5, 6, 7, 8, 10, 21
Black Magic, 200
Blackmore, R. D., 79
The Black Museum, 207–8; select episodes from, 208
Blake, Nichols, 146
The Blessed and the Damned, 201
Blitzstein, Marc, 33, 34, 42, 66
Blue, Howard, xv
Bogdanovich, Peter, xii, 151, 169, 198; and conversations with Welles, 20, 22, 27, 53, 98, 145, 156, 170, 178
Boston Post, 99
Bounty, 35
Bourbon, Diana, 133, 137, 138
Bowles, Paul, 23, 24
Boyd, James, 162
Boyer, Charles, 136
Bradbury, Ray, 78
Brady, Frank, 32, 61, 91, 160, 174, 175
Brazil, 176
Break of Hearts, 184
Brecht, Bertolt, 33
The Bridge of San Luis Rey, 118
Bright Lucifer, 11
Bringing Up Baby, 124, 152
Broadway, 40, 41, 43, 116, 132; and *Julius Ceasar*, 57; and Welles, 16, 129
Brook, Peter, 196
Broom Stages, 144–45
Brown, Bill, 59, 118
Brown, John, 10, 130
Brown, Johnny Mack, 198
Brown, Porter Emerson, 130
Buchan, John, 62, 63
Bücher, George, 116
Buchman, Sydney, 144
Buck Rogers, 30
Burgess, Meredith, 27–28, 31

Burlesque, 134
Burnett, Murray, 110
Burns, George, 152
Burroughs, Edgar Rice, 78
Bushman, Francix X., 186

Call It a Day, 123, 134
Cameron, William, 158
Campbell Playhouse, xiv, xvi, 4, 37, 40, 63, 121, 165, 186; debut of, 118–20; first season, 122–44; performers, 122, 154; second season, 144–50; and sponsorship, 118, 119
Cantor, Eddie, 36
Cantril, Hadley, 107, 108–9, 111
Capra, Frank, 145
Carringer, Robert, 169
Carroll, Madeleine, 126, 142, 150
Carson, Johnny, 60
Casablanca, 79, 110, 120, 137
Casablanca: Script and Legend, 110
Cassini, Giovanni, 76
Catholic Legion of Decency, 106
Catlett, Walter, 148
Cavalcade of America, 17, 173, 174, 176
CBC (Canadian Broadcasting Corporation), 64
CBS (Columbia Broadcasting System): and *Campbell Playhouse*, xiv, 4, 123; and *Columbia Workshop*, 39–40, 46, 90, 214; and Herrmann, Bernard, 80; and *Mercury Theatre on the Air*, xiv, 4, 45–50, 52, 81; and Reis, Irving, 30, 46–47, 90; and *War of the Worlds*, 82, 85, 87, 94, 96–99, 101–5, 111; and Welles's early work on radio, 17, 18, 21, 24, 25, 34
Ceiling Unlimited, 147, 174
Chambrun, Jacques, 99, 104–5
Chaplin, Charlie, 137, 138
Chapple, Earnest, 121, 134, 137, 138, 144
Chase and Sanborn Hour, 65, 81, 183

Chesterton, G. K., 65
Chicken Wagon Family, 124, 134
Chimes at Midnight, 4, 129, 167, 191, 213
Christie, Agatha, 142
A Christmas Carol, xvi, 123, 134, 143
Christopher, Percival, 127
Cimarron, 152
The Citadel, 144
Citizen Kane, xiv, xv, 16, 20, 30, 52, 115, 143; cast, 5, 67, 80, 98, 154, 170, 171; and Herrmann, Bernard, 47, 50, 67, 108, 150, 154; legacy, 57, 151, 212, 215; and Mackiewicz, Herman, 142, 147–48; the making of, 154–56; scenes from, 19, 157–63; similarities to *Marching Song*, 10; and *Treasure Island*, 59; and Wells, H. G., 100
civil rights, 64
Clarence, 69, 118, 139
Close Encounters of the Third Kind, 75
Clurman, Harold, 116–17
CNN, 102
Cohn, Harry, 193, 197
Collins, Ray: and *Citizen Kane*, 154, 162; and *Magnificent Ambersons*, 14, 165, 167, 169; and Mercury Theater, 20, 53, 64, 67, 69, 70, 150, 180, 186; and *War of the Worlds*, 80, 90
Colman, Ronald, 127, 176
The Columbia Playhouse, 40
Columbia Presents Corwin, 187
Columbia Records, 43
Columbia Workshop, 16, 24, 29, 30, 32, 40, 90, 157; and Ries, Irving, 39, 46–49
Colbert, Claudette, 144
Come and Get It, 144
Comingore, Dorothy, 154
commercials, 119, 136
Connell, Richard, 165
Conrad, Joseph, 115
Conried, Hanz, 183

Cooper, Bobby, 166
Cooper, Gary, 127, 135, 145
Cooper, Jackie, 147
Corell, Charles, 212
Cornell, Katherine, 12, 13
Cortez, Stanley, 165
Corwin, Norman, 39, 48, 59, 120, 157, 195
Cosmopolitan, 99
Costello, Dolores, 165, 166
Cotton, Joseph, 169, 201; character references, 23, 124, 126, 139, 154, 178; and *Magnificent Ambersons*, 165, 166, 169; and Welles, 17, 42
Cotton Blossom, 129
Coulouris, George, 53, 54, 59, 64, 66, 126, 150, 154
Counselor-at-Law, 124
The Count of Monte Cristo, 37, 53, 64–65, 102, 136, 194
Coward, Noel, 120, 129
Crabbe, Buster, 97
Cradle Will Rock, 33, 43
The Cradle Will Rock (film), 33–34
Craig's Wife, 147
Crespin, Lucilla, 126
The Critic, 99
Cromwell, John, 64
Cronin, A. J., 144
Crosby, Bing, 152, 184
Cullow, Simon, 108
Curtain Time, 38
Cyrano de Bergerac, 200

Daily Worker, 42
Dane, Clemence, 144
Danton's Death, 61, 65, 68, 69, 93, 96, 116, 139
Dark Room, 11
The Dark Town, 183
Dark Victory, 38
Davies, Marion, 161
Day, Clarence, 115, 116

The Death Triangle, 28–29
Dekker, Thomas, 42, 126
Delmar, Kenneth, 85, 103
Denning, Michael, 41, 212
Denny, Roger Quayle, 171
De Mille, Cecil B., 38–39, 46, 47, 51, 118, 184
A Diamond as Big as the Ritz, 186
Dickens, Charles, 118
Dietrich, Marlene, 178
Dietz, John, 80, 85, 108
Dillaway, Don, 166
Dinner at Eight, 146, 147
Dodsworth, 142, 153
Donovan's Brain, 178, 184
Don't Catch Me, 187
Doone, Lorna, 79
Douglas, Susan, xiv, 78
Doyle, Arthur Conan, 79
Dozier, Julia, 129
Dracula, xvi, 11, 52–53, 58, 120; comparisons with *Citizen Kane*, 57; and the novel, 53; synopsis of, 54–56
Dreathnach, Lormach, 8
Dreiser, Theodore, 140
Dressler, Marie, 146
Drinkwater, John, 11, 63
Dukes, Ashley, 9
Dumas, Alexander, 65, 66
du Maurier, Daphne, 118, 120, 125, 135
du Maurier, George, 120, 134, 135
Dunning, John, 37

Eddy, Nelson, 82
Edwards, Cliff, 164
Edwards, Hilton, 8, 13, 201, 202
Edward the Earl of Langford, 8
Eighteenth Brumaire of Louis Bonaparte, 213
Entrinken, Knowles, 17–18
Epstein, Julius and Philip, 110
The Escape, 138
Euwald, Carl, 171

Evans, Maurice, 127
An Evening with Orson Welles, 202
Everybody Comes to Rick's, 110
Everybody's Shakespeare, 11, 17
Ewald, Carl, 63
Exploring Music, 48
extraterrestrial life, 75–76, 77–78, 81, 84, 111

facism, xv, 42, 176
Fadiman, Clifton, 173
The Fall of the City, 16, 25, 28, 29, 39, 47, 91, 157; synopsis of, 30–32
Famous Musical Evenings, 48
Farewell to Arms, 123
Farrell, Elizabeth, 55
Faustus, xv, 21, 24, 25, 116
FCC (Federal Communications Commission), 19, 58, 104, 106
Feder, Abe, 22, 24
Federal Theater Project, 68
Ferguson, Perry, 155
Ferner, Edna, 128, 134, 144, 146
Ferrer, José, 200
Ferry to Hong Kong, 117
F for Fake, 111
Field and Fair, Travels with a Donkey in Ireland, 8
film, 151–52; and influence of radio, 151–52; and sound, 152
The First Nighter, 37–38
first person narration, 121, 150, 172, 174, 184. *See also* narration
First Person Singular, 91, 120, 147, 150, 204; beginnings of, 47, 50–51; description of, 53; first broadcasts, 60, 61–66
Fitzgerald, Geraldine, 144, 171
Fitzgerald, Scott F., 186
Five Kings, 60, 116, 126–27, 128, 129, 131
Flanagan, Hallie, 22, 23, 33, 34, 40
Flaubert, Gustave, 160

Fletcher, Louise, 164
Fletcher, Lucille, 120
Flying Dutchman, 117
Flying Fortress, 175
Follow the Boys, 178
Fonda, Henry, 64
Ford, John, 21, 64, 142, 155
Forward, Jean, 161
Foster, Norman, 171
Four Saints in Three Acts, 13
Fox, 19
France, Richard, 42
Francis, Arlene, 70
The Fred Allen Show, 191
The Free Company, 162, 163
French Press: The Liberation of Paris, 187
Freud, 49
Froelich, Ann, 71, 109
funding, 24, 127; and *Faustus*, 24

Gabel, Martin, 20, 36, 37, 42, 53, 54, 55, 66
Gable, Clarke, 144
Galileo, 76
Galsworthy, John, 40, 138
Garbo, Greta, 20
Garde, Betty, 36, 62, 175, 194
The Garden of Allah, 153
Garfield, John, 162
Gate Theater, 8–10, 12
Gaudet, Hazel, 107
Gauthierre, Henry, 59
Geduld, Harry M., 83, 89, 109, 110
Geiger, Milton, 187
Geiger, Miriam, 153
Germany, 102
Gershwin, George, 48
Geste, Beau, 127, 128
Gibbs, Wolcott, 19
Gielgud, John, 209, 213
The Gift of the Magi, 115
Gillette, William, 60
Gludskin, Lude, 178

God and Uranium, 187, 195
Goddard, Paulette, 137, 138
Godsen, Freeman, 212
Goetz, Bill, 188
Golden Age of Radio, 81, 120
Golden Honeymoon, 194
Goodbye Mr. Chips, 134
Gordon, Flash, 97
Grant, Cary, 124
The Grapes of Wrath, 156
The Great Dictator, 137
Green, Graham, 201, 203
Green, Johnny, 48
Green, Paul, 162
The Green Goddess, 63, 126, 131
Griffith, D. W., 64, 213–14
The Group Theater, 117
Grover's Mill, 79, 84–85, 87, 88, 92–94, 103, 109
Guernica, 90
Gunsmoke, 48
Gwenn, Edmund, 162

Hall, James Norman, 124, 141
Halloween, 82, 94, 99, 111
Hamlet, 23, 47, 148
The Happy Prince, 184
Hardwicke, Cedric, 40
Hardy, Ann, 135, 147
Harlow, Jean, 146
Harmetz, Aljean, 110
Harpers, 111
Harris, Phil, 149
Have Gun Will Travel, 48
Hawks, Howard, 147
Hayword, Susan, 182
Hayworth, Rita, 165, 178, 183, 184, 186, 187, 197
Hayes, Helen, 119, 125, 134, 135, 136, 139, 142, 144, 145
Hearst, William Randolph, 100, 105, 161, 162, 163
Hearst Metrotone News, 19

Heartbreak House, 43, 171
Heart of Darkness, 115, 147, 186
Hearts of Age, 61, 153
The Helen Hays Theatre, 136
Hello Americans, 174, 176, 194
Hell on Ice, xvi, 57, 68–69, 97, 124, 139, 194, 195
Hell's Angels, 89
Hemingway, Ernest, 123
Henry, O., 115
Henry IV, 126
Henry V, 126, 199, 213
Henry VI, 127
Hepburn, Katherine, 123, 124
Herman, Victor, 184
Herrmann, Bernard, 24, 141; and CBS, 30, 154; and *Citizen Kane*, 150, 160–62; and *The Columbia Workshop*, 39, 48–49; and *Magnificent Ambersons*, 165, 166, 169; his music, 58–59, 67, 70, 80, 108, 117, 121, 123, 135, 142–43, 172; and Welles, 47, 49–50, 176, 193
Herschel, Sir William, 77
Hershel, Sir John, 77
Herzog, Herta, 107
Hichen, Robert, 142
Hill, Edwin C., 120
Hill, Roger "Skipper," 6, 7, 8, 10, 11–12, 20
Hilmes, Michelle, xiv, 38
Hilton, James, 142
Hindenberg, 86
His Girl Friday, 158
His Honour the Mayor, 162
Hitchcock, Alfred, 62, 63, 119–20, 121, 123, 126, 171; *Psycho*, 48, 49, 195; *Vertigo*, 48, 195
The Hitch Hiker, 164, 183, 194
Holiday, 124
Holland, Joseph, 66
Hollywood, 116, 137, 138; and Hitchcock, Alfred, 120, 123; and

Welles, 40, 108, 112, 125, 132–33, 135, 140, 148
Hollywood Hotel, 118
Holmes, Sherlock, 7, 67; and the Todd School, 7, 67
Holt, Tim, 69, 141, 165, 166, 170
Hoover, Edgar J., 162
Hope, Bob, 152
Hopkins, Arthur, 41
Hopkins, Miriam, 144
Hopper, Hedda, 180, 182
Horse Eats Hat, 23, 60, 69, 191
Houghton, Norris, 174
Houseman, John (née Haussmann): and *Campbell's Playhouse*, 132, 134, 139, 142–43; and *Mercury Theater*, 36, 76, 183–84, 194; and *Panic*, 15–16; and *War of the Worlds*, 79, 80, 85, 92, 95–96, 98; and Welles, 13–14, 20–23, 27, 33–34, 40–41, 63, 64, 118, 162; and writing, 46, 52, 57, 58, 66, 68, 90
Houseman, Laurence, 131
How Green Was My Valley, 38
How to Raise a Child: The Disturbing Life—to Date—of Orson Welles, 145
Hughes, David Y., 99
Hugo, Victor, 34
The Hurricane, 141
Husing, Ted, 19
Huston, John, 68, 79
Huston, Walter, 64, 130, 134, 140, 142
Huygens, Christiaan, 75

Ibert, Jacques, 199
I'll Not Go Back, 187
Illustrated World, 78
I Lost My Girlish Laughter, 124–26, 134, 202
I Love Lucy, 212–13
I'm a Fool, 63
I'm a Fool/The Tell-Tale Heart, 199
The Immortal Story, 57

improvisation, 9, 60, 70
Independence Day, 75
Information Please, 173
Inner Sanctum, 178, 184
Inquirer, 156
In the Garden of Allah, 142
The Invasion from Mars: A Study in the Pschology of Panic, 107
The Invisible Man, 26
Ionesco, Eugene, 128
iris-out, 168
It Happened One Night, 144
It's All True, 33, 169, 172, 173, 176
Ives, Beatrice, 3–4, 5, 21
Ives, Charles, 48

Jane Eyre, 38, 67, 121, 150, 177, 184, 188, 194, 195
The Jell-O Program, 148
Jew Süs, 9
Joan of Arc, 128
Johnson, Alva, 145
Johnstone, William, 25, 36
Jolson, Al, 46
Journey into Fear, 55, 124, 171, 177
Juarez: Liberation of Mexico, 173
Juarez: Thunder from the Hills, 173
Julius Ceasar, 12, 43, 60, 161, 182; radio version, 66, 67; stage version, 16, 32, 41, 42, 57
June Moon, 148, 149, 150
Jürgens, Curt, 117

Kael, Pauline, 153
Kaltenborn, H. V., 32
Kane, Charles Foster, 152
Kane, Whitford, 7
Karas, Anton, 203
The Kate Smith Show, 184
Kaufman, George S., 59, 128, 146, 148, 183
Kelley, George, 147
Kemp, Hugh, 194

Kennedy, Joseph P., 152
Kent, Amelia, 153
King, Henry, 200
King Cole trio, 182
King Kong, 56, 152
King Lear, 40, 194, 196
Kitt, Eartha, 202
Kitty Foyle, 152
Knickerbocker Playhouse, 38
Knox, Father Ronald, 111
Koch, Howard, 36, 57, 68, 69, 70, 71, 83, 139; and *War of the Worlds*, 78–80, 84, 98, 107–11, 115, 117, 119, 124
Koerner, Charles, 173, 197
Korda, Alexander, 200, 201, 203
Korngold, Erich, 154
Kremer, Ray, 59
Kurosawa, Akira, 57

La Barthe, Henri, 137
Labide, Eugene, 23
La Carta, James, 25
Ladd, Alan, 137
Lady from Shanghai, 167, 193, 195, 197–98
Lamarr, Hedy, 136–37
Landi, Elissa, 128
Lang, Fritz, 97
Larder, Silvia, 124
Lardner, Ring, 148
Larson, Roy Edwards, 18
Laughton, Charles, 37, 182
Lawrence, Gertrude, 129, 145
Lazarsfeld, Paul, 97
Leaming, Barbara, 10, 20–21, 131, 212
Lee, Annabel, 164
Lee, Canada, 162
Lehman, Gladys, 142
Leigh, Janet, 16
Les Bravades, 5
Les Misérables, 34, 35–37, 39, 46, 64, 120, 130, 147, 191, 192, 204, 210,
215; connections with *The Shadow*, 36
The Letter, 79
Lewis, Sinclair, 125, 140, 142
Lewis, William B., 30, 46
Life with Adam, 194
Life with Father, 115, 116
Light Programme, 204
Liliom, 138–39
Listening In, xiv
The Little Boy, 63
Lives of Noble Grecians and Romans, 67
live studio audience, 118, 149, 164, 177, 185
Living Dramas of the Bible, 25
The Lonely Man, 68
The Lone Ranger, 34, 35
The Long Voyage Home, 156
Lost Horizon, 142
The Lost World, 79
Lowell, Percival, 77–78
Loy, Myrna, 39
Luce, Henry, 18
Lugosi, Bela, 52
Lupino, Ida, 130
The Lux Radio Theatre, 137, 150, 184, 186; beginnings of, 38–39; and *Campbell's*, 132; and CBS, 46; and De Mille, Cecil B., 65, 118

Macbeth, 4, 50, 145, 148, 213; and film version, 57, 198, 199–200; and play, 22, 42; and radio version, 32, 47–48; and Voodoo *Macbeth*, 56, 186–87
MacLeish, Archibald, 14, 15–16, 25, 30, 32, 90, 91, 162
MacLiammóir, Micheál, 8–9, 13, 201
The Madison Journal, 6
magic, xii, 5, 24, 51, 60, 78
The Magnificent Ambersons, 5, 47, 69, 125, 136, 139, 163; influence on radio play, 141; and novel, 169; and radio version, 168, 169; synopsis of, 165–71

The Magnificent Ambersons: A Reconstruction, 169
Mankiewicz, Herman, 142, 143; and *Citizen Kane*, 108, 111, 125, 147, 148, 153, 156, 163
A Man Who Was Thursday, 60, 65, 66
Marching Song, 10–11, 131; similarities with *Citizen Kane*, 10
The March of Time, 21, 22, 23, 89, 199; and radio, 18–20; and Welles, 19
Marconi, 78, 152
Markle, Fletcher, 194, 195
Marlowe, Christopher, xv, 21, 24
Maro, Michel, 23
Mars, 76–77, 78, 83, 84, 87, 97, 103, 109
Mars and Its Canals, 77
Mars as an Abode of Life, 77
Martian Chronicles, 78
martians, xv, 56, 71, 75, 89, 107, 109, 111; and *War of the Worlds*, 77–83, 86–89, 91–97, 101–4
Marx, Groucho, 180
Mason, Sarah Y., 184
Massenet, Jules, 160
Massey, Richard, 64
The Master of Ballantrae, 186, 187
Masterson, Whit, 11
Mathews, Grace, 194
Maxine Elliot Theater, 23, 25, 34
McBride, Joseph, 197
McCambridge, Mercedes, 194, 195
McCarthy, Charlie, 65, 81, 82, 84, 85, 164, 183. See also Bergen, Edgar
McClintic, Guthrie, 12, 13
McClintic-Cornell Company, 12–14
McCormick, Harold, 161
McIntire, John, 186
McLendon, Rose, 22
McLuhan, Marshall, xv, 22, 213
media event, 95
Meincken, Helen, 40
The Melians, 8

Meltzer, Robert, 174
Mencken, H. L., 41
The Merchant of Venice, 12
The Mercury Company Remembers, 21
The Mercury Shakespeare, 12
Mercury Summer Theatre, 193, 194, 195, 196
Mercury Theater on the Air, xiv, xvi, 4, 45–71, 80, 139, 214; *Abraham Lincoln*, 63–64; beginnings of, 41–43, 53; to *The Campbell Playhouse*, 118, 124, 136; ensemble, 20, 25, 28, 154; first broadcasts, 26, 47; life after *War of the Worlds*, 115–20; and novel adaptations, 147; and *War of the Worlds*, 81–94, 96, 98, 104, 105; and Welles's radio debut, 17
Meredith, Burgess, 127, 162, 175
Metropolis, 97
Mexican Spitfire Sees a Ghost, 173
MGM, 152
A Midsummer Night's Dream, 4
Miller, Arthur, 173, 175
Miranda, Carmen, 176
Miss Dilly Says No, 186
The Moat Farmer Murder, 194, 195
Moby Dick, 194, 195–96
Moby Dick: Rehearsed, 196
Mod Squad, 212
Molnár, Frederick, 138
Moorehead, Agnes, 5, 20, 178, 186, 196; character references, 36, 53, 56, 67, 121, 135, 138, 164–65; and *Citizen Kane*, 154, 162; and *First Person Singular*, 150; and *Magnificent Ambersons*, 141, 166, 167, 170
Morgan, Brewster, 40
Morgan, Heather, 128
Morrison, Brett, 25
Morrison, Herbert, 86
motion pictures, 147, 151
Mott, Robert, 59
Movietone News, 19

Mr. *Arkadin*, 57, 205, 214
Mr. *Deeds Goes to Town*, 145
Mumford, Lewis, 41
Muni, Paul, 162
The Murder of Roger Ackroyd, 142, 153
Murrow, Edward R., 32, 48, 102
Muse, Clarence, 148
Museum of Television and Radio, 19
music, 58, 59, 64, 65, 108, 134, 142, 154, 169; and *Citizen Kane*, 153, 154, 160. See also Herrmann, Bernard
Musical Reviews, 21
Musician's Union, 34
Music in the Manner, 48
Mutiny on the Bounty, 124, 134
Mutual Broadcasting Network, 23, 25–26, 33, 34, 35, 38, 64, 68
My Little Boy, 171, 172
My Little Margie, 212

Nachman, Gerard, xiv
Naremore, James, 199
narration, 31, 35, 47, 56, 58, 64, 67, 79, 92, 147, 148, 173
Nathan, George Jean, 41
Native Son, 129, 162, 163
Natwick, Mildred, 121
NBC, 92, 152, 173, 187; and Benny, Jack, 32; NBC Red, 38; and radio plays, 37, 65, 81, 92, 148; and *War of the Worlds*, 102, 112; and Welles, 17, 19, 25, 34, 46
Negro Theater Project, 22, 23
New Jersey, 79, 82, 84, 86, 87, 88, 92, 96, 101, 102, 103, 118
New Masses, 16
newscasting, 18
Newsweek, 52, 212
New Theater, 16
news radio, 95, 101, 102, 105, 108, 111; and *The March of Time*, 18–20; and *War of the Worlds*, 85, 86

New Yorker, 19, 45
New York Evening Journal, 99, 100
New York magazine, 110
New York Post, 192
New York Sun, 77
New York Times, 10, 12, 41, 42, 46–47, 77, 104–6
New York Tribune, 106
Nichols, Ora, 59
Nicolson, Virginia, 13, 21, 23, 36, 37, 65
The Night That Panicked America, 111
Nolan, Jeanette, 186, 199
Nordhoff, Charles, 124, 141

Oboler, Arch, 59
O'Brien, Emuch, 176
O'Callaigh, Cathral, 8
Olivier, Laurence, 127, 128, 199
Omnibus, 196
O'Neill, Eugene, 136
Only Angels Have Wings, 147
The Open Window, 63
The Orson Welles Almanac, 161, 163, 164, 165, 171, 178, 180, 183, 187, 191–94
Orson Welles Commentaries, 192, 193
Orson Welles's Almanac, 146, 161
The Orson Welles Show, 163
Orson Welles: The One Man Band, 22
Orson Welles Today, 192
Orwell, George, 174
Ory, Kid, 182
Othello, 4
Our Town, 12, 130

Paine, Thomas, 180
Paley, Bill, 38, 45, 46, 48, 49
panic, 76, 82, 89, 95, 98, 99, 102–5, 111, 112
Panic, 14, 15, 16, 19, 20, 91; synopsis of, 14; and Welles, 15, 19

Panic Broadcast, xv, 78, 99, 106, 112, 161; reactions to, 95–97, 102–3, 126; and realism, 95, 98, 101, 111; and Welles, 118, 123; and Wells, H. G., 100
Panic Broadcast: Portrait of an Event, 109
Papashvily, George and Helen, 187
The Paper Chase, 13
Parker, Dorothy, 164
Parsons, Louella, 118, 197
Parted on Her Bridal Tour, 25
Passenger to Bali, 117, 118, 124, 194
Pearson, Bud, 187
Pearson's Magazine, 83, 99
Peter Ibbetson, 135
The Philco Radio Hall of Fame, 184
Phoenix Theater, 14, 15, 21
Pickwick Papers, 118, 147
Pierson, Richard, 79
The Player, 124–25
Plutarch, 67
Pratt, Theodore, 186
Price, Vincent, 126
Private Lives, 129, 130, 145
Poe, Edgar Allen, 164
Porter, Cole, 193, 194
Powell, Jane, 186
Powell, Richard, 187
Powell, William, 39, 144
Project 891, 23, 24, 33
Publishers Weekly, 119
puppet theater, 5
Purple Cloud, 79

Rabble at Arms, 147
racism, xv, 42, 129, 142, 162
Radio and the Printed Page, 107
Radio Days, 81, 95, 214
radio vérité, xv, 85
Radio Voices: American Broadcasting, 1922–1952, xiv

Raised on Radio, xiv
Raphael, John Nathaniel, 135
Rashomon, 57
Rathbone, Basil, 13, 67
Ratoff, Gregory, 200
RCA, 152
Readick, Frank, 25, 27, 36, 80, 84, 139
Reading Out Loud, 178
realism, 120, 136, 158. See also *War of the Worlds*
Rebecca, xvi; and series broadcast, xvi, 118, 119, 125, 134, 135; synopsis of, 121–23
Regina, Victoria, 131, 134
Reis, Irving, 59, 120, 157, 187; and *The Columbia Workshop*, 30, 39, 46, 90; and *Hamlet*, 23; and Herrmann, Bernard, 47, 48–49; and Welles, 25, 32
Rennie, Michael, 202
Republic Pictures, 198
Rhinoceros, 128
Rice, Elmer L., 124
Richard II, 126
Richard III, 42, 127, 213
Richardson, Ralph, 209, 213
Riefenstahl, Leni, 42
RKO (Radio Keith Orpheum), 126, 131, 169–88; and *Citizen Kane*, 52; and *Magnificent Ambersons*, 140–42; and Schaefer, George, 130, 131; and Welles, 36, 40, 115, 132, 139, 147, 148, 150, 151–88
Robert, Kenneth, 147
Robinson, Edward G., 175, 191
Rockefeller, Nelson, 172
Rodenberry, Gene, 75
Rogan, Jim, 59
Rogers, Buck, 97
Rogers, Ginger, 152
Rogers, Roy, 198
Romeo and Juliet, 12, 13

Roosevelt, President Franklin Delano, 105, 184, 187, 192
Rosenbaum, Johnathan, 17, 169, 173
Roses and Drums, 25
Run-Through, 111

Sabotage, 29, 175
Saki, 63
Sanford, Erskine, 154, 162, 165, 199
Sarnoff, David, 152
Saturday Evening Post, 145
Scarlet Pimpernel, 26
Schaefer, George, 130, 131, 132, 143, 153, 154, 166, 173
Schiaparelli, Giovanni, 77
Schnitzler, Arthur, 64
School of the Air of the Americas (*The American School of Air*), 17, 48
Scientific American, 78
Scorsese, Martin, 48, 49, 84
screwball comedy, 128, 138, 146, 152, 158, 194
Sea Hawk, 79
The Search for Henri Le Fevre, 194
Secchi, Father, 77
Selznich, David O., 119, 123, 124
Semmler, Alexander, 65, 66
Sergeant York, 79
Seventeen, 69, 70
Seymour, Dan, 53, 54, 56, 61, 65, 66, 81, 94, 120
The Shadow, 5, 24, 25–28, 34, 36, 45, 68, 120, 175; connections with *Les Misérables*, 36; and death, 28; origins of, 26
The Shadow Detective Magazine, 26
Shakespeare: *Chimes at Midnight*, 4; *Five Kings*, 60; *Hamlet*, 23, 47, 148, 199, 213; *Julius Ceasar* (*see Julius Ceasar*); *King Lear*, 40, 194, 196; *Macbeth* (*see Macbeth*); *The Merchant of Venice*, 12; *A Midsummer Night's Dream*, 4; *Othello*, 4, 200, 201, 202, 203, 207, 213; *Romeo and Juliet*, 12, 13; *Twelfth Night*, 12, 40
Shaw, George Bernard, 43
Sherlock Holmes, 67, 209
Sherman, Jason, 33
Shile, M. P., 79
Shining Victory, 79
Shirer, William, 102
The Shoemaker's Holiday, 42, 43, 126, 191
Showboat, 128, 134
Signs, 75
Sight and Sound, 48, 151
Siodmak, Curt, 184
Sinatra, Frank, 182
Sloane, Everett, 36, 117, 150, 154, 156, 162, 198
The Smiler with a Knife, 146, 147
Smith, Fred, 18, 145
Snow White and the Seven Dwarfs, 186
socialism, 15
social justice, xv, 15
The Song of Bernadette, 201
Song of Solomon, 164
Sorry, Wrong Number, 120, 164, 170
sound, 30, 65, 156, 157, 158
sound effects: and *Algiers*, 137–38; and *The Death Triangle*, 28–29; and *Dracula*, 54–56; and *Les Misérables*, 37, 39; and *A Tale of Two Cities*, 62; and *Treasure Island*, 59
Special Bulletin, 112
Spiegel, Sam, 188
Spielberg, Steven, 76
Spier, William, 184
sponsorship, 19, 123; Campbell Soup, 51, 60, 104, 122; Chapple, Earnest, 121; Crest Blanca wine, 185; Lear Radios, 192, 193; Mobile Oil, 164, 178; Pabst Blue Ribbon Beer, 193, 194, 195
Spreaight, Robert, 129

Stafford, Anna, 36, 65. *See also* Nicholson, Virginia
Standard Brands Presents, 25
Stanton, Frank, 107
Stanwyck, Barbara, 121
stars, 118, 152
Star Trek, 75
Steinbeck, John, 175
Steiner, Max, 154
Stevenson, Robert, 67, 186
Stevenson, Robert Louis, 58
Stewart, James G., 154–55, 165, 168
Stewart, Paul, 17, 57, 80, 84, 85, 162; and *Campbell Playhouse*, 119, 132; and *Citizen Kane*, 154; and *War of the Worlds*, 108, 111
St. Joseph, Ellis, 117
Stoker, Bram, 11
Stoney Creek Connecticut Summer Theater, 61, 63
The Strange, 188
The Strangers, 57, 196–97
Strasberg, Lee, 117
Street and Smith's Detective Story Magazine Hour, 25
Sturges, Preston, 211
Sullavan, Margaret, 121, 128, 134
Sunderland, Nan, 140, 142
Suspense, 164, 165, 178, 183
Suthern, Ann, 186
Swenson, Karl, 53, 64
Swing Time, 152
Syms, Sylvia, 117

A Tale of Two Cities, 38, 53, 60, 61–62, 186, 194
Tallman, Robert, 186, 187
Tarkington, Booth, 3, 16, 136, 139–40; and *Magnificent Ambersons*, 166, 168, 170; and *Mercury Theatre*, 118; *Seventeen*, 69
Taxi Driver, 48, 84

Taylor, Davidson, 46, 50, 51, 56, 87, 108
Taylor, Mary, 62
Teichman, Howard, 128
television, 112, 148, 151
Terry, Ruth, 182
Tesla, Nikola, 78
Texaco Star Theatre, 174, 191
Thackeray, William Makepeace, 144
Thaïs, 160
theater, 23, 24–25, 116, 117; and politics, 33, 34
Theatre Guild, 127
Theodore Goes Wild, 144
There Are Frenchmen and Frenchmen, 165
There's Always a Woman, 142
The Things We Have: An American Cavalcade, 130, 131
The Thin Man, 39
The Third Man, 27, 124, 196, 200–201, 202, 203
The Third Man: The Lives of Harry Lime, 204–6
The Thirty-Nine Steps, 54, 62–63, 126
This Above All, 38
This Is My Best, 115, 185, 186, 187
This Is Orson Welles, 109
This Is Radio, 161
Thompson, Dorothy, 106
Thomson, David, 32, 124, 212
Thomson, Virgil, 22, 23
Time, 18, 43, 45, 52, 78, 91, 106, 211, 212
Time Runs, 201, 202
'Tis a Pity She's a Whore, 21
Todd, Mike, 70
Todd School, 6, 7, 10, 12, 22, 67, 153
Toland, Gregg, 155, 157, 165
Tomorrow Is Forever, 188, 191
The Tonight Show, 60, 124
Too Much Johnson, 52, 60, 61, 63, 67, 68, 153, 193

Towers, Harry Alan, 202, 203, 209
The Town Crier, 12
Town Meeting of the Air, 187
Touch of Evil, 11, 167, 169
Tragical History, 202
The Tragical History of Doctor Faustus, 24
Trauffaut, François, 211
Treasure Island, 52, 53, 56, 57–60, 62, 104, 118
Triumph of the Will, 42
Tschaikovsky, 81, 115, 120, 196
Tune, Franchot, 162
Turl, Conway, 40
Turner, Lana, 182
Tussler, John, 124–25
Twelfth Night, 12, 57
Twentieth Century, 128
Twilight Zone, 164

Un Chapeau de paille d'Italie (*An Italian Straw Hat*), 23
Understanding Media, xv, 213
The Unthinking Lobster, 201–2

Vallee, Rudy, 161
Vanessa, 142
Van Gogh, Vincent, 66
Vanity Fair, 144, 153
Vassar's Experimental Theater, 22
Velez, Lupe, 173
Verne, Jules, 69, 193
Voodoo *Macbeth*, xv, 22, 23, 33, 56, 162, 176, 186–87
Voorhis, Westbrook van, 19

Walker, Vernon L., 165
Walpole, Hugh, 142
Walska, Ganna, 161
Walter Wagner Productions, 137
War and Peace, 57
War of the Worlds: and academics, 106–7; aftermath, 95–98, 101–4, 109; and audience, 100–101, 102–4; and Halloween, 82; and novel, 98, 99, 105, 109, 110; and the popular press, 105–6; and realism, 85, 88, 89; synopsis of, 83–90
Warwick, Ruth, 154, 171
Waxman, Franz, 121, 154
Webb, Roy, 169
Weissberger, Arnold, 104
Weissberger, Augusta, 52, 53
Welles, Orson, xii–xvi, 3–14; career, xiv, 60–61, 97, 126; and directing, 36, 40, 41, 45, 46, 47, 53, 120, 174, 187, 188; his early years, 3–4; and guest appearances, 173, 183, 184, 187, 191; legacy, xvii, 25, 151, 212; and magic, 24, 51, 60, 163, 200; and producing, 46, 147, 154, 174; radio debut, 17, 120; reputation, 46, 145; as stage actor, 8–10, 13, 41, 43, 45, 97; and theatre, 24, 45, 116, 117, 126–27; and Todd School, 6, 7, 10, 12; and voice, xiv, 9, 12, 13, 14, 31, 52; and writing, 36, 46
Welles, Richard Head, 3–4, 5, 6
Wells, H. G., 76, 78, 81, 83, 93, 161
What Every Woman Knows, 136
Wheelock, Ward, 119, 120, 132, 134, 143, 144, 146–47
White, Les, 187
Widmark, Richard, 36
Wilde, Oscar, 184
Wilder, Thorton, 12, 118, 130
Wilson, Mary, 142
Wilson, Richard, 59, 173, 214
Winchell, Walter, 102
Wind, Sand, and Stars, 175
Wise, Robert, 165
The Wonder Show, 23
Wood, Brett, 67, 69

Woodbury Playhouse, 136
Woodward, Isaac, Jr. 192
Woollcott, Alexander, 12, 98, 183
Words at War: World War II Era Radio and the Postwar Broadcasting Industry Blacklist, xv
World War I, 78, 90, 102
Wrath, Jay, 11
Wray, Fay, 56
Wright, Richard, 129, 162

Wuthering Heights, 155
Wyatt, Eustace, 145

Yates, Herbert, 198
Young, Loretta, 144, 184, 196
Young Mr. Lincoln, 64

Zatkin, Nathan, 14
Zell, Harry von, 19
Zorina, Vera, 52

About the Author

Paul Heyer is professor of communication studies at Wilfrid Laurier University, Waterloo, Ontario, Canada. After pursuing graduate degrees in anthropology at the New School for Social Research and Rutgers University, he developed an interest in media history. He is coeditor (with David Crowley) of the introductory textbook, *Communication in History: Technology, Culture, Society*, and author of *Communications and History: Theories of Media, Knowledge, and Civilization; Titanic Legacy: Disaster as Media Event and Myth;* and *Harold Innis*. His most recent project is editing and preparing Harold Innis's "History of Communications" manuscript for publication.